Autistic Spectrum Disorders

An Introductory Handbook for Practitioners

Rita Jordan

David Fulton Publishers
London

David Fulton Publishers Ltd
Ormond House, 26–27 Boswell Street, London WC1N 3JD
http://www.fultonbooks.co.uk

Published in Great Britain by David Fulton Publishers 1999
Reprinted 2000

Note: The right of Rita Jordan to be identified as the author of this work has been asserted by her in accordance with the Copyright, Designs and Patents Act 1988.

British Library Cataloguing in Publication Data
A catalogue record for this book is available from the British Library

ISBN 1-85346-666-2

Typeset by FSH Print and Production Ltd, London
Printed in Great Britain by the Cromwell Press Ltd, Trowbridge, Wilts.

618 928

618.928

T025595

Autistic Spectrum Disorders

This book is to be returned on or side College
Centre

Contents

Acknowledgements   vii

Preface   ix

Introduction   1

1   The Nature and Definition of Autism   7

2   The Importance of Diagnosis in Education and Care   29

3   Autism and Behaviour   35

4   The Biological Bases of Autism   49

5   Psychological Theories on the Nature of Autism   59

6   The Individual with an Autistic Spectrum Disorder   113

Appendices   131

References   139

Index   163

Acknowledgements

The author wishes to acknowledge the contribution of Francesca Happé, whose original handbook, for the autism ACE course in Birmingham, formed the basis for this current edition. Thanks are also due to Marion Glastonbury for her careful reading of an earlier draft of this handbook and whose insightful comments have, the author hopes, resulted in this improved edition. Thanks are also due to colleagues on the Birmingham courses whose helpful comments on earlier editions, and practical support of the author's work, have helped the handbook take its current form. These are: my fellow tutor, Glenys Jones; the knowledgeable and supportive band of regional tutors; the hard-working staff in the distance education unit; and the many past and current professional students on the courses themselves. This book could not have been written without their support, but neither are they responsible for its contents. That responsibility lies with the author alone. Finally the author wishes to acknowledge her debt to the many professionals, parents and, above all, adults and children with autistic spectrum disorders who have helped shape her thinking over the years.

Preface

This handbook was written to accompany course texts for those taking distance education courses in autism at the School of Education, the University of Birmingham, UK. It will, therefore, from time to time refer to such course materials but it is also written to stand alone, and does not depend on course material for its interpretation.

Although described as a handbook, it is the work of a single author with that author's view and knowledge alone, and it does not claim to be comprehensive in its coverage of the field of autism. What it does aim to do is give an overview of the main landmarks in the field at the time of writing and to put them into some sort of coherent frame for the reader. Where what is written is based on judgement or opinion there is an attempt to make this clear. However, the whole process of selection, and consequent omission, is itself a reflection of a judgement of what is important (or a reflection of the author's ignorance). It is hoped that there is no systematic bias, other than clearly expressed opinions.

It is assumed throughout that the main audience for the book is practitioners in the field of autism, and this has influenced the selection of topics and the way they are presented. However, theories and academic perspectives on autism are presented because it is the author's contention that effective practice depends on understanding the condition. That does not mean that every practitioner needs to engage with each theory or academic position, but they should be aware of current thinking on the nature of autism and they should have the chance to reflect on these theories in the light of their own experience. It is a further contention of the author that theories of autism and its nature should not just emerge from academic research and then be applied to practice, but should be informed by those with daily practical experience. Practitioners need to be involved in research and the formulating and testing of theories, but to do so they need to be informed of the process and the current state of play. It is hoped that this book will contribute to the involvement of practitioners in this research.

Throughout this handbook, children's ages are written as 2; 4, 3; 1, 11; 8 etc. to indicate years; months.

This book is dedicated to Christina Tilstone, who started the autism studies courses at Birmingham, persuaded me to take over, and has been a source of support and inspiration ever since.

Introduction

Overview of the handbook

This handbook should acquaint you with one view of the current research and thinking about autism. Clearly, this book cannot be exhaustive in this respect, since space, and the author's knowledge, are obvious limits. Research in autism is vast and expanding, but it is hoped that the selection here will be relevant to those who work with individuals with autism. Even within that constraint, this book can only provide an outline and so, in addition to the normal academic references in the text, suggestions are also given for further reading, which may or may not appear as in-text references. This is a particular convention of a teaching text and should not provide a model for referencing essays in courses. References in the text are given at the end of the handbook in the normal way, but suggestions for further reading (usually in the form of books or review articles) appear at the end of each chapter. This allows the reader to broaden knowledge of the whole area covered by that part of the handbook. Throughout, the discussion of points has been kept as brief as possible, as the purpose of the book is to provide an overview of autism, tying together a number of quite different areas. The density of the handbook means that it is not meant to be read and absorbed at one sitting; it should serve as a reference text for the reader.

Explaining autism: types of explanation

The term 'autism' is used in this book (and in most of the texts in the Birmingham distance education courses, unless otherwise indicated) to mean 'autistic spectrum disorders' as a whole. The nature of the range of this spectrum will become apparent later in this handbook and through the courses. The point is that it covers a number of different diagnostic categories in medical terms (such as Asperger's syndrome, Kanner's autism, 'atypical' autism) describing the commonality of all those diagnoses. The aim is to arrive at a 'practice' definition of autism, which will refer to conditions that require specific treatment approaches in both lifetime education and care. For some purposes, most notably that of research, finer medical diagnoses will be needed. However, it is the contention of the author, followed in the courses to which the handbook relates, that it is the commonality of autistic spectrum disorders that needs to be addressed, as well as individual needs, in provision for people with autism. The question then arises of how this commonality is best expressed.

In the study of any condition, such as autism, three kinds of explanation in particular are useful: the biological, the psychological, and the behavioural. There could also be a political and sociological perspective, but they are beyond the scope of this text. The first three kinds of explanation will be discussed more fully below, but it is useful to understand that these provide distinct models of autism. As a psychiatric condition, autism is defined and diagnosed medically from its characteristic pattern of behaviours, yet there are no behaviours that of themselves will unequivocally indicate autism. Concentration on the behaviour alone will often lead to misleading interpretations of its meaning and thus to inappropriate treatment. Behaviour, then, is essential in our recognition of autism but, by itself, it does not help us understand the condition or decide how to approach it.

As will be shown later in the handbook, autism is undoubtedly rooted in biology yet, again, our current state of knowledge does not allow us to pinpoint any single causative biological factor. Indeed, it may be that different combinations of factors are differentially important in different cases. That is, one individual may develop autism primarily through a genetic link with a small part played by the environment (such as an infection *in utero*) in triggering the genetic factor. Other cases may arise primarily through environmental factors (such as birth trauma or foetal injury) with a genetic predisposition playing a relatively minor role. The point is, there may well be more than one biological 'cause' of autism so our understanding of the condition at the practical level is not much helped by understanding biological causation, although there will be some direct effects of biology on behaviour which may be more relevant. There may also be some treatments (such as diet and/or drugs) arising from this model, but these are only mentioned insofar as they have a direct effect on the education or care of individuals with autism; this is a handbook for education and care practitioners.

The third model of autism operates at the level of brain functioning, the psychological level. This is the level at which biological factors are translated both into overt behaviour and into ways of thinking and feeling and seeing the world. A model at this level should help us see why the characteristic pattern of autism exists and to make sense of the behaviours that characterise autism. It should also incorporate what is being discovered about the biology of autism, although much of this is still speculative. Above all, this handbook argues for the importance of understanding autism at this psychological level, if treatment and care are going to address the fundamental needs.

Frith (1989a) and Happé (1994a) have preferred to use the term 'cognitive' rather than 'psychological' to cover the level of explanation to do with the functioning of the brain. This is because the term 'psychological' has been associated with the view that autism is an emotional disorder – a kind of mental illness in response to poor parenting or early childhood emotional trauma. This author would strongly disassociate herself from these latter views but feels that 'cognitive' suggests (in spite of attempts by Frith and others to widen its meaning) a too narrow focus on functions of perception and thinking whereas she would want to include emotional and motivational functions.

About this handbook

This handbook will cover models of autism at behavioural, biological and psychological levels. In Chapter 1, the history of the diagnosis of autism is discussed, focusing on the behavioural level, since autism is currently recognised on the basis of behavioural features rather than, for example, biological aetiology. Chapter 2, however, makes the case for the importance of recognising the psychological level in the treatment of autism. Chapter 3 shows the range of behaviours which are covered in the 'triad of impairments' (Wing 1988) underlying autistic spectrum disorders and examines some of the issues in differential diagnoses. Chapter 4 gives an outline of the biological understanding of autism, but only to show the way research is progressing and to pick out any practical implications. In Chapter 5 the psychological model is discussed as a kind of 'theory' about the existence of a condition of 'autism', and the role of psychological theories in understanding autism is illustrated with examples from current theorising. Chapter 6 looks at developmental issues in autism and the nature of the interactions over time with the social environment. The transactional nature of development is explored and the question raised of primary and secondary symptoms in autism. Finally, this section reasserts that it should be the individual who is the focus of treatment, education and care and makes the claim that people with autism are even more 'individualistic' than others, in spite of the commonality of any 'deficits' or differences from normal development.

Some questions about autism

Are we all 'a bit autistic'?

It often happens when first reading about autism that readers can see that they share many of these 'autistic' symptoms, or can see them in their family and friends. Of course, the reader may have autism and so may his/her family and friends but that does not follow from noting that we all share certain behaviours. Remember there is no one behaviour that is 'autistic' and it is the total pattern of our behaviour, plus the reasons that underlie it, that indicates autism. That is one of the reasons why professionals cannot just operate at this behavioural level. However, at the biological level people with autism may well be different from people who do not have autism – something in the anatomy, neurophysiology or chemistry of their brains may be responsible for their condition, which is not present in non-autistic people. Or it may be that differences are ones of degree, rather than specific pathology, so that the 'symptoms' of the disorder shade into normality, as in a continuum.

At the psychological level, too, people with autism may be quite distinct, and not simply at one end of a normal continuum, although this is a matter of current debate (Jordan 1998; Lesser and Murray 1998; Walker 1998). So, for example, very different reasons may underlie apparently similar behaviour by the individual with autism and by the 'normally developing' person. The autistic individual social difficulties probably have a quite different cause (at the psychological level) from the 'normal' shy person's – although the behaviours produced (avoiding people, social anxiety, inappropriate social behaviour such as avoiding eye contact) may be very similar. On the other hand, many apparently 'autistic' behaviours can be seen in anyone under a sufficient degree of stress and this will be relevant later in the discussion of what is primary and what is secondary in autism.

Can parents cause autism?

Unless one is talking about genetics, the answer is 'no'. The myth of 'refrigerator parents' (especially mothers) has been shown to have no basis in fact but continually resurfaces in new guises (Hocking 1990). Its roots lie at least partly in the false analogy made by Bettleheim (1967), who had witnessed the horrific traumas suffered by the inmates in concentration camps in the Second World War and saw that the results were often social withdrawal, anxiety, depression, stereotyped behaviour and a loss of the ability to communicate. When he later saw this same pattern of behaviour in children in America, he falsely jumped to the conclusion that they too must have suffered a similar 'trauma'. Since their only incarceration had been with their mothers in their own homes, Bettleheim located the source of the trauma as the rejecting parent. There is no evidence that parents of children with autism are more rejecting than others (bearing in mind the effects of having a non-responsive child) nor that grossly abused and neglected children develop autism (Clarke and Clarke 1976). It may, however, be the case that severely traumatised children may present with behaviours that are initially compatible with a diagnosis (Rutter *et al.* 1999). Such children would be expected to respond to loving care and to reveal that they did not in fact have autism, although they might, of course, suffer other emotional and behavioural difficulties as a result of their experiences.

Can one 'grow out of' autism?

The idea that autism is a childhood disorder probably arose from early misunderstandings and the nature of some of the labels that followed, such as 'early infantile autism' (Kanner 1943). There will also often be accounts of autism, either by the individuals themselves (Williams 1996), by their parents (Kaufman and Kaufman 1976; Kaufman 1994) or by practitioners (Lovaas 1987; Tinbergen and Tinbergen 1994) that claim 'cures' or 'near normal functioning' in at least a proportion of individuals with autism undergoing a particular therapy. None of these claims have been completely validated, although some are currently under attempted replication and evaluation (Jordan *et al.* 1998). There are also anecdotal reports of young infants who appear at eighteen months or so to have the symptoms of autism, but then to 'grow out of it'; this is particularly likely where the child has been premature or suffers from a sensory loss. Possible reasons for this will be discussed later. All we can say for certain is that autism is a life-long condition but that there may, of course, be considerable improvement over time, especially with appropriate education. It is also true that some more able individuals do learn to function in ways that may be indistinguishable from the norm. It is a moot point whether they can then be said to be 'cured' of their autism. In this author's experience there is little point in labelling them at this stage, but we should recognise that they may still need to work much harder than others to maintain this 'normal' existence.

Is autism always characterised by special, or 'savant', skills?

The film *Rainman* did a lot to increase awareness of autism, but also gave the impression that all people with autism could display a marvellous and even mystical talent. Sadly this is not the case. There are some who do have truly savant abilities (usually in music, art or calculation) but they are in the minority. Those who are most able may pursue a very narrow interest to such an extent that they do develop enormous expertise, but often this is just in the collection of facts and has little practical value. Other 'special' skills may arise in a difference in the way information is processed, but again this may be very context-dependent and may have limited value because the individual is unable to exercise conscious control and adapt and apply his or her skill. The author once knew a forty-year-old man with autism who was placed in a secure psychiatric unit, for arson. He was able to perform marvellous feats of mental arithmetic but could not remember the simple steps of the process necessary to operate an electronic calculator. No employer would take him on in a retail outlet or working with figures as a bookkeeper or in a bank because his mental 'workings out' were not trusted and he could not slow them down to reflect on them or to check them on a calculator. It is this patchiness and lack of adaptability of the skills of people with autism that provides a key challenge in their education. Autism is, in fact, found at all IQ levels, but is often accompanied by general learning difficulties and, the more profound the general learning difficulties, the more likely that the individual will also have autism. Such individuals may have a characteristic unevenness in their skill development but they seldom have abilities that are remarkable in themselves, when compared to a normally developing population.

Is autism just a 'shell' within which a 'normal' person is waiting to get out?

This is often the feeling that professionals get when working with individuals with autism, especially when they are young, but it is not a very helpful way of approaching autism. Autism is a severe disorder of communication, socialisation and flexibility in thinking and behaviour which involves a different way of processing information and seeing the world. People with autism may make great strides in seeing the world as we see it and in understanding us, but it is an effort and they do not always see why they should make the effort (Sinclair 1992) or think that it is automatically better to be 'non-autistic' (Grandin, cited Sacks 1995). As a very able woman with autism, Temple Grandin, (cited Sacks 1995) has said, autism is another way of being a person. It is not so much that people with autism are abnormal as that our concept of what is normal may need to be enlarged to encompass these fascinating and different ways of being.

The author recently came across a hair dryer with two possible settings: 'normal' or 'healthy'. This gave much pause for thought but it is a distinction that may be of value when we consider autism and the question of what is normal. Too often 'normal' is equated with 'healthy' so that those who do not fit the norm become automatically 'abnormal', even 'pathological' or 'diseased'. But what if 'normal' is equated instead with 'ordinary', 'average' or even (as many of those with autism choose to call those without) 'neurotypical'? Suddenly it does not seem so wonderful to be normal or so terrible to differ from the norm; one can be different without necessarily being unhealthy.

Further reading

Baron-Cohen, S, and Bolton, P. (1993) *Autism: The Facts*. Cambridge: Cambridge University Press.
Gerland, G. (1997) *A Real Person*. London: Souvenir Press.
Wing, L. (1996) *Autistic Spectrum Disorders*. London: Constable.

Chapter 1

The Nature and Definition of Autism

Identification of a new syndrome

He wandered about smiling, making stereotyped movements with his fingers, crossing them about in the air. He shook his head from side to side, whispering or humming the same three-note tune. He spun with great pleasure anything he could seize upon to spin...When taken into a room, he completely disregarded the people and instantly went for objects, preferably those that could be spun...He angrily shoved away the hand that was in his way or the foot that stepped on one of his blocks...' (Kanner 1943; reprinted in Kanner 1973 pp. 3–5)

This description, of a five-year-old boy called Donald, was written over 60 years ago. Kanner saw Donald and made these observations in 1938, and they appear in his landmark paper, published in 1943. That paper was based on a study of 11 cases that Kanner had encountered in his work as a child psychiatrist in the USA. He decided, as a result of this study, that these children had enough in common, and were sufficiently different from other children he saw, to warrant the identification of a separate condition.

Autism, then, has only been defined as a condition since the early 1940s although, as Frith (1989a) has shown, it is likely that people with autism have always been with us. Given its complex manifestations and the controversies over aetiology, it is not surprising that there have been, and continue to be, controversy and misunderstandings over diagnosis and treatment as well. Wing (1997) gives an overview of the history of ideas in autism. Kanner, while describing the features of the disorder with an accuracy and a perceptiveness that has largely stood the test of time, came to think the condition was an emotional illness with a psychogenic origin. Mothers of children with autism were described as 'refrigerator mothers who had only managed to defrost long enough to have a child'. Some workers in this area have defended this position (e.g. Bettleheim 1967) but research and clinical experience over the years has failed to provide any evidence that mothers (or indeed fathers) 'cause' autism. If parents of children with autism appear odd in any way, it is more likely to be an effect of having such a child (or a mark of a broader genetic phenotype) rather than a cause.

At almost the same time, Asperger was also identifying a group of four children as having autism (Asperger 1944, translated Frith 1991a). Kanner's work became well known and had great influence throughout the world, but it is only comparatively recently that Asperger's work has been taken up internationally. As we shall see, this has led to questions about the exclusivity of the two 'syndromes' or indeed whether there are two separate syndromes at all. The earliest confusions, however, were between autism and childhood psychoses. For many years the terms 'childhood psychosis' and 'childhood schizophrenia' were used as synonyms for 'early infantile autism', even though autism was not a deterioration in social functioning but an 'autistic' aloofness from the start.

Kanner's description

Kanner saw the 'defining' features of the syndrome as being:

- a profound autistic withdrawal;
- an obsessive desire for the preservation of sameness;
- a good rote memory;
- an intelligent and pensive expression;
- mutism, or language without real communicative intent;
- over-sensitivity to stimuli; and
- a skilful relationship to objects.

A profound autistic withdrawal

The children failed to relate to people normally, especially other children, and appeared to be happiest when left alone. This lack of social responsiveness appeared to Kanner to start very early in life, as shown by autistic infants' failure to put out their arms to the parent who was about to pick them up, or to mould themselves to the parent's body when held.

An obsessive desire for the preservation of sameness

The children were abnormally upset by changes of established routine, or in familiar surroundings. A different route to school or a rearrangement of furniture would cause a tantrum, and the child could not readily be calmed until the familiar order was restored.

A good rote memory

The children Kanner saw showed an ability to memorise large amounts of effectively meaningless material (e.g. an encyclopaedia index page), which was out of line with their apparent severe learning difficulties in other respects. This good memory is tantalising – leading one to feel that if only it could be turned to some practical use, the child might learn well. However, as later modules in the courses will show, even this is limited to certain aspects of memory.

An intelligent and pensive expression

Kanner believed that the outstanding memory and dexterity shown by some of his cases reflected a superior intelligence, despite the fact that many of the children had been considered to have severe learning difficulties. Certainly, an impression of intelligence is given by the lack of any physical stigmata in most cases of autism. Unlike individuals with many types of severe learning difficulties, individuals with autism usually look 'normal'. Kanner remarked on his cases' 'intelligent physiognomies', and other authors have described children with autism as unusually beautiful. The strong impression of intelligence (that an individual, with autism, *could*, if only they *would*) is often felt by parents and teachers. This may reflect the fact that intellectual development is patchy or it may be to do with the difficulty experienced in autism of initiating spontaneous behaviour without a clear (usually visual) prompt. It is this lack of spontanous behaviour, which nevertheless can be elicited by the correct prompt, which furthers the impression that the individual could do it if s/he wanted to. Professionals, parents and researchers have all debated whether it is a deficit or a problem in motivation. When we look at the nature of some of the difficulties in more depth later we will see how there are difficulties in functioning which are to do with the ability to intend actions and thus to perform actions spontaneously. In other words, as a parent once put it: '*I used to wonder whether it was that he* can't *do something or that he* won't *do something until I finally realised that he can't help* won't.'

Mutism, or language without real communicative intent

This includes children without speech but also those that only used echolalia. Kanner was particularly struck by the phenomenon of 'delayed echolalia' whereby the children repeated language they had heard some time before (even years before), but failed to use words to communicate beyond their immediate needs. Kanner also remarked upon what he termed 'the reversal of pronouns' so that the children would use 'you', when referring to themselves and 'I' when referring to the other person. This usage would sometimes follow from a direct repetition of the other speaker's remark (immediate echolalia) and so appeared to be an echo. Later texts in the courses will show that this is not quite the case, but confusion with pronouns is certainly characteristic of autism (Jordan 1989). In the same way, the individual with autism commonly uses the whole of a question as a request for the item which usually follows (e.g. 'Do you want a sweet?' meaning, 'I want a sweet'). Again, this might not be a true request in the usual sense of the term, but it can come to function as a request if it is responded to as such.

Oversensitivity to stimuli

Kanner noticed that many of the children he saw reacted strongly to certain loud noises and to objects such as vacuum cleaners, lifts and even the wind. Some also showed feeding problems or extreme food fads. These phenomena pose a 'chicken and egg' problem. Is perceptual or even sensory oversensitivity one of the core features of autism, or does it result from a failure to analyse input and to perceive social meaning? This issue has not been resolved to date, and informs the debate about some of the psychological theories of autism.

A skilful relationship to objects

Kanner noted the contrast between the very good manipulation of objects that the children showed and the uses made of those objects. The actions they performed were often advanced in terms of manual dexterity, but they did not create new ways of using the objects or engage with others in social play activities with objects. On the contrary, their activities were characterised by repetition and the rigid performance of set routines.

Other characteristics

Kanner also remarked that all his cases had intellectual parents. However, this is probably due simply to a referral bias; Kanner's sample is unlikely to have been representative. Parents who persist in trying to obtain a diagnosis for their children are likely to be well educated and know the system. Kanner also described the parents as cold, although in this first paper his was very far from a psychogenic ('refrigerator mother') theory. Instead he states, '*These children have come into the world without the innate inability to form the usual, biologically provided affective contact with people*' (p. 242).

Later Kanner views

A further study of 23 children in 1946 led Kanner to elaborate on these characteristics, particularly in relation to language. He noted then how apparently mute children might, under conditions of stress, utter complete and well-articulated phrases. Many of the children with language showed both immediate and delayed 'echolalia' (the parroting of phrases – using the exact intonation of the speaker) far in excess of any found in normal language development, both in the amount echoed and in the developmental period over which it occurred. They were also characterised in the following ways:

- their language was also extremely literal;
- they used simple negation to avoid unpleasant events but not to deny;
- they did not affirm by saying 'yes' but by repetition;
- they showed metaphorical substitutions, transfer of meaning by substitute analogy of the whole for the part and the part for the whole; and
- their speech showed 'pronominal reversal' (referring to themselves as 'you' and the person being spoken to as 'I').

By the 1950s Kanner was being influenced by the current ideologies of attachment theory (Bowlby 1969) and had moved away from detailed descriptions of deviant behaviour to produce broader defining characteristics (Eisenberg and Kanner, 1956) which were:

- extreme isolation;
- obsessive insistence on the preservation of sameness;
- onset of the condition within the first two years of life.

The other symptoms he considered to be both secondary to, and caused by, these two elements (e.g. communicative impairments), or non-specific to autism (e.g. stereotypies).

This has moved from the previous emphasis on the language and communication characteristics, to omission of language features from the defining criteria. The rare 'odd' phrases occasionally seen in otherwise mute children led to the belief that there was an elective element in the muteness and the child's parroting of heard expressions was seen as cruel mimicry. Bettleheim (1967) even claimed that pronominal reversal could not be explained by linguistic or pragmatic confusion on the part of the child, or by the child's exact parroting of the phrases he heard addressed to him, but instead resulted from a refusal to use 'I' – a denying of self.

Diagnostic criteria

All this may seem very messy and vague compared with, say, the diagnosis of measles, but it is not uncommon in medicine, and very common in psychiatry, for conditions to be defined by, and diagnosis based on, sets of behavioural characteristics that cluster together often enough to form a 'syndrome'. Of course there has to be more to it than that or we might have 'syndromes' of all fair-haired blue eyed people, or chance associations of big noses and musical talent or whatever. The features defining a syndrome should be pathological or deviant from normal development, and there is the assumption that they reflect some underlying common cause, or at least a common pathway.

Thus, there began to appear lists of 'points' for the diagnosis of autism, although it was often called 'childhood schizophrenia' at this stage. Sometimes these 'points' (referring to aspects of abnormal behaviour or development) were merely seen as descriptive i.e. 'salient features'. Thus, there was no clear prescription of which features had to be present in order to make the diagnosis of autism and which were merely features that frequently accompanied autism but were not essential criteria. Creak's nine points (1964) were of this nature, whereas O'Gorman's six points (1967) were described as 'essential' and so presumably all six needed to be present before a diagnosis could be made. Rendle-Short (1971, cited Newson 1979) came up with 14 points, seven of which had to be present in order for a diagnosis to be made. There were misgivings about the nature of some of these points themselves, some of them in Rendle-Short's list, for example, seeming contraindicative of autism. This points system, also led to a confusing and unacceptable, situation. Under this system, two children might be diagnosed as having autism, and yet not have a single 'defining feature' in common!

Rutter *et al.* (1971) reformulated these lists to give the following four essential diagnostic criteria:

- delay in speech and language development;
- an 'autistic-like' failure to develop interpersonal relationships;
- ritualistic and compulsive phenomena; and
- onset before 30 months.

The four points were reformulated in 1978 (Rutter 1978) to include a description of these social abnormalities and to take account of greater understanding about the nature of the difficulties in communication and behaviour. The 'autistic-like' failure in interpersonal relationships was spelt out as:

- failure to come for comfort or a cuddle;
- lack of eye gaze giving the appearance of aloofness or distance;
- relative failure to become attached to parents;
- little or no separation anxiety;
- sometimes little variation in facial expression;
- apparent lack of interest in people;
- tendency when a toddler to treat all adults in the same way; and
- failure to make friends and join in group activities.

These amended criteria formed the basis of the diagnostic criteria accepted by the World Health Organisation and were very similar to American formulations under DSM. The four criteria were:

- delayed and deviant language development, which has certain defined features and is out of keeping with the child's intellectual level;
- impaired social development, which has a number of special characteristics and is out of keeping with the child's intellectual level;
- insistence on sameness, as shown by stereotyped play patterns, abnormal preoccupations, or resistance to change; and
- onset before the age of 30 months.

Newson (1979) modified Rutter's criteria to spell out some of the 'special characteristics' and to emphasise communication deficits. Her reformulation kept the same four points:

- impairment of language and all forms of communication, including gesture, facial expression and other 'body language', and the timing of these;
- impairment of social relationships, in particular a failure of social empathy;
- evidence of rigidity and inflexibility of thought processes; and
- onset before 30 months.

Newson also points out that each impairment interacts with every other, so that they overflow and pervade each other; it is the interaction between different parts of the syndrome which is most characteristic of autism.

Volkmar (1998) describes the process behind the setting of the diagnostic criteria of DSM-IV (American Psychiatric Association 1994) and compares it to the system used by the World Health Organisation (WHO 1993) in ICD-10. He makes interesting points about the different purposes of classification and shows how in America (and this is increasingly the case in the UK) services depend on categorical diagnoses. He suggests that it is these service requirements for a specific diagnosis that determine the categorical nature of the diagnostic system.

The triad of impairments

Each of the attempts at diagnosis so far looked for features that would pick out autism as a separate syndrome. However, there are other interactions, which make this process even more difficult. Kanner had originally supposed that all children with autism were fundamentally intelligent and that apparent delays in development were a direct result of the autistic condition. Sadly, this is one of the 'facts' about autism that Kanner got wrong and *Rainman*-like autistic individuals are very rare indeed, even within the autistic population. Many individuals with autism have additional learning difficulties. In fact, the more severe the general learning difficulties the more likely it is that the person will have autism, although it becomes increasingly difficult to separate out the effects of autism from the effects of having profound learning difficulties.

Wing and Gould (1979) conducted research in Camberwell, looking at all the children referred for psychiatric help. They were able to select a group of these children who were socially impaired compared to others who had equally severe learning difficulties but without social impairment. They also found that three areas of development were associated with this social impairment, forming a cluster of features that provide diagnostic criteria for autism.

Table 1.1: Wing's triad of impairments in autism	
Social	Impaired, deviant and extremely delayed social development – especially interpersonal development. The variation may be from 'autistic aloofness' to 'active but odd' characteristics.
Language and communication	Impaired and deviant language and communication – verbal and non-verbal. Deviant semantic and pragmatic aspects of language.
Thought and behaviour	Rigidity of thought and behaviour and impoverished social imagination. Ritualistic behaviour, reliance on routines, extreme delay or absence of 'pretend play'.

All the above behaviours should be out of keeping with the child's mental age.

Most people would also want to limit the diagnosis to conditions with an onset before 36 months of age, although Lorna Wing herself feels there may be late onset autism and this should be included in a broad view of the diagnosis of autism.

This became the triad of impairments by which autistic-like conditions were diagnosed. Some of these characteristics are out of keeping with Kanner's original description and so children so diagnosed may not have what is known as Kanner's syndrome but they do fall into what Wing (1988) has described as 'The Autistic Continuum' and later 'the Autistic Spectrum' (Wing 1996). Wing based her broader classification on assuming that social effectiveness (or what Gillberg (1992) feels could best be seen as 'empathy') is normally distributed in the population with the majority having a medium level of social effectiveness or empathy and a small minority at either end of the distribution. Presumably those at the high end are no problem, unless super-sensitivity to others can be seen as such. However, at the low end there will be groupings of individuals where the boundaries of the groups are not set, but fade into one another – in effect *forming a continuum*. At the far end of the continuum will be the classically autistic group merging into other groups such as those with Asperger's syndrome who might merge with some other psychiatric disorders and/or with the 'normal' group. The overlapping nature of these conditions and their variation on dimensions other than empathy suggests that a 'spectrum' is a better model of the condition than a 'continuum'.

Necessary and sufficient features to diagnose autism

When we ask what are the defining features of a disorder, we are asking something about the symptoms that are necessary and sufficient for the diagnosis to be made. Any disorder will have core features, which a person must show to receive the diagnosis. But there will also be non-necessary features that a person may or may not show. The core features alone will be sufficient for the diagnosis, and will distinguish the disorder from other disorders. Since autism commonly occurs with associated disorders, such as general learning difficulties or a specific language disorder, it is particularly important to 'unpack' those difficulties that are due to autism alone from difficulties common to other groups. However practitioners, especially, cannot ignore associated difficulties and, where these are common associations with autism, Rutter and Bailey (1993) have pointed out that they should also be considered when defining the nature of autism.

In order to count as a 'core' or 'sufficient' symptom of autism a feature must be universal among all those with the autistic syndrome and must not be present in other groups (i.e. it must be specific to autism). Sometimes, non-essential symptoms have even been put forward as candidates for the fundamental 'cause' (i.e. the underlying psychological factor) of autism. Such an example is the 'stimulus over-selectivity hypothesis' of Lovaas *et al.* (1971), which suggested that the difficulties in autism were caused by over-focused attention. This promising theory floundered when research showed that a failure to pay attention to multiple aspects of the environment is associated with severe learning difficulties in general and is not specific to autism. Similar criticisms have been made about more current candidates for the fundamental 'deficit' in autism such as an executive function deficit (Bishop 1993), although there is evidence on either side and the issue is not yet settled (Ozonoff 1995). Even more recently, strong candidates for autism specificity such as difficulties in developing a 'theory of mind' have also been shown to be a feature of other disorders (Peterson and Siegel 1995; Ashford *et al.* 1999).

Some reviews of the epidemiological work conclude that, of the host of symptoms shown by people with autism, many are not specific to autism. So, for example, Wing and Wing (1971) found that, while more than 80 per cent of children with autism in their sample showed a preference for the proximal senses, this preference was also seen in 87 per cent of partially blind and deaf children, 47 per cent of subjects with Downs syndrome and 28 per cent of normally developing children. Since features such as language problems, stereotypies and general learning difficulties can be found in other, non-autistic, people they cannot be primary causes of the specific problems of the individual with autism. Whether there is any single underlying deficit will be discussed later in this handbook.

The autistic spectrum of disorders

Apart from its use for including a number of conditions that may or may not be separate syndromes (such as Asperger's syndrome and Rett's syndrome), the notion of an autistic spectrum also covers the fact that even Kanner's syndrome may not represent a 'pure' and simply defined condition. Kanner's original description of autism has been modified over time with the recognition that the same fundamental disability will have different effects in different individuals in different circumstances and even in the same individual over time. So, while some individuals with autism avoid social contact, like Kanner's cases, others are merely passive, or even actively sociable in an 'active but odd' way (Wing and Gould 1979). The clinical picture of autism has been found to vary between and even within individuals, according to intellectual ability and age. The picture that autism presents, then, varies greatly, and Wing (1988; 1996) introduced the concept of a spectrum of disorders in autism to capture this idea of a range of manifestations of the same fundamental disorder.

This broad definition of autism, based on the triad of impairments, can be seen to underlie the two penultimate versions of the common world systems of classification – ICD-9 (WHO 1978) and especially DSM-IIIR (APA 1987). The most recent systems of classification support a separation out of certain diagnostic categories (such as Asperger's syndrome) from this spectrum (IC-D10 – WHO 1993 – Appendix 1; DSM-IV – APA 1994, Appendix 2). The broad definition is, however, the one most appropriate for education and care, and it is the one followed in the courses associated with this handbook, as indicated above. An international study of the current behaviours and developmental history of a large sample of individuals diagnosed as having high functioning autism or Asperger's syndrome

(Prior *et al.* 1998) concluded that subdivisions within this spectrum were not justified.

Semantic-pragmatic disorder

Before looking at the diagnostic systems that are currently used, it is worth looking at another group that has emerged as a proposed 'diagnostic label' and which is causing more confusion over diagnosis in autism. This group consists of children with a complex language disorder referred to as 'semantic-pragmatic disorder' (Rapin and Allen 1983). Following the naming of this disorder, in 1984 and 1985, letters and reports appeared in the College of Speech Therapists Bulletin, describing groups of children with severe language problems such as comprehension problems, echolalia, verbal conceptual deficits, and an inability to use gestures. In addition, some of the children showed severe early behaviour problems and a lack of symbolic play. Despite obvious similarities, many speech therapists insisted that at least some of these children did not have autism. However, it is not clear to what extent this judgement was based on the claim that the children were not withdrawn, and were affectionate. This suggests that too narrow a conception of autism, or too strong an adherence to a Kanner-type stereotype, may have led these authors to discard a diagnosis of autism prematurely. The fact that they report the children to be egocentric, with poor social skills, so that they are incapable of getting on with their peers, showing affection only to adults, suggests a picture reminiscent of Asperger's original cases. Nothing in the exploration of these children by Bishop and Adams (1989) (and Adams and Bishop 1989) contradicts such an idea.

The author has seen two children diagnosed as having 'semantic-pragmatic disorder' (out of some 40 seen in total) whom she felt had a qualitatively different condition to that of autism, but also one that was different from the usual language-disordered child. In both cases, what was striking (and different from autism) was that both children were aware of their communicative failure, were frustrated by it, and were trying to repair the conversation. To do this, they used rudimentary gestures and mime. They also manipulated the adult in the way that individuals with autism often do but it differed in that they would continually check the results of their manipulations by looking at the adult's face and in particular their eyes. Thus, the distinguishing features from autism appeared to be that the disorder was limited to language functions and the children had an understanding of what communication was and how it worked. They also appeared much more socially aware than children with autism and, although wary, able to join in play with others. It would seem that there might be a language disorder that affects the semantic and pragmatic aspects of language alone. However, if it is accompanied by difficulties in understanding communication itself and a lack of social empathy and restricted imagination, then such individuals would meet the criteria for autism.

Bishop (1989) suggests that a continuum approach should be taken in this area. She suggests not just a single continuum of severity, but two dimensions, in order to capture the differences in the pattern of symptoms between the disorders (see Figure 1.1). This is an advance on other approaches, and Bishop shows great sensitivity to the issue of the diverse manifestations of social handicap. Autism, Asperger's syndrome and semantic-pragmatic disorder can, for her, be represented as different but overlapping areas on a graph where the x-axis is 'meaningful verbal communication', and the y-axis represents 'interests and social relations' (both ranging from 'abnormal' to 'normal'). In this model, autism generally shows severe impairment in both verbal communication and social interests. Asperger's syndrome, on the other hand, shows little impairment of verbal communication but more severe impairment in social behaviour and interests, and semantic-pragmatic disorder shows the reverse – little impairment of social behaviour and interests but relatively severe impairment of verbal communication.

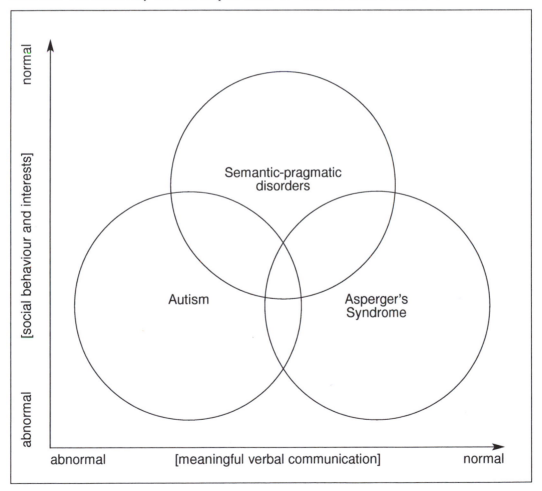

Figure 1.1: Bishop's (1989) model of the relationship between social communicative disorders

However, this presupposes that there is no necessary relation between social and communicative competence – since such a graph would be pointless if all subjects with mild social deficits necessarily had mild communicative deficits and so on. Lister-Brooke and Bowler (1992) have examined this issue and conclude that semantic-pragmatic disorders do not exist as a separate condition outside of the autistic spectrum. Gagnon *et al.* (1997) come to much the same conclusion.

There are continuing arguments within the profession of speech and language therapy about whether the linking of semantic with pragmatic difficulties in this way is helpful for any child (Ripley 1996). If we concede, however, that some children do suffer from both semantic and pragmatic disorders, how does this relate to autistic spectrum disorders? As Wing (1996) suggests, the confusion only exists in diagnosis if we look solely at the language features of the two groups. The semantic-pragmatic group would not be expected to feature in the autistic spectrum as an identified group since the social skills on which the spectrum is based are not central to the condition; semantic-pragmatic children may have good or poor social skills. It is likely that some social skills will be affected by the language impairment, but these are secondary to that impairment and in any case result in a different kind of social impairment to that found in autism.

Other related conditions

There are other conditions that are diagnosed as separate conditions but appear to have similar overlaps with autism and are likely to feature within the autistic spectrum of disorders. Gillberg and Rasmussen (1982) have identified a group of children suffering from disorders of attention, motor coordination and perception (DAMP). These are clearly symptoms that many children within the autistic spectrum (especially those with a diagnosis of Asperger's syndrome) would share, and the question arises of whether one is just talking about a collection of symptoms shared by a number of different diagnostic groups, or a separate syndrome. The same questions could be asked about those people said to be suffering from attention deficit disorder (ADD) or attention deficit hyperactivity disorder (ADHD) (Gordon 1994). In the author's experience, many of the children so diagnosed do suffer also from the social and communicative difficulties that characterise autism (even though the impairments may be subtle) and so they would be classified as being within the autistic spectrum. As with the semantic-pragmatic disorder controversy, if it can be shown that children do have these difficulties without the social and communicative impairments that characterise autism, then there would be a case for saying that those particular individuals do not have autism. That does not mean, however, that they have a separate syndrome of ADD or whatever. The same justification for a syndrome would apply to them as to those with autism – that the symptoms should not only be common to all the members of the group, but should distinguish those members from others i.e. should be specific to the syndrome. It does not seem to this author that the case has been made for any of these conditions, yet, in that respect.

Rett's syndrome (Rett 1966) is a condition where the child shows the diagnostic criteria for autism in the early years (up to and around two years of age) and then appears to become more sociable as a progressive deterioration in mental and physical abilities occurs. Most people would want to include such children within the spectrum, since teaching approaches that are helpful for autism will also apply to this group, but it may be a less useful classification as the child grows to adulthood and the physical and mental limitations are more dominant. This condition, unlike autism, is largely, if not entirely, confined to girls.

People with William's syndrome (Wang and Bellugi 1993) also show a pattern of overlaps with autistic spectrum disorders and, again, might also benefit from being treated as part of the spectrum for treatment purposes. Superficially they have very good language skills but much of it is empty of content and their speech usually exceeds their understanding of language. Social difficulties seem to come from intellectual failures rather than a specific social impairment and yet there are signs of difficulties in seeing social meaning and communicating effectively.

Heller's syndrome is used to describe children who appear to develop normally for at least two years and then suffer a loss of skills, from which they never fully recover, then showing clearly autistic characteristics. This condition may also be referred to as 'disintegrative psychosis'. Again, there is doubt about its status as a separate syndrome (Wing 1996).

Newson (1983; Newson and Le Marechal 1998) has also identified a group she sees as being within the autistic spectrum (at least for treatment purposes) but who have a separate condition she describes as 'pathological demand avoidance syndrome' (PDA). She describes this group as socially aware but unable to tolerate or respond to social demands. She reports that they have good, if not advanced, conversational skills and pretend play but that both these skills are used to divert the need for compliance. The evidence for this syndrome remains at present anecdotal and it is difficult to distinguish this behaviour from learnt avoidance of difficult social demands by the more able child with autism. Some practitioners report that the clinical descriptions given help them make sense of some children in a way that the broader 'autism' diagnosis does not, but the question of reliability and validity of such a syndrome remains unanswered.

For a long time autism was believed to have strong links with schizophrenia, and indeed up to the late 1960s was used interchangeably with a diagnosis of childhood schizophrenia (see Rutter 1978, for a review of this confusion). Since then, it has been shown that autism is not connected with schizophrenia in any straightforward way (Kay and Kolvin 1987). Schizophrenia may share some of the same behavioural features as autism, especially in an adult, but the course of the illness will be very different from the developmental pattern of autism. The key distinguishing feature is the hallucinations and delusions that characterise schizophrenia but not autism. Certainly, it is not the case that people with autism are more likely to become schizophrenic, nor is schizophrenia particularly prevalent among the relations of people with autism. However, links between research into schizophrenia and into autism still exist. Frith and Frith (1991) have pointed out the similarities between the negative symptoms of schizophrenia and the developmental difficulties seen in autism. They suggest that a similar psychological deficit might underlie both disorders. The great differences in appearance of the two disorders would be expected; breakdown of a mature psychological system will not have the same effects as the lack of (or disturbance in) a psychological component from the start of development.

A second link between schizophrenia and autism has come about through Asperger's syndrome. Wolff and her colleagues have studied a group of children with what they call 'schizoid personality disorder', who are oversensitive, emotionally detached, solitary, rigid/obsessive, lacking in empathy, and prone to bizarre thoughts. They claim that these are the sort of children Asperger was describing in his 1944 paper. Wolff argues, therefore, that Asperger's syndrome does not belong within the autistic spectrum, but rather is part of a group of schizotypal or schizoid disorders.

Wolff's initial description of schizoid personality disorder, in 1964, did not refer to Asperger's paper (Wolff and Chess 1964). However, she was careful to distinguish her group from children with autism on the basis of three features. She claimed that the schizoid children – unlike those with autism – did *not* show any of the following: late/poor language acquisition with echolalia; a lack of emotional responsiveness and gaze avoidance; and ritualistic behaviour. It is not clear, however, precisely how her group could fit her criteria for schizoid personality disorder without any of the above problems. Her criteria include 'emotional detachment' and 'rigidity, sometimes to the point of obsession', and she describes the children as using odd 'metaphorical' language. As before, the terms are too vague to allow a principled distinction to be made. The difference between the groups, then, appears to revolve around severity and age of onset – two factors which are intimately connected (since milder impairments take longer to reach parents' attention) and which provide no evidence of qualitative rather than quantitative differences.

It is hard to see anything in the diagnostic criteria which Wolff and Cull (1986) propose for the disorder, which could in principle distinguish schizoid personality disorder from autism (at the higher ability end of the spectrum). They list core features of schizoid personality disorder as follows:

- solitariness;
- impaired empathy and emotional detachment;
- increased sensitivity, amounting to paranoia;
- unusual styles of communication; and
- rigidity of mental set e.g. single-minded pursuit of special interests.

Only 'increased sensitivity' from the list above would look out of place in a description of an able child with autism. Wolff and Cull claim that Asperger's syndrome is a severe form of schizoid personality disorder, the latter being a broader category covering cases not fitting Asperger's syndrome, and overlapping with ICD-9's 'schizoid paranoid personality disorder'. An important question, then, is how are the schizoid personality disorder children who *do not* have Asperger's syndrome different from those who *do*? This is not made clear, and the implication is once again that the difference is in severity. The question remains, however: does Asperger's syndrome belong with schizoid personality disorder or with autism? To decide this we need to look at the implications of both possibilities. Schizoid personality disorder is seen by Wolff as a personality variant, rather than a pathology (a view interestingly similar to Asperger's own, concerning his cases, and echoed by the author in pleading for differences rather than defects (Jordan 1998; Jordan and Powell 1995a). However, the diagnosis suggests connections with schizophrenia or a milder, but characteristically similar, disorder. Research is currently being conducted on the differential diagnosis of individuals with Asperger's syndrome, autism (without additional learning difficulties) and schizoid personality disorder. Wolff (1995), in her latest description of the individuals she now refers to as 'loners', accepts that they would fall within the autistic spectrum of disorders.

As Wing (1984) says, while making links between Asperger's syndrome and autism has useful implications for management, a diagnosis of schizoid personality disorder is 'distressing without being constructive'. She also makes the important point that the latter diagnosis is as yet vague and while it may include some people with Asperger's syndrome it also includes many with quite different disorders. An interesting point arises here concerning whether individuals with Asperger's syndrome can develop paranoia. Paranoia would seem to indicate some awareness of mental states (both one's own and other people's) in order to feel that one is being persecuted. However, the author has witnessed a young man with Asperger's syndrome develop paranoia and it seems to her to differ from the kind of paranoia found in schizophrenia. In the case of the young man with Asperger's syndrome, his paranoia stemmed not so much from his own feelings of persecution or his imaginings of another's wish to persecute him as from his own lack of understanding of mental states and consequent inability to predict behaviour.

One of his classmates had once attacked him (not very seriously) but this had been very frightening. He then began to watch this other lad very carefully, trying to see from his behaviour when such an attack might occur again. His fear increased, fed by his inability to make meaningful connections between behavioural acts and thus he saw many behaviours as potential precursors to an aggressive act. He thus built up a pattern of wariness and unreasonable expectations in relation to this other lad that looked on the surface very like the behaviour of someone with classically paranoid delusions. His 'delusions', however, did not arise from his imagination but from his inability to understand the motivations of others and so predict their behaviour.

Many of the symptoms of clinical depression can appear to be like those of autism, although it is perhaps more common to have the autism missed in favour of a diagnosis of depression, rather than the other way around. What is even more common is the failure to entertain a dual diagnosis. In that case, the adult with autism may suffer from clinical depression (more common it is thought in the

Asperger's group, or perhaps just easier to recognise in that group), but not have it treated, because symptoms are put down to autism. Able people with autism are also often misdiagnosed as having obsessive compulsive disorder (OCD), although, again, this can co-occur with autism. It can be difficult to recognise when the autistic routines have switched to being compulsions but the key difference lies in the 'driven' nature of a compulsion. An individual with autism who is engaging in an obsessive ritual will find the ritual calming, although they may have difficulty in moving to something else and will become very anxious if the ritual is disturbed. A compulsion, however, is not soothing in any way and the person appears unhappy and worried even during its performance. They often welcome help at this stage in 'freeing' themselves from its tyranny.

Wing (1996) feels that diagnoses such as 'schizoid personality disorder' may be alternative ways of looking at autistic spectrum disorders, especially in adults, although there is not a complete overlap between 'schizoid disorder' and autism. It is also difficult to see the difference (from the clinical descriptions given) between this category and Newson's PDA. It may be that different clinicians are using different terms for very similar, if not identical, conditions. In practical terms, as discussed below, this handbook and the associated courses take the position that the broad definition of autistic spectrum disorders is the most helpful one to consider when looking at practical implications.

Asperger

As discussed above, at the same time that Kanner was identifying a new 'autistic' syndrome in America, an Austrian physician Hans Asperger was also identifying a similar group. In 1944 he published a dissertation concerning 'autistic psychopathy' in childhood. Because he published in German and in the middle of the Second World War, it has taken nearly 50 years for Asperger's original paper to appear in translation in English (Frith 1991a), although his work attracted interest, following a publication by Wing in 1981. Asperger, however, did not just duplicate the insights of Kanner (1943), but produced striking ones of his own.

Nevertheless, Kanner's and Asperger's descriptions are surprisingly similar in many ways, especially when one considers that each was totally unaware of the other's work. Their choice of the term 'autistic' reflects their common belief that the child's social problems were the most important and characteristic feature of the disorder. This term comes from Bleuler (1908) who used the word, from the Greek 'autos' meaning self, to describe the social withdrawal seen in adults with schizophrenia. Both Kanner and Asperger believed the social handicap in autism to be innate (in Kanner's words) or constitutional (as Asperger put it) and to persist through life into adulthood. In addition, Kanner and Asperger noted the children's poor eye contact, their stereotypies of word and movement, and their marked resistance to change. The two authors report the common finding of isolated special interests, often in bizarre and idiosyncratic objects or topics. Both seem to have been struck by the attractive appearance of the children they describe.

Kanner and Asperger make a point of distinguishing the disorder they describe from schizophrenia, on the basis of two features:

1. Autism starts from poor or absent interpersonal skills and usually improves over time, whereas schizophrenia represents a period of normal development followed by deterioration.

2. Autism is characterised by the absence of hallucinations, whereas this is a key positive symptom in schizophrenia.

Both Kanner and Asperger also believed that they had observed similar traits – of social withdrawal or incompetence, obsessive delight in routine, and the pursuit of special interests to the exclusion of all else – in the parents of many of their patients. As a matter of interest, Kanner identified interpersonal difficulties primarily in mothers, whereas Asperger noted them in fathers and saw autism as reflecting an extreme version of traits found primarily in males.

Asperger was particularly interested in a group of able young men with good structural language skills, whom he followed into adulthood. Thus, although he identified the same group as Kanner, his name has come to be associated with this latter group and it is the more able who carry the label 'Asperger's syndrome'. The differential diagnosis of this group (and some of the controversy surrounding it) will be covered in other parts of the courses.

Wing (1981) introduced the diagnosis of Asperger's syndrome in an attempt to gain recognition for those very able people with autism who do not fit the Kanner stereotype of being silent and aloof. She listed six diagnostic criteria based on Asperger (1944):

1. Speech – no delay, but content odd, pedantic, stereotyped;

2. Nonverbal communication – little facial expression, monotone voice, inappropriate gesture;

3. Social interactions – not reciprocal, lacking in empathy;

4. Resistance to change – enjoys repetitive activities;

5. Motor coordination – gait and posture odd, gross movements clumsy, sometimes stereotypies; and

6. Skills and interests – good rote memory, circumscribed special interests.

In addition to these, she reports Asperger's claim that this disorder is more frequent in males than females, and rarely recognised before the third year of life. Wing modified these criteria, according to her own clinical experience, making three changes:

1. Language delay – only half of the group Wing would label, 'Asperger's syndrome' developed language at the normal age;

2. Early development – before the age of three years, the child may be odd, e.g. no joint attention; and

3. Creativity – Wing claims these children are not creative, and for example do not show true pretend play. Rather than being original, their thought is simply inappropriate.

Asperger's syndrome, then, for Wing, forms a means of extending the autistic spectrum to previously unrecognised, subtle degrees. Her paper suggested that the differences between Kanner-type autism and Asperger's syndrome were to be explained by a difference in severity alone; that is, those with Asperger's syndrome are the same as those with high ability and autism. Some authors have denied the need for the label Asperger's syndrome (e.g. Volkmar *et al.* 1989), on the grounds that forming subgroups within autism does not aid the recognition of the range of manifestations of autism. However, a number of clinicians have adopted the label, and found it useful practically if not theoretically. Most researchers have followed Wing's suggestions fairly closely in their diagnostic criteria for Asperger's syndrome. By the end of the 1980s, something of a consensus seemed to have emerged. Burd and Kerbeshian (1987) offered five features of Asperger's syndrome subjects:

1. Speech – pedantic, stereotyped, aprosodic[1];

2. Impaired nonverbal communication;

3. Social interaction – peculiar, lacks empathy;

4. Circumscribed interests – repetitive activities or savant skills; and

5. Movements – clumsy or stereotyped.

Tantam (1988a; 1988b), looking at adults with Asperger's syndrome, proposed the same core disabilities in communication, socialisation, and nonverbal expression, with conspicuous clumsiness and special interests. Gillberg (1989) required all six of his criteria for a diagnosis of Asperger's syndrome to be made. These criteria are broadly the five used by Tantam and Burd and Kerbeshian, plus a tendency for the individual to impose routine or their special interest on their entire life (recalling Wing's fourth criterion, resistance to change).

The diagnosis of Asperger's syndrome has been discussed largely by clinicians, and this may explain the loose approach to the specification of diagnostic criteria. Interest in this diagnosis began primarily in its use as a label for a type of person who had hitherto been hard to fit into existing categories, but whom the clinician felt was an easily recognised type. A parent explained why she liked the label by saying that before that, her son had been described as having 'mild autism' and she felt that was a very misleading description for the severity of his difficulties. The diagnosis is as yet quite poorly defined, making it hard to assess the results of experimental studies (e.g. Ozonoff *et al.* 1991a) investigating differences between so-called 'Asperger's syndrome' subjects and subjects with autism who do not receive this diagnosis. With the two classification systems (see Appendix 1 and Appendix 2) now defining Asperger's syndrome separately, this objection will no longer hold, although arguments about the validity of the diagnosis remain. As the

---

[1]aprosodic: speech lacking the musical qualities of stress, intonation and rhythm.

reader will note, the two systems are not entirely in agreement over the diagnostic criteria, and this remains a problem.

The criteria for Asperger's syndrome in ICD-10 (WHO 1993) seem to define Asperger's syndrome as autism without the language and cognitive impairments. This carries the theoretical implication that the language and cognitive impairments in autism are not fundamental to the disorder and do not arise from the same psychological deficit as the social difficulties. The implication is that the language and cognitive impairments are additional handicaps, which can be present with or without autism, and leave the picture of core (i.e. social?) handicaps unchanged in their absence. This is a rather large assumption and goes against what this author has argued in terms of the pattern of disabilities defining the autistic spectrum. Of course, a clearer distinction between structural language skills and those associated with communication (i.e. the pragmatic aspects of language) would remove much confusion. For example, the phrase 'communicative phrases' begs the question of whether language phrases used non-communicatively (as is often the case in autism) would count or not.

At present, then, Asperger's syndrome is probably a term more useful for the practical needs of the clinician, parents and/or the individuals themselves. If the individuals in question were simply given a diagnosis of autism, and turned to the literature on the subject, they may find that the picture given (especially in terms of likely prognosis) is unnecessarily gloomy. Moreover, this does not reflect the real prognosis for individuals with good structural language skills and no additional learning difficulties. As the term becomes more widely used, there is a more representative literature emerging that reflects the wide spectrum of ability within the autistic spectrum. Experimental work to date (Kugler 1998) would seem to indicate that the Asperger's syndrome label is used to mark a subgroup of autism which is at the more able end of the spectrum in terms of social and communication handicaps. How distinct the subgroup is remains a matter for debate and research. In general, it can be said that the evidence for a clear distinction between children with autism and those with Asperger's syndrome in terms of cognitive and social functioning is not entirely convincing (Gillberg 1992; Wing 1996) although others would argue that it was (Trevarthen *et al.* 1996). In spite of distinctions made by the two current diagnostic systems, many would feel that the main differences at a practical level between those with Asperger's syndrome and other autistic conditions lie in the good intellectual ability and structural language skills of the former group. Certainly, most would feel that treatment approaches would be similar (e.g. Jordan and Powell 1995a), while taking account of these individual differences in general and linguistic ability.

A definition for practice

When we consider the special needs of individuals, whether for educational placement or adult care, we need to consider all those who will have specific needs in relation to the curriculum or programme offered, the teaching approach and the environment. As indicated above, this should cover all those who fall within the spectrum of autistic disorders. There will be a great range of intellectual ability within this group, from those who have additional profound and multiple learning difficulties through to those within the normal range of intelligence and who would be described as having Asperger's syndrome or as being 'more able'. The range of difficulties in the triad of impairments would then be:

1. Difficulties in interacting with both carers/teachers and peers. This will include the classically 'aloof' individual, but also those who respond to social interaction, although they may be unable to initiate it, through to the 'active but odd' individual who seeks social interaction but is socially naive and cannot quite 'get it right'.

2. Difficulties in all aspects of communication. The autistic problem concerns communication rather than language *per se*. At one end, this will mean an individual who has good grammar and phonology and may speak fluently, but whose speech has odd intonation and may show echolalia (repeating) and 'reversal' of pronouns (at least when young) and whose understanding of speech is literal. There will be difficulties in holding conversations, with the individual with autism talking 'at' rather than 'to' or 'with' people. There will also be difficulties in understanding and using facial expressions, body postures and communicative gestures. At the other end of the spectrum, the individual will have the same difficulties in understanding all forms of communication, but will have no speech and will not easily compensate with sign or communicative gesture. Communication, at all levels of ability, is directed at having needs met, rather than sharing information or interests.

3. Difficulties in flexible thinking and behaviour. This is shown in repetitive stereotyped behaviour and, in some individuals, an extreme reaction to change in expected situations or routines. Play is not socially creative or symbolic (although symbolic play acts may be copied or developed in isolation from others) and tends to be isolated, often involving spinning objects or a fascination with light or angles. The more able show these difficulties in their development of obsessive interests or 'hobbies' that are pursued at the expense of everything else. Understanding of fiction is minimal, even in the more able. Learning is by rote.

The special needs of any individual will, of course, not be determined solely by developmental difficulties but will be the result of interactions between abilities and disabilities and the learning environment. As the child grows to adulthood, the effect of education and the kind of experiences the person has had will have an increasing role in determining his current behaviour and ways of thinking.

Range of 'labels'

Because of these difficulties in diagnosis, professionals might use a range of descriptions for someone classified as being on the autistic spectrum. Such descriptions will include 'autistic tendencies', 'autistic features', 'Kanner's syndrome', 'Asperger's syndrome', 'autistic behaviours', 'atypical autism' and so on. Sometimes, one of the diagnostic features is emphasised ('semantic pragmatic disorder', for example, or 'rigid and obsessional behaviour'). In such cases, it will be necessary to look at the other two classifying features to determine whether this is an autistic spectrum disorder, or whether difficulties are limited to that one area of functioning. It must be remembered that autism is diagnosed by the existence of the full triad of impairments (although the diagnosis of 'atypical autism' may be given with just two of the triad of symptoms present) and the particular manifestation of the triad will vary among individuals. There are no behaviours *per se* that, by their presence or absence, indicate autism; it is the overall pattern and the underlying difficulties that define autism. All the symptoms and behaviours, as has been noted, modify with time and so the diagnosis of an adult cannot be made reliably on the basis of current behaviour alone. It is important to note the developmental path and to look for the possibly more subtle difficulties that will remain even after a lifetime's learning and adjustment.

Conclusion

Autism, as we have seen, is a relatively 'new' diagnosis, although the disorder itself has probably always existed. A great deal has been learnt about the syndrome over the last decades, but much still remains to be understood. In the next sections, the current state of knowledge concerning the biological, behavioural and psychological understanding of autism will be reviewed, and the effects this knowledge should have on provision for the person with autism will be discussed. The value of a diagnosis of an autistic spectrum disorder, in making that provision, will be argued, but the case for remembering that each person is an individual will also be made.

Further reading

Bishop, D.V.M. (1989) 'Autism, Asperger's syndrome and semantic-pragmatic disorder: Where are the boundaries?' *British Journal of Disorders of Communication* **24**, 107–21.

Frith, U. (1991a) 'Asperger and his syndrome', in Frith, U. (ed.) *Autism and Asperger Syndrome,* Cambridge: Cambridge University Press.

Kanner, L. (1943) 'Autistic disturbances of affective contact', *Nervous Child* **2**, 217–50.

Kanner, L. and Eisenberg, L. (1956) 'Early infantile autism 1943–1955' *American Journal of Orthopsychiatry* **26**, 55–65.

Nagy, J. and Szatmari, P. (1986) 'A chart review of schizotypal personality disorders in children' *Journal of Autism and Developmental Disorders* **16**, 351–67.

Volkmar, F. R. (1998) 'Categorical approaches to the diagnosis of autism', *Autism: the International Journal of Research and Practice,* **2**, 45–59.

Wing, L. (1991) 'The relationship between Asperger's syndrome and Kanner's autism', in Frith, U. (ed.) *Autism and Asperger Syndrome.* Cambridge: Cambridge University Press.

Wing, L. (1996) *The Autistic Spectrum.* London: Constable.

Chapter 2

The Importance of Diagnosis in Education and Care

The medical model and inclusion

In education in particular, but also in social services practice, there has been a move away from what is called the 'medical model'. This reflects a move towards a view of disability as arising not so much from 'within-person' factors but from the way people are treated. The argument is that, if we try to look for explanations of behaviour and development solely in terms of the characteristics of a condition such as autism, this will lead us to ignore individual characteristics (treating the person as 'autistic' rather than a person with autism, in effect). Even more importantly, we may ignore the fact that the social situation and attitudes of others may be creating the difficulties we observe. Not being able to speak Japanese is not a learning difficulty or a special need in England, but can become one if we move to Japan (which the author can verify from her recent experience!).

This is an important perspective that we must consider. Later modules on the courses will explore ways in which teaching or treatment approaches can and do affect the behaviour and learning potential of individuals with autism. Yet autism is one condition where observation of behaviour as the basis for treatment is likely to mislead. As this handbook will show, the professional and the carer need to have some understanding of what is underlying the behaviour if treatment is to be effective. Each individual will react differently according to his/her own pattern of strengths and weaknesses, but, as the author hopes to show, knowing about autism will help put those individual aspects in the correct explanatory context.

It has been argued (Booth 1991) that the very act of diagnosis in education is discriminatory, and locates the difficulties the child experiences in school to within-child factors, rather than to the wider interactive context to which they belong. One presumes the same arguments would be made for adults in service provision. The basis of this argument is that diagnosis automatically sets an individual apart and as such is inimical to inclusive policies. However, Jordan and Powell (1994) have argued that there can be no true inclusion that does not include the needs of all from the start; it is not a matter of trying to integrate a group into a system whose very nature has excluded them. Inclusion, therefore, depends on recognising and allowing for differences in the way individuals think and learn and it is only when these differences are addressed in autism that true inclusion can be attempted.

Recognition of needs, then, should lead to the provision of 'prosthetic environments' for autism. The term 'prosthetic environment' applies to one that favours normalisation. Prosthetic devices are ones that do not alter the fundamental disability but enable the person to act as if it were not there, and thus prevent disabilities from becoming handicaps. The most obvious and common example is a pair of spectacles. Prosthetic organisation of the environment for someone with autism might include:

- optimum room size with flexible use of space;
- flexible timetables and programme content, in a communicable form;
- monitoring and 'trouble-shooting' of problems; and
- accessible communication systems.

The use and misuse of labels

Booth (1983) offers two justifications for segregated provision in schools: the mental/physical characteristics of the pupils and their learning needs; and that specialised resources need to be centralised.

Autism might (although, not inevitably) require specialist provision on both those counts, both at school and in later adult provision. However, as later texts will emphasise, it is not location or segregation itself that is important, but how needs are identified and met and the most appropriate setting for this to occur in each individual case (Jordan and Powell 1995b).

There is a case to be made against the use of labels. The term 'diagnosogenesis' has been used to describe a process of labelling whereby ascription of deviance or disorder to a person creates or exacerbates that disorder or deviance. Yet a young man with Asperger's syndrome (Exley, personal communication) has described the misery of his school and college days where his needs were not recognised or met and makes an equally powerful plea for the use of the diagnosis of autism. He argues that it is not a label, but a signpost. In other words, knowing that someone has autism will not tell you exactly how to treat that person or what and how to teach them, but it will give a signpost to where one can look.

Diagnosis as a clue to fundamental psychological functioning

An understanding of the fundamental difficulties faced by individuals at the psychological level is crucial in developing a programme for them and a teaching approach that addresses each individual's needs (Powell and Jordan, 1993a). Here, the assumption is made that all those who work with individuals with autism (whatever their professional background) are in effect 'teachers' and are engaged in 'education' whether this takes place in a school, a college, a residence or in the community. Responding at the level of behaviour only may lead to unhelpful or even damaging misinterpretations of the individual's behaviour and a consequent failure to identify true needs. Each individual will still be an individual and will need careful observation to determine his/her level of understanding and capacity, but that observation needs to be informed by the knowledge of what particular difficulties the individual is facing in making sense of his/her world.

One way of exploring the importance of identifying diagnostic features at the level of psychology rather than behaviour is to look at how behaviour can be illuminated by one such possible 'explanation' at this level. A possible contender for a fundamental psychological difficulty was identified by Frith (1989a) as a problem in developing understanding of their own and others' mental states. It was not just that they did not understand what people were thinking or feeling (which would be true of individuals with emotional and behavioural difficulties) but that they did not understand that people *are* thinking and feeling i.e. have a mind. In individuals with Asperger's syndrome, this may still be an area of difficulty but the more able might come to that understanding, albeit at a much later stage than in normal development (nine-14 years as opposed to four in normal development: Happé 1995a). However, the route by which they reach this understanding may be different to the normal developmental route and the development may stop short of the next stage of understanding – that people can have thoughts or feelings about their (or others') thoughts or feelings.

This is not to accept the argument that people with autism have a 'theory of mind' deficit (that will be discussed in later sections). It is simply to show that looking beyond behaviour to psychological functioning may be a much more reliable guide to the nature of autism and to its treatment. It may be that there is an even more fundamental difficulty in searching for meaning, or seeing coherence, or establishing intersubjectivity or agency, underlying autistic difficulties (Frith 1989a; Hobson 1993a; Russell 1996). It remains true, however, that difficulties in understanding mental states still offer a coherent explanation for many of the problems in autism, even though there are arguments (which will be explored later) about how truly fundamental this difficulty is, and whether or not it depends on other factors.

A fundamental difficulty in understanding thoughts and feelings would lead to:

- difficulty in predicting behaviour → finding people aversive;
- difficulty understanding emotions → lack of empathy, poor emotional expression;
- no understanding of what others can be expected to know → language pedantic or ambiguous;
- no idea that one can affect how others think or feel → no conscience, no motivation to please, no communicative intent;
- no sharing of attention → idiosyncratic reference; and
- lack of understanding of social conventions including conversational strategies → no signalling with eyes, poor interaction, poor turn-taking, poor topic maintenance.

If one is to affect the way an individual thinks, as well as behaves, there is a need for a remedial approach as well as a compensatory one. A remedial approach is one that helps the individual to learn and think more effectively and does not just teach compensatory skills or provide 'access' to (in the case of school-aged children) the National Curriculum or a programme of 'normal' activities or pursuits as an adult. The key aspects of a specialist programme that would take account of these fundamental difficulties might be that it:

- demonstrates an understanding of the condition;
- has special provision, such as teaching for integration, or specialist content (e.g. a communication rather than a language focus, helping to create a self-identity); or
- includes a specialised environment (e.g. visual structure to minimise stress, as in TEACCH).

Its aim would not be to remediate in a biological sense i.e. 'to cure' but to provide compensatory routes to learning at a psychological rather than a behavioural level. Fundamental to a 'remedial' approach or an effective compensatory one, is the recognition of the importance of understanding the way the 'autistic' learner learns and understands the world.

The central role of education

Whatever biological disturbances are uncovered in autism, there must be a route through which behaviour, and the way individuals perceive, think and learn, is affected. Even if in the future diets or drugs are completely effective in restoring normal brain functioning, there will be sequelae in the results of the disturbed perceptions and cognitions that have gone before. Education will be needed to address those disturbances. The fact is that biological research, while exciting, is a long way from offering a 'cure' for autism and education remains the one treatment approach with the best track record for dealing with the difficulties associated with autism. Thus access to education is not just a statutory right for people with autism, but it also can have a central role in remediating the effects of autism (not curing it) and improving the quality of life for individuals with autism throughout their life span.

Of course, there are reasons why education often seems to have a Cinderella role in the treatment of individuals with autism. Prime among these is the fact that some form of education is a statutory right for children with autism and so, while searching for the right education for their child is a constant and pressing preoccupation of parents, education as such is not seen as a treatment for the condition. There is also the confusion between education and schooling and the situation where services for children carry the label 'education' whereas those for adults have the label 'care', as if the two processes were not (or should not be) features of all services for individuals with autism, throughout life. Certainly there is evidence that individuals with autism continue to learn and to make cognitive gains throughout life and the role of 'care' staff must surely include an educational bias in enabling this process.

The final reason has more to do with the fundamental nature of education and the fact that most systems of education (in the UK, at least) are modest in the claims they would make in respect of what can be achieved with pupils with autism. It may be honest and realistic to point to the fact that education can be (and usually is) successful in building up skills and diminishing unwanted behaviour. However, at the end of the educational process, the individual will still be an individual with autism, albeit a more skilled and less disturbing one. However honest or realistic, such claims may seem a little inadequate to parents, when they realise the millions of separate skills that will need to be taught. This is apart from the difficulties of teaching some of those skills, such as social skills or communication, without the understanding to underpin them and the problems of predicting adaptations that will be needed for all future environments.

The educational challenge

'Deficits' or 'challenges'?

As indicated above, it has become part of educational orthodoxy in the UK that the 'medical model' of education is outdated and that teachers do not need to consider within-child factors (in some cases, at all) related to psychological functioning but should instead base their teaching on observable behaviour. This is problematic for any kind of teaching, but it is disastrous for autism. In the latter case, the teacher will be misled by using his/her own understandings of the world to intuit those of the person with autism, and assumptions that similar behaviour requires similar treatment may lead to potentially damaging approaches. In autism effective teaching and care must be based on a thorough understanding of the condition. There will still be a need to study each individual to determine his/her special needs (a product of abilities as well as disabilities, alongside personality and history and current situation) since there is such a wide variety of needs among those with autism. Unless the practitioner is informed about the likely areas of difficulty in autism, however, s/he is unlikely to hit upon these by chance or merely by observing behaviour.

While recognising the very profound nature of the difficulties faced by people with autism in living in our socially dominated and culturally biased world, it is fundamentally '*un*educational' always to talk of 'deficits', which conjure up images of irreversible damage or absences. However, if instead of a 'social deficit', for example, we talked of the individual with autism being 'socially challenged' then the image alters to one of a situation where a challenge (at least in principle) can be overcome. This may be clumsily 'politically correct' (and for an alternative view of the problems of 'politically correct' language in autism, see Wing 1996), however, it is not only more optimistic about what might be done educationally (and thus much more in the spirit of education itself) but is actually a better reflection of the true state of affairs. It is seldom, if ever, the case that an individual with autism has a complete deficit in any area of development; rather, it is the case that they do not do things spontaneously or naturally or intuitively (e.g. joint attention, spontaneous play,) but they can do so (or they can perform with very similar behaviour) if prompted, cued or taught.

The real deficit may not be the absence of any particular skill or ability, but a more fundamental problem that prevents the child from developing this skill or ability naturally, without having to learn it. Practitioners need to move from a situation where they are 'allowing' for these deficits in their teaching to one where they recognise the 'challenge' that these difficulties present to the individual's learning but they also try to identify ways of helping the individual meet and overcome those challenges. We know many able individuals with autism overcome or meet these challenges more or less unaided, so we know that autism itself is not a barrier to this being done, although the presence of additional difficulties, such as general learning difficulties, will make an already difficult task far more difficult. If we succeed in our teaching, we will not have 'cured' autism, because the original difficulty or deficit remains. The many ordinary everyday aspects of living which are accomplished by us without effort or thought, will still require considerable amounts of both by the individual with autism and his/her 'teacher'.

The development of principled strategies

If it is necessary for the practitioner to work at the level of psychological functioning, then it is important to see how knowledge about such functioning (allied to the psychological 'explanations' that are associated with them) can be translated into more effective strategies for teaching. This will be done later in this handbook when considering psychological understandings.

Further reading

Jordan, R.R. and Powell, S.D. (1994) 'Whose curriculum? Critical notes on integration and entitlement', *European Journal of Special Needs Education*, **9**, 27–39.

Jordan, R.R. and Powell, S.D. (1995a) *Understanding and Teaching Children with Autism*. Chichester: John Wiley and Sons.

Morgan, H. (1996) *Adults with Autism*. Cambridge: Cambridge University Press.

Powell, S.D. and Jordan, R.R. (1993a) 'Diagnosis, intuition and autism', *British Journal of Special Education*, **20**, 26–9.

Chapter 3

Autism and Behaviour

Behavioural criteria for diagnosis

As indicated in the Introduction, autism is defined on the basis of behaviour. This is essential in a condition where there is no (at least as yet) identifiable biological marker for the condition. As we will see below, the evidence for a biological base for autism is increasingly certain. Yet this evidence also suggests that there is unlikely to be a single biological factor accounting for all autistic spectrum disorders, and so diagnosis will depend on these behavioural criteria, at least for the foreseeable future.

Defining a condition on the basis of behavioural criteria, however, does not mean that there are particular behaviours that are, of themselves, 'autistic'. There is nothing that someone with autism does that is not also found in other groups, including groups of people with normal development. It may be that there are some things that they do *not* do, however, and the absence of these 'key' behaviours may be an effective indicator of autism, as we will see in the section on diagnostic instruments below. It is important to note that one cannot look at any single behaviour, or even any single absence of a behaviour, and use this to decide whether someone does or does not have autism. One cannot say, for example 'He does not look at people, therefore he has autism' or conversely, 'He makes good eye contact, so he cannot have autism'. Lack of eye contact is common in autism but it is also a feature of other conditions such as fragile-X (with or without associated autism) or clinical depression. Equally, some children with autism only go through a fleeting phase of avoiding eye contact, and many are subject to training that encourages them to make eye contact. One cannot then use the fact that an older child or an adult makes eye contact to say anything about the existence of autism. It would be more pertinent to ask whether their use of eye contact is appropriate and whether they appear to understand *why* they are making eye contact.

It follows from the above, then, that what one is looking for in autism is a particular pattern of abilities and disabilities, all of which must be present for a correct diagnosis. Since this is the case, it makes no sense to talk of 'autistic features' and still less of 'autistic tendencies', whatever they might be. The fact that these labels appear in the diagnostic notes of many professionals may be because they have misunderstood the nature of the diagnostic process and its basis in the overall pattern of behaviour, or it may be that they are uncertain of the diagnosis (either in reality, or because they judge that it would not be helpful to make a full diagnosis at this time). The safest assumption for the practitioner, faced with such a 'diagnosis', is to assume the individual is within the autistic spectrum. To treat someone without autism as if they had it is likely to be less damaging in most cases than to ignore someone's very real difficulties because their diagnosis is not secure. There will be exceptions to this rule, usually among the most able, where the individuals themselves or their families find it easier to conceive of themselves (or their children) as having certain 'traits' or 'features' rather than having a definite label of 'autism'. Even then, it will be worth the practitioner looking at the supposedly 'non-autistic' areas of the triad, since there may well be subtle difficulties that have been overlooked in the diagnostic process.

Epidemiological issues

The epidemiological basis for autism

The evidence for autistic spectrum disorders at a behavioural level, then, depends on this pattern of characteristic features (as exemplified by the triad of impairments) occurring at more than chance level in the population. The fundamental work in establishing that this was the case, and the work that led to the formulation of the triad, was done by Wing and Gould (1979) who conducted an epidemiological survey of all children living in the Camberwell area. From the total population aged under 15 years (35,000), all children known to the social, educational or health services (914 in all) were screened. They used a behavioural screening battery collecting key information in all-important areas of development. Children were selected from this group if they had severe learning difficulties and/or if they showed one of the following: social impairment, verbal and non-verbal language impairment, and repetitive/stereotyped activities.

The screening resulted in a group of 132 children, all of whom attended special schools, and who ranged in age from two to 18 years. The children were observed

---

Table 3.1: Subject breakdown in the Camberwell study

Total pop. <15 yr.	Known	SLD/triad
35,000	914	132
		58 = Socially appropriate
		74 = Socially impaired

and given medical and psychological tests, and their carers were interviewed with the Handicap, Behaviour and Skills Schedule (Wing and Gould 1978). The group was divided on the basis of social behaviour. Fifty-eight children were judged to have appropriate social interaction (for their mental age) and 74 to be socially impaired (of whom 17 had classic autism, by Kanner and Eisenberg's (1956) criteria of social aloofness and elaborate routines). The groups did not differ significantly in age, but there were significantly more males in the socially impaired group than the sociable group. In addition, there were significant differences in communicative and play behaviours in the two groups. Ninety per cent of the impaired group (versus only 50 per cent of the sociable subjects) were either mute or echolalic at the time of the interview, and 97 per cent of the impaired group (versus 24 per cent of the sociable group) showed no, or only repetitive, pretend play. In the sociable group, all subjects showed pretend play except those with a language comprehension age below 20 months – a mental age below which pretence would not be expected, since normally developing children only manifest this ability at that age.

By contrast, the socially impaired subjects with a language comprehension age over 20 months still showed language deficits and poverty of pretend play. Wing and Gould also concluded that all the children with social impairments had repetitive stereotyped behaviour, and found that almost all had absence, or abnormalities, of communication (although the authors do not distinguish language from communication very well) and pretend activities (although, again, the authors do not use the term 'pretend play' and classify both functional and true symbolic play as 'symbolic'). The differences between the sociable and non-sociable groups with these other behaviours were highly significant. Thus the study showed a marked tendency for these problems to occur together. The association between these three areas of disability also emerges if the Camberwell sample is divided on the basis of types of play shown (Wing *et al.* 1977: Table 3.2 below) rather than social functioning.

This association between deficits in socialisation, communication and imagination (in the terms used by the authors) was also found in a group of 761 adults in a mental subnormality hospital (Shah *et al.* 1982: Table 3.3, below). Abnormal speech was shown by 75 per cent of those with social impairment, versus 14 per cent of those showing social interaction appropriate for their mental age.

Table 3.2: Association of social disability with communication impairments and rigidity in thinking and behaviour, in Wing and Gould's (1979) sample

Subject group	Mute/Echolalic	No/repetitive pretend play
Socially impaired	90 %	97 %
Socially appropriate	50 %	24 %

Lack of symbolic or functional activity – including lack of interest in books and films, lack of concern for others, and lack of mental age-appropriate play – was found in 73 per cent of the socially impaired group, and only 8 per cent of the sociable group. It appears, then, that difficulties in social understanding, in communication, and in flexibility in thinking and behaviour tend to co-occur in the same individual, and do not simply arise together by chance in individuals diagnosed as suffering from autism.

Table 3.3: Association of social handicap with communication impairments and rigidity in thinking and behaviour, in Shah *et al.'s* (1982) sample:

Subject group	Abnormal speech	Lack of 'symbolic' activity
Socially impaired	75 %	73 %
Socially appropriate	14 %	8 %

Epidemiology of autistic spectrum disorders

The incidence of any condition refers to the number of new cases occurring each year, but this is difficult to assess in a condition like autism where there is no diagnosis at birth and where age of onset is uncertain. Epidemiological studies of autism instead rely on prevalence rates, which are counts of the total number of existing cases in a specified time period in a specified place and for a specified age range. Sometimes these are quoted as incidence rates, but the distinction is important when planning services. Nevertheless, prevalence will give a rough indication of incidence and the earlier diagnosis is made, the truer this will be.

The prevalence rate for autism also depends crucially upon how it is diagnosed and defined. The rate in early studies appeared to be around four to 10 children with autism in every 10,000 (e.g. Lotter 1966) but these studies all looked at typical or Kanner's autism, rather than the broader definition of autistic spectrum disorders. Wing and Gould's study (1979) also found a rate of five per 10,000 for this group but reported an incidence of 22 per 10,000 for 'the triad of social, language and behavioural impairments'. Gillberg *et al.* (1986) found similarly high rates of the triad and mental retardation in Swedish teenagers. Other studies report a prevalence of between three and 16 per 10,000 (e.g. Bryson *et al.* 1988; Burd and Kerbeshian 1988; Ciadella & Mamelle 1989; Tanoue *et al.* 1988). Ehlers and Gillberg (1993) found the rate for Asperger's syndrome to be 36 in 10,000. Wing (1996) adds this prevalence data to that of her own of 22 per 10,000 from the special school population in Camberwell and comes up with a prevalence rate of 58 per 10,000 or almost six in every 1,000. This perhaps represents the full range of autistic spectrum disorders, but it is not clear that all the cases represented by these figures would fit the treatment definition of autism given above. In other words, from the practitioner's viewpoint, one needs to ask whether all of this group will have needs severe enough to warrant special treatment. It may be that this will be the case, not necessarily in terms of specialised provision, but in terms of recognition and understanding of their differences.

While the reported prevalance of autism has increased in recent years (e.g. in Gillberg's Swedish population), the reasons for this are not clear. This is probably due to better information, a wider conception of autism, and possibly (in Sweden) the rise in numbers of immigrants from tropical countries, who may be more susceptible to infectious diseases during pregnancy (Gillberg 1991). There are other more controversial views about possible causes for an increase in reported prevalence (Knivsberg *et al.* 1991; Shattock *et al.* 1998; Williams 1991) but it should be emphasised that there is as yet no proof of an actual increase to require an explanation. Studies of identified cases (Jordan and Jones 1996) show that these lag behind estimates from even the lowest prevalence rates, so it is clear that many people with autism remain unidentified.

All the epidemiological studies show a significantly greater number of boys than girls with autism. Male:female ratios vary from 2:1 (Ciadella and Mamelle 1989) to almost 3:1 (Steffenburg and Gillberg 1986). The sex ratio seems to vary with ability; most girls with autism are at the lower end of the ability range, while at the most able end (including those with Asperger's syndrome) boys may outnumber girls 5 to 1 (Lord and Schopler 1987). Szatmari and Jones (1991) have suggested some possible reasons for the lower IQ of females with autism but there is no real evidence for this to date. It may be that, whatever area of brain function is disturbed in autism, it is more localised in males than in females, thus it would be more likely that males would only have autistic problems, whereas females would only have autism if they suffered greater areas of brain damage and would thus be more likely to have additional learning difficulties. Alternatively, the sex linkage may indicate a genetic link and the genetic factor may be more influential in some cases of autism than in others. Thus, cases of 'pure' autism will be more likely to result from a genetic factor whereas those with associated general learning difficulties may result from more global brain damage, perhaps with a genetic factor but also from viral infections in the foetus or from birth trauma.

Both Kanner (1943) and Asperger (1944) remarked on the intelligence and high social standing of the families whose children had autism, and this has given rise to the idea that autism is more prevalent among the higher socioeconomic classes. There is little support for such an idea since only one epidemiological study (Lotter 1966) has shown any evidence of a social class bias. A number of reports have suggested that the association with social class may be an artefact caused by, for example, the greater likelihood that a middle class parent will be able to get their child seen by a specialist (Schopler *et al.* 1979).

The association of autism with major organic conditions, with severe learning difficulties and with epilepsy will be discussed in Chapter 4, which discusses the biological basis of autism.

Differences in behaviour between individuals with autism

Problems of socialisation, communication and rigidity are sufficient and necessary to describe much of the behaviour found to be specific and universal to autism, provided they all occur together. However, the way each area of impairment manifests itself in any individual will differ both between individuals in the spectrum and in the same individual over the course of time (or even in different contexts). This emphasises the point that diagnosis rests on a pattern of behaviour and not any particular behaviours.

A person with autism may have no speech or communicative gestures whatsoever, or they may have well articulated speech but only use it as echolalia, or they may have fluent speech but have difficulty using it flexibly or to engage appropriately in social communication. All of these variations can be seen as manifestations of a communication handicap. The actual amount and structural quality of the language used is a poor guide to the difficulties experienced, and autism is often a situation where speech may be greater than understanding. Some individuals with autism are so talkative, but in such a repetitive and obsessive way, that the impression they give is that speech is used to avoid communication rather than to effect it. Those who are mute (have no effective speech) may be suffering from an additional specific language impairment. If they have severe learning difficulties, on the other hand, their communication difficulties may have made it impossible for them to learn language (either spoken or signed) in the way that others without autism may often manage.

In the same way, the toddler with autism may spin the wheels of a toy car or line it up in the same ritualistic way, instead of pretending to park or clean it, or may have an obsessive interest in Thomas the Tank Engine. The adult with autism may show no interest in fiction in the form of drama (although the repetitive and stereotyped nature of many TV soaps can make them attractive to the more able individual with autism) or novels, preferring to read telephone directories. Both of these pictures reflect an underlying impairment in spontaneous or flexible thinking and behaviour. Some authors, such as Wing (1988, 1996) refer to this aspect of the triad as a failure in imagination, but this author feels this can be misleading. To begin with, the term 'imagination' suggests creativity and so the practitioner may be misled about the fundamental difficulties experienced in this area. It is not just that the individual cannot be creative in an artistic sense, but that their behaviour is almost entirely habitual. They are dependent on cueing and prompting to start behaviours or trigger thoughts and feelings and have little sense of self-autonomy or the planning or reviewing of their actions or thoughts. Their understanding is rooted in the external context and the more able may exhibit forms of imaginative behaviour (creating an 'imaginary' town drawn from innumerable perspectives, composing music or poems, writing science fiction plots) but still often lack a full understanding of the 'imaginary' status of their creativity. In other words, they may imagine but have difficulty distinguishing this from their experience of reality. This can lead (in the more able) to confusion with schizophrenia, but the difference is that there is no elaborate delusion. The difficulties in this area of the triad are fundamental and, as yet, ill understood.

Similarly, the difficulties in interpersonal engagement will always be present in autism but will be manifest in different ways. A person with autism may run away from social approaches, or may cause others to leave them alone through their apparently 'antisocial' behaviour. They may seem cut off and passive, content to twiddle by themselves but not resisting when others approach (especially a familiar carer or key worker) and insist they join in. Others may appear at first to be very sociable, even socially indiscriminate. They may pester people (even strangers) with questions and monologues and approach people too closely, making no distinction for different levels of intimacy. Far from avoiding others, such individuals, especially as young adults, may be desperate for friends and may make themselves vulnerable to abuse in their eagerness to have a 'friend' at any cost. These behaviours are clearly very different, almost opposites in some cases, yet they all demonstrate a fundamental lack of social understanding (Wing 1988).

Diagnostic systems

As indicated above, the set of three core impairments, which has become known as Wing's triad, is the basis for the diagnosis of autism today (Rutter and Schopler 1987). Appendix 1 contains the full criteria from ICD-10 (WHO 1993) and Appendix 2 contains the full, diagnostic criteria from DSM-IV (APA 1994). As with all psychiatric diagnostic criteria, they are meant to guide a trained and experienced clinician and not to act as a kind of 'checklist' for autism. For that to happen, there would have to be very specific behaviours that were unequivocally associated with autism, whereas, as we have seen, that is not the case. Once there has been training, however, Rutter and Schopler (1987) and Bailey *et al.* (1996) report that the diagnosis of autism is one of the most reliable and valid diagnoses in child psychiatry. That may be a surprise to parents, and even some professionals, who have spent a long time fighting for an appropriate diagnosis. Difficulties in obtaining a diagnosis, however, say more about attitudes to diagnosis (in education especially), and the availability of trained and experienced diagnosticians, than they do about the quality of the criteria themselves.

CHAT (Checklist for Autism in Toddlers)

While there may not be specific behaviours that can be used to denote autism, the lack of certain behaviours at expected times in development may be a more promising approach to diagnosis at the behavioural level. This is the approach adopted by Baron-Cohen and his colleagues (Baron-Cohen *et al.* 1992; 1996a) in trying to find early indicators of autism in 18-month-olds. They have devised a screening device for this age group based on both questions and structured observations to be performed by general practitioners or health visitors as part of a developmental check. As a screening device, it is not meant as a complete diagnostic tool for autism. One might expect a number of both 'false positives' (infants who appear to have autism at 18 months but do not have this confirmed at later diagnostic assessment) and 'false negatives' (infants who are not diagnosed as having autism at 18 months but where later diagnosis reveals its presence). However, the number of these in trials has, in fact, been very low. More than 80 per cent of a randomly selected control group passed all items, showing normal development of imaginative and social abilities at 18 months. No child from the control group showed problems in more than one of the five key areas. By contrast, four of the 41 high-risk children failed on two or more of the key items. Follow-up at 30 months found that these four children, and only these four, had received a diagnosis of autism. This study, then, suggests that we may be able to detect autism at 18 months by looking for deficits in specific areas of social, communicative and imaginative competence.

These five key behaviours are:

- protodeclarative pointing (i.e. pointing to comment rather than to request);
- joint attention;
- interest in, and emotional engagement with, others;
- social play; and
- pretend play.

Rating scales/checklists and questionnaires

Trevarthen *et al.* (1996) reviewed some of the most frequently used rating scales and checklists for autism. There was an earlier review by Parks (1983). This covered the following:

1. The Diagnostic Checklist for Behaviour-Disturbed Children, Form E-1 and Form E-2 (Rimland 1964; 1971) which are in the form of retrospective questionnaires for parents.

2. The Behaviour Rating Instrument for Autistic and Atypical Children, BRIAACC (Ruttenburg *et al.* 1966; 1977) which is an observation schedule based on a psychodynamic view of autism.

3. The Behaviour Observation Scale for Autism, BOS (Freeman *et al.* 1978) which is also an observational schedule based on a computer-coded analysis of videoed sessions.

4. The Autism Behaviour Checklist, ABC (Krug *et al.* 1980), which is a checklist completed by professionals with weighted scores for certain behaviours noted, and

5. The Childhood Autism Rating Scale, CARS (Schopler *et al.* 1980), which is also a checklist divided into 15 scales with a rating for each of these scales.

Of these early checklists, the CARS appears to have best stood the test of time, with generally acknowledged good reliability (over different raters and at different times) and validity (it distinguishes those who present a clinical picture of autism from those who do not).

Other checklists have been developed for more specific purposes. Barthelemy *et al.* (1989) developed the Behavioural Summarised Evaluation (BSE) for looking specifically at the severity of behaviour problems. This has been adapted for use with younger children and the new version (the Infant Behavioural Summarised Evaluation (IBSE): Adrien *et al.* 1992) is intended to assess infants from six months old to four years. Early results suggest it may be valuable in distinguishing autism from other conditions, but this needs replication. A more general diagnostic tool which is increasingly used in the UK and elsewhere is the Autism Diagnostic Interview (ADI) (Rutter *et al.* 1988; LeCouteur *et al.* 1989) which is more a form of structured interview than a checklist, as the name suggests. It was developed to overcome the problem that earlier checklists increased the likelihood of positive responses to certain behavioural categories simply by asking about those particular behaviours. It builds a picture of how the child functions in the areas of language and communication, social development and play. It does, however, need training to administer and evaluate the responses.

Lord and her colleagues (Lord *et al.* 1989) have devised a developmental 'test' for the diagnosis of autism based on standardised observations. This is the Autism Diagnostic Observation Schedule (ADOS) and charts communication and social behaviour in a 30 minute observation period using standardised tasks and attempts to elicit certain key behaviours. At the moment this schedule is only applicable to those with a mental age over three years, but a version for those with lower mental ages has also been developed. The Pre-Linguistic Autism Diagnostic Observation Schedule (PL-ADOS) (DiLavore *et al.* 1995) also involves structured observation of play situations. In this schedule, however, the play is freer, with the elicitations merging more naturally into the child's play activity, and the key behaviours looked for are earlier-occurring ones such as imitation, joint attention and social routines. Lorna Wing is currently developing yet another diagnostic tool (Diagnostic Interview Schedule and Childhood Observation or DISCO) but this has not yet been standardised for general use.

How early can autism be diagnosed?

Until recently the generally accepted view was that a reliable diagnosis of autism is rare before the age of 3 or 4 years (Stone *et al.* 1999). This was primarily because the types of behaviours which are impaired in autism (according to the diagnostic criteria used) do not emerge reliably in normal children until this age. However, there is growing recognition that many of these later behaviours have precursors in earlier developmental steps and, as we have seen above, there is a growth of diagnostic instruments attempting to detect autism at ever-earlier ages. The difficulty with autism has always been that there are no biological markers for autism at birth (unlike, for example, Down's syndrome), so that information on the child with autism (prior to diagnosis at, say three or four years of age) had to be obtained from retrospective studies. This was usually done by getting the parents to recall their child's earlier history, and these parental reports will vary in a number of ways.

Parents will have different degrees of knowledge about normal development (depending in part on whether or not this is their first baby), different expectations of how babies should behave, and different degrees of tolerance of deviations from this norm. The author once knew a parent who had married late and then given birth to what turned out to be triplets, all with autism. The triplets had varying degrees of autism and accompanying learning difficulties but the behaviour of all three would have been enough to send most mothers to their nearest source of help from an early age. But this mother was so happy to have been 'blessed' with children at a late age, that she did not complain and their problems were not recognised until they were presented for schooling, where the teacher took a somewhat different view! This brings us back to the point made earlier that a 'handicap' is only partly defined by factors within the individual.

A more satisfactory and useful approach has developed from the pioneering work of Baron-Cohen and his colleagues. The difficulty in collecting prospective data on autism (i.e. observing or assessing infants early on and then later to see what key behaviours at the first observation lead to a diagnosis of autism at the later one) is that it is a comparatively rare condition. Thousands of babies would need to be screened in order to pick up any children with autism at a later stage. Baron-Cohen *et al.* tackled this difficulty by selecting a population to study where the incidence of autism was much more common than in the general population. This was a population of families who already had a child with autism, since we know from genetic studies that there is a fifty-fold increase in the chance of having a child with autism if there is already one in the family (Rutter 1999). By screening a volunteered population in this way, Baron-Cohen *et al.* (1992) were able to isolate the key behaviours mentioned above and to develop their CHAT instrument, which could be validated on a larger sample on an international basis.

Age of onset

At the present time, the overall picture concerning the age of onset is confused. There is evidence from the use of CHAT that there are reliable indicators of autism at 18 months, and yet there are some children who appear to have all the classical symptoms of autism at 18 months but then 'grow out of them' in some way. We do not know whether this is because the 'symptoms' are not really symptoms of autism until they appear out of keeping with later stages of development, or whether something happens to bring these children back onto a normally developing path. There is a suggestion (tied into some diagnostic criteria, e.g. ICD-10 and DSM-IV) that for some children there is normal development up until the age of two years or so, followed by a period in which skills are lost and autism becomes apparent. Wing (1996) suggests that this idea of a disintegrative psychosis as part of the autistic spectrum is confusing, although she recognises that there is a group who do start to develop language skills (or at least, speech) and then lose them at around this age. This loss of speech is often accompanied by a loss of involvement with others, and a loss of functional play behaviour. Again, there is not usually any further deterioration, unless the child has a progressive condition. It is not clear whether this does represent the onset of autism, or whether the difficulties that were there all along only manifest themselves as the child attempts to engage in more socially directed play and language. Certainly, Trevarthen *et al.* (1996) favour the latter explanation and tie it into their model of how brain functioning and organisation changes over time.

Parents certainly find it particularly distressing when their child appears to develop normally for the first year or two of life and then shows symptoms of autism. Sometimes this is after an illness of some kind, but more often there is no discernible cause. Again, there is the query of how 'normal' the early development was in retrospect, and more stringent research is needed. With the growth of video recording of babies by parents (Bernabei *et al.* 1998; Osterling and Dawson 1994) there will be increasing opportunities to examine the early development of individuals with autism to attempt to identify any deviations from the normal course of development and to gauge the significance of these.

It should be remembered that the actual symptoms of autism do not include completely abnormal behaviours in themselves. A proportion of normally developing children will use echolalia in the course of developing language and this is a very common feature in the language of children with a visual impairment. Many normally developing children may become withdrawn, may develop an attachment to a piece of cloth, may rock or head-bang, may want the same story over and over again and so on. Almost all behaviours that are seen in autism can be seen in normal development at some time, and even the more marked 'symptoms' may be caused by illness or temporary stress in a young child's life (Rutter 1999). What makes behaviours 'autistic' is their persistence, the overall pattern of these behaviours, the lack of any alternative 'normal' behaviours, and the situations in which they occur. Thus, to reiterate a point already made, you cannot diagnose autism on the basis of the presence or absence of certain behaviours (and this applies even more when considering diagnosis in adults) but only on the total pattern of behaviour and developmental history.

Methods of studying early development

Early indicator studies were of two major types: retrospective and prospective. Retrospective studies work backwards, taking a population and looking at their developmental history. Such studies are open to all the factors about parents mentioned above and to the criticism that remembering may be influenced by subsequent outcome – remembering with the benefit of hindsight may be unreliable. In order to avoid such unintentional bias, researchers may look back at reports written at the time about the child's development for example, medical or school records. These records will not be biased by subsequent outcome, but they may instead be scanty or deal with matters not of interest to the researcher. Prospective studies allow the researcher to decide which early behaviours to monitor, and are free from memory biases. However, if the disorder of interest is rare, an enormous initial sample may be needed in order to be sure that some of the infants will later prove to have the condition, hence the approach adopted by Baron-Cohen *et al*. in relation to the CHAT study.

Many parents of children with autism report that they suspected something to be wrong from the first months onward although this must be seen against the background of the many parents of normally developing children who also suspect problems (in most cases unnecessarily). It may also be that what such parents notice in infancy is not the autism but the additional severe learning difficulties which their child also has. The search for an early indicator of autism must therefore compare the early development of children with autism with the early development both of normally developing children and of children with severe learning difficulties but not autism.

Apart from the CHAT study, there have been other attempts to look at the early development of children with autism in a less biased way than by using parental reports. A follow-up study by Lister-Brook used data from the Camberwell study (Wing and Gould 1979), to look at whether problems at 12 months (assessed by health visitors using a specially devised questionnaire) predict the triad of impairments at 12 years. Preliminary analyses suggest that nothing is picked up at one year which would differentiate those children who later receive a diagnosis of autism from those who do not.

Johnson *et al*. (1992) looked back at the infant health screening records of children who were subsequently diagnosed as suffering from autism, and compared them with the records of children who grew up to be normal or to have mild/moderate learning difficulties (but not autism). They found that the group with learning difficulties showed impairments in many of the areas tested (motor, vision, hearing and language) as assessed at their 12-month screening. By contrast, the children with autism had shown very few problems at this age. At their 18-month assessment, however, many of the infants who were later diagnosed as having autism showed problems in social development. While a few of the children with learning difficulties also showed social problems at 18 months, these were part of a more general delay across all areas of functioning. In the children with autism, by contrast, the health visitors noticed social deficits in the absence of other problems. This would support the findings from the CHAT study. The Johnson *et al*. study suggests that it is not until during the second year that these children show social impairments – at 12 months the children in this study were judged to be normally sociable by health visitors (on items such as smiling and responsiveness to people). However, one needs to be careful about making such sweeping judgements over what may be very subtle disturbances at this stage. The measures of interpersonal development taken at these infant screenings were very crude and cannot be used to assert that individuals with autism develop normally in their first year. There may be problems in interpersonal development that are there from birth but are not evident in gross measures of social behaviour until much later.

Other studies have explored possible early indicators of autism through rather different techniques. Single case studies have been reported, concerning children who for one reason or another were closely monitored in their early years before autism was suspected (e.g. Sparling 1991). Home movies and, as has been mentioned, the use of video cameras may also be good sources of information about the early years of the development of an individual with autism (Adrien *et al.* 1991; Bernabei *et al.* 1998). Both types of study suggest very early but rather subtle abnormalities, with 12 to 18 months being the age when the abnormalities become apparent. However, the lack of control subjects makes it hard to know which, if any, of these early features might be specific to autism. It remains a possibility that early problems are merely due to attendant learning difficulties, or that the developmental histories of many 'normal' children may contain such apparently odd behaviours.

Conclusion

It is the behaviour of people with autism which leads to their diagnosis, and it is only their behaviour that can be observed, and that must be coped with directly, therefore it is clearly important to know about the behavioural nature of autism. Behavioural techniques also have a role to play in the building of basic skills and in the management of behaviour problems, as course texts will show. However, we cannot really deal effectively with autism by simply reacting to the behaviours shown. We need to understand the way the person with autism is thinking and feeling if we are to work out what those behaviours mean; we cannot assume they have the same root or the same meaning as similar behaviours seen in normal development. We can gain insight into these behaviours and better understand their cause and nature if we also know about autism at the psychological level. This will, in turn, lead to more effective ways of managing behaviour and encouraging development. Chapter 5 considers this aspect of our understanding of autism.

Further reading:

Rutter, M. (1999) 'Autism: two-way interplay between research and clinical work', *Journal of Child Psychology and Psychiatry* **40**, 169–88.

Rutter, M. and Schopler, E. (1987) 'Autism and pervasive developmental disorders: conceptual and diagnostic issues', *Journal of Autism and Developmental Disorders* **17**, 159–86.

Trevarthen, C., *et al.* (1996) *Children with Autism: Diagnosis and Interventions to Meet their Needs.* London: Jessica Kingsley.

Wing, L. (1988) 'The continuum of autistic characteristics', in Schopler, E. and Mesibov, G.B. (eds) *Diagnosis and Assessment in Autism.* New York: Plenum Press.

Wing, L. (1996) *The Autistic Spectrum: a Guide for Parents and Professionals.* London: Constable.

Chapter 4

The Biological Bases of Autism

Psychogenic theories

Psychogenic theories are those that attribute the cause of autism to faulty upbringing, rather than to a biological cause. As was discussed earlier in this handbook, Bettelheim (1956; 1967) was the source of the 'refrigerator mother' theory (the idea that children become autistic as a maladaptive response to a threatening and unloving environment) based on the false analogy from his own experiences in a concentration camp. Kanner originally saw autism as a biological deficit within the child, but later he became influenced by the dominant ideas of the time, and believed that the mild autistic features of detachment and social difficulty that he saw in the parents of the children he treated could account for autism in their children. Originally, Kanner had interpreted these same parental traits as signs of a genetic component to autism (Kanner 1943) and this highlights one of the difficulties in determining aetiology (causation) – the same information can be interpreted in different ways according to one's theoretical viewpoint.

No evidence has emerged to support the psychogenic explanations of autism, and yet they can persist, in different forms, supported by anecdotal experiences. Hocking (1990), for example, blames herself for her child's condition because of her maternal depression in the first year or so of his life. This is not an entirely whimsical view, given the effect that maternal depression can have on the early interactions between mother and child (Trevarthen *et al.* 1996), yet it is clear that children can suffer extreme emotional trauma in infancy without developing autism (Clarke and Clarke 1976; Curtiss 1977) and there is no evidence that children with autism have been treated any differently by their parents than their non-autistic siblings. It is easy to see, especially if the baby is a first baby, how parents may be made to feel responsible for their baby's difficulties. This is even more likely if the only treatment offered is some form of 'family therapy', as it still is in some countries, and even in some parts of the UK. There may also be the attraction that if you feel you have caused the problem it gives more hope of being able to 'cure' it. In spite of this, most parents do not feel this way and they welcome the scientific evidence that will help them better understand the condition and offer more realistic hopes of treatment.

Evidence for an organic cause

Reviews of the biology of autism conclude that evidence for an organic cause is overwhelming (Bauman and Kemper 1994; Coleman and Gillberg 1985; Gillberg 1991; Gillberg and Coleman 1992; Schopler and Mesibov 1987; Trevarthen *et al.* 1996). A study by Steffenburg (1991), for example, found that almost 9 per cent of her sample (35 autistic and 17 autistic-like children) showed some evidence of brain damage or dysfunction. She presents the pie chart in Figure 4.1 to show the relative incidence of different sorts of brain abnormalities in their sample.

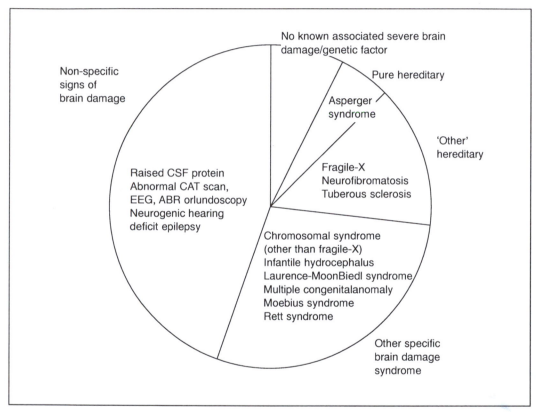

Figure 4.1: Sub-groups of autism. From Steffenberg (1991)

One indication that brain damage or dysfunction is at the root of autism is the high incidence of epilepsy in people with autism (Olsson *et al.* 1988; Gillberg 1991; Volkmar and Nelson 1990). Autism, unlike other conditions involving epilepsy, is associated (especially in the group without severe learning difficulties) with late-onset epilepsy (in late teens or early adulthood). This may also have some significance in the biology of the disorder, although it is not clear at present what this might be (Goode *et al.* 1994). Another pointer to brain damage is the tendency for general learning difficulties to accompany autism; if one excludes the population with Asperger's syndrome, around three quarters of the remainder with autism have additional learning difficulties (IQ < 70) (Rutter 1979). As mentioned above, as one looks at groups of people with severe learning difficulties with progressively lower IQs, the incidence of autism increases (Smalley *et al.* 1988). This is easily explained if autism is caused by damage to a particular brain region or to the control of a particular brain function. Widespread damage to the brain, such as causes general severe learning difficulties, will be more likely to affect this particular component, the more of the brain it affects. While no unambiguous and universal findings have emerged to suggest the site of the lesion, or the precise nature of the neurochemical pathway disrupted in autism, we can be confident that autism has a primary cause at the level of the brain (Steffenberg and Gillberg 1990).

What must be remembered is that it is at the psychological level (the level of brain *function*) that autism exists as a syndrome, thus, there may not be a single organic cause. As suggested earlier in this handbook, current research findings make it likely that autism will turn out to be more like cerebral palsy in this respect than like Down's syndrome, for example. Cerebral palsy can result from infections in the womb, birth trauma, or post-natal infections and brain damage. What makes it cerebral palsy is not the particular insult to the brain, but the area of brain function that is affected (in this case control of movements). Like autism, cerebral palsy is diagnosed at the level of behaviour but it is the disordered function that makes it cerebral palsy rather than, for example, polio. Cerebral palsy exists as a syndrome regardless of the precise behavioural manifestations (for example, athetosis or spasticity) and regardless of whether it was caused by lack of oxygen at birth or a fall on the head at one month old. So, the existence of autism as a syndrome does not depend on finding a single organic cause. There may be several different causes that all lead to autism by affecting the same area of brain functioning.

Is there a gene for autism?

Overall the evidence for a genetic component in autism is weighty, although the exact role of the genetic factor is not clear (Bailey *et al.* 1995; Rutter 1999; Rutter *et al.* 1990) and, as explained above, it may have more of a role in some cases than in others. Rutter *et al.* (1997) suggested that the best estimate so far is that there are between three and 10 genes involved and that it is most likely to be three or four. There are a number of factors pointing to this multiple genetic role, explaining why (given that most individuals with full-blown autism will not have children) autism continues to exist. As Baron-Cohen *et al.* (1997) point out, there are probably evolutionary advantages to some of the genes which, in combination, lead to autism. They show, for example, that engineering is far more common in the fathers and grandfathers of children with autism than in other groups and this helps to account for the range of other characteristics (sometimes, but not always, difficulties) that appear in the families of people with autism.

There is a significant familial loading for autism; autism is 50 times more frequent in the siblings of people with autism (Smalley 1997; Smalley *et al.* 1988;

Szatmari *et al.* 1993). There is also an increase of other conditions in siblings, especially language disorders (August *et al.* 1981; Bolton and Rutter 1990; Bolton *et al.* 1994) and social impairments (Macdonald *et al.* 1989). Identical twins also have a far higher concordance (that is, if one has the condition, the other will) for autism than non-identical twins (Folstein and Rutter 1977; Le Couteur *et al.* 1996; Rutter 1999), showing that familial loading is not simply due to a mother's tendency to experience difficult pregnancies. Nevertheless, although the concordance rate in identical twins is high, it is not 100 per cent, so it is possible to be the identical twin of someone with autism, and yet not have autism.

One possibility is that there may be a genetic predisposition for autism, but it is only fulfilled if triggered by pre- or peri-natal difficulties. Mothers of children with autism report more problems during pregnancy and delivery than mothers of, for example, children who later develop schizophrenia (Green *et al.* 1984). Folstein and Rutter (1977) also found that where non-identical twins had one twin with autism and one without, it was only the one with autism that had experienced a difficult delivery. This suggests, in turn, that it was not necessarily the difficult birth that gave rise to the autism, but, rather, the autism that gave rise to the difficult birth, as has been found with other conditions. As can be seen, it is precisely how these 'chicken and egg' situations are interpreted in autism that leads to so many contrary views of its aetiology.

In some cases, there is a definite link with a known genetic disorder. Fragile-X syndrome, phenylketonuria, and tuberous sclerosis all carry an increased risk of autism (Blomquist *et al.* 1985; Cohen *et al.* 1989; Friedman 1969; Gillberg 1992; Gillberg and Forsell 1984; Gillberg *et al.* 1986; Hunt and Dennis 1987; Reiss *et al.* 1986; Smalley *et al.* 1992). For example, 26 per cent of the fragile-X population, who have severe learning difficulties, also have autism, yet fragile-X cannot be 'the gene for autism'. This is not only because not all those with this condition have autism, but also because only 8.1 per cent (or, from later studies [Bailey *et al.* 1993] only 5 per cent) of the population with autism, who have been screened, are found to carry the fragile-X gene (Trevarthen *et al.* 1996). With regard to tuberous sclerosis, Gillberg *et al.* (1994) estimated that 9 per cent of individuals with autism also have this disorder, thus there is a significant connection, but not enough to account for the genetics of autism. This is especially likely to be the case since autism is associated mainly with tuberous sclerosis where there is also additional epilepsy and general learning difficulties; this suggests the connection with autism may be through brain damage rather than genetics, even though tuberous sclerosis is itself a genetic condition.

The incidence of psychological and social-communicative impairments in the non-autistic siblings of children with autism (August *et al.* 1981; Bolton *et al.* 1994) has led to the suggestion of an 'extended phenotype' in autism (LeCouteur 1996). Thus, the suggestion is that the genes responsible for autism may in some cases produce far milder disorders in other family members. Szatmari and Jones (1991) discussed the types of inheritance that might be involved in autism. They conclude that cases of autism may be divided into three aetiological groups:

1. Exogenous (caused by external factors such as prenatal accidents, including infections while in the womb);

2. Autosomal recessive gene (carried on non-sex chromosomes, but not dominant, so that it is only expressed if it is inherited from both father and mother);

3. X-linked gene (carried on the female sex chromosome). The latter case would offer another explanation of the greater preponderance of autism in males and the fact that females with autism may be more severely affected. This would occur because females would have an extra X-chromosome to counter the defective one, and would only become affected when both X-chromosomes carried the gene for autism.

However, they stress that more data needs to be collected concerning the pattern of occurrence of autism in families and the severity of attendant general learning difficulties, in order to explore the possible modes of inheritance.

Skuse *et al.* (1997) provide evidence (from a study of Turner's syndrome) that suggests that a location on the X-chromosome that is inherited from the father could be linked to autism. They hypothesise that it may be responsible for social cognitive skills and that it is significantly related to the executive functioning skills of behavioural inhibition and (to a lesser extent) planning. Since all X-chromosomes in males are naturally inherited from the mother, they would miss this site. It cannot be solely responsible for social cognition (or all males would have autism) but it does help to explain the sex bias in autistic spectrum disorders. Skuse is quoted in Schmidt (1997, p. 50) as saying, 'I suggest that girls are genetically pre-programmed to learn almost by instinct to interpret social cues; boys on the other hand do not have this advantage and have to work harder to get to the same point.' Such a sex-linked view of the genetics of autism harks back to the view of Asperger (1944) that autism represented the extreme form of maleness.

The only other indication of an 'autism-specific' gene connection has been the work on chromosome 15. Here there have been some reports that autism is associated with an extra portion of chromosomal material translocated from chromosome 15 (Gillberg *et al.* 1991; Hotopf and Bolton 1995). Media reports of the location of an 'autism-specific' gene, followed a report by Cook *et al.* (1997) but this supposed association was subject to refutation (without the media attention) a few days later (Klauck *et al.* 1997). In general, more work needs to be carried out, but we are not yet at the stage of knowledge where diagnosis should automatically be accompanied by gene investigations, unless there are other indications of a likely positive outcome.

There has also been some work on the biology of autism (Shattock and Lowdon 1991; Waring and Ngong 1993; Williams *et al.* 1991) that suggests that what may lie at the heart of autism is not a gene for the condition itself, but one that affects food metabolism. This would, eventually, affect the chemical environment of the brain. In one such model, the child would inherit certain food intolerances from both parents (a pattern of migraine from the maternal side and excema and hay fever from the father's side is one linkage that has been found) which would result in an inability to metabolise certain foodstuffs adequately. This in turn would lead to harmful toxins entering the blood through the gut wall and, through a possible weakening of the blood-brain barrier due to a viral infection or some other agent, through into the brain (Sun and Cade 1999; Sun *et al.* 1999). In one theory the sulphurinase system is affected (the child not being able to eat, for example, bananas, chocolate or fruits without being affected). Another theory is that it is the endogenous opioid system that is affected (the child not being able to tolerate casein from milk or gluten from wheat, or both). It should be emphasised that these theories are still just that, although some parents and some individuals with autism have adopted diets to eliminate the supposedly guilty foodstuffs and have claimed positive results (Whiteley *et al.* 1999). Nevertheless, they are far from showing that they can produce effects when compared to a control group, or even that any effects are autism-specific. This is mentioned here to show that a genetic defect can work indirectly to bring about autism (at least in theory) and to reemphasise that there may be more than one biological cause, even at the genetic level.

Recent advances in molecular genetics give rise to the possibility of finding susceptibility genes for autism (Rutter 1999) and this is likely to change the picture dramatically in the next few years.

Brain abnormalities

Structural differences

A general consensus at present is that a number of rather different biological causes may result in autism (Coleman and Gillberg 1985; Rutter 1999; Schopler and Mesibov 1987). It may not, therefore, be useful to think of a common biological insult to the brain or to brain functioning that would lead to autism. There has been evidence of brain abnormalities in autism but, unfortunately, no agreement has yet emerged concerning the area of the brain which is damaged. Localising higher psychological functions (such as the social, communication and imagination skills impaired in autism) is always problematic and such functions may be widely disbursed in the brain. To date a number of different brain regions have been suggested as the site of damage in autism (on the basis of neurochemical investigations, autopsy examinations, and *in vivo* brain imaging). In each case, however, there has been a disappointing failure to replicate findings, or the discovery that such damage is not specific to autism but merely associated with attendant general learning difficulties. While abnormalities are usually found in any such study, few specific differences have been discovered in the brains of autistic people. Courchesne and his colleagues (Courchesne 1989; Courchesne *et al.* 1994; Courchesne *et al.* 1995) have suggested more consistent findings with respect to cerebellar damage or dysfunction, but this was not confirmed by Bailey *et al.* (1996).

Courchesne and his colleagues suggested that there is no single abnormality of cerebellar function disturbed in autism, but rather two different kinds of disturbance; in some cases of autism there is an abnormally large cerebellum and in others an abnormally small one. Kemper and Bauman (1993) and Bailey *et al.* (1998) found increases in brain size generally in autism, but with structural abnormalities in the brain stem and in the cortex. There may also be a disturbance in the Purkinje cells that are sited in the cerebellum (Bauman and Kemper 1994), although Bailey *et al.* (1996) only found this in the brains of adults with autism and not in those of children. The significance of this distinction is not clear, except that it may indicate a secondary, rather than a primary, effect. Traditionally, the cerebellum has been seen as the site of motor control in the brain and so finding abnormalities in this region in autism has led to an increased interest in motor disturbance in autism. In extreme cases, these findings have been used to support the ideas of Biklen (1990) that autism is not a disorder of social and communication impairments but rather a form of cerebral palsy that can be remediated through the use of 'facilitated communication'. All scientific studies of this treatment have failed to validate those claims and so treatment cannot, in this instance, support the biological theory.

The other main candidate for the locus of an autism-related brain abnormality has been the left temporal horn alongside abnormalities in the underlying sub-cortical structures, including the hippocampus (Bauman and Kemper 1994; Hauser *et al.* 1975). As with all other studies of brain structure abnormality in autism, the results of attempts to replicate these findings have been inconsistent. Attempts to find consistent cortical abnormalities have been equally disappointing (Bailey *et al.* 1996).

There are four factors to consider in the interpretation of findings. In the first place, similar behaviour does not necessarily imply a similar cause. Secondly, even where abnormalities in brain functioning are established, these tell us nothing about how those abnormalities came about either in terms of their timing (in a developmental sense) or in terms of the specific brain abnormalities that led to them. For example, they may represent a disorder fundamental to autism or they may represent a secondary effect of another more general disorder. The third point is that even a structural abnormality in the brain tells us little about the brain functions that will be disturbed, since we do not have accurate mappings of brain function onto structure. We also know that some brain functions can be taken over by other parts of the brain, especially when the damage occurs early enough in brain development. Finally, finding many different sites of abnormality does not necessarily mean there are many different causes at the biological level since a single cause may have a widespread effect, especially if it occurs in the developing brain. Morton and Frith (1995) suggest some of the different models for mapping the connections between biology, psychology and behaviour.

Functional abnormalities

Many researchers, discouraged by their failure to find obvious brain damage or abnormality in all people with autism, have begun to look for the damaged function with neuro-psychological test batteries. Minshew (1991) has shown that there are EEG abnormalities in around 50 per cent of the tested cases of individuals with autism. Naturally, there is an association of abnormal EEGs with general learning difficulties, but abnormalities are found in autism even when there are no additional general learning difficulties and no definite epilepsy. Nevertheless, there was no particular abnormal brain pattern that was found in autism.

Imaging techniques (Rugg 1997), such as PET and MRI scans have been used to try to determine abnormalities of function. Again the results have not been consistent and abnormalities found in one study have failed to be replicated by others. In all studies, it should be remembered that small groups of subjects are involved and so the risk of chance or idiosyncratic findings is increased. Rumsey *et al.* (1985) have even suggested that what may be of interest in autism is the fact that results are far more idiosyncratic between individuals than with other groups, with those with autism showing more extreme effects than any other group. Other studies have supported this and showed less coordination between the different regions of the brain in subjects with autism (Horwitz *et al.* 1988).

Subjects with autism have tended to perform poorly in tasks which people with frontal lobe damage also fail (Rumsey and Hamburger 1988; Prior and Hoffman 1990; Ozonoff *et al.* 1991b). However, as indicated earlier, this may not mean that people with autism and individuals with frontal lobe damage necessarily fail these tasks for the same reasons. The picture is further complicated by the fact that performances on different tasks, that all supposedly involve functioning of the frontal cortex, do not correlate well. Patients can be found who clearly show loss of frontal tissue in brain scans, but still perform well on these tasks, as well as patients who fail despite no obvious damage to these brain areas. These are not patients with autism; but they, nevertheless, cast doubt on the findings in relation to autism. As remarked above, it is also important to recognise that not all brain function is neatly localised to discrete areas of the brain and social behaviour, in particular, may well be controlled by the coordination of many different brain functions including perception, emotion and physical action. A lack of the coordination between different areas of functioning in the brain might be more significant in autism than failure in the functioning of any one area.

Brain chemistry

Most studies of brain chemicals in autism are not able to study brain levels directly, for ethical reasons, and so have to infer brain levels from blood or urine studies. This will mean that the theories about the significance of any differences that are found will also have to include some indication of the way these differences are translated across the blood-brain barrier. Cook (1990) and Narayan *et al.* (1993) have reviewed the studies on neurotransmitters in autism. Again, many of the studies have produced inconsistent results both with respect to opioids and, to a lesser extent, with serotonin. Attempts in the 1970s to improve autism through reducing serotonin levels with the drug fenfluramine, have not been validated

(Geller *et al.* 1982) and the drug has now been withdrawn, following toxic side effects. Similar reports have appeared about another serendipitous 'medication' for autism, secretin (Horvath *et al.* 1998). Once more, evaluative studies have not been carried out and past experience suggests caution.

More recent work with diets, in a study reducing peptide levels in autism, have shown more promising results, although there was no control group (Knivsberg *et al.* 1990). Parental surveys of parents whose children with autism have been placed on gluten-free diets (Whiteley *et al.* 1999) also show reports of positive results but also require a cautious interpretation, given likely Hawthorne effects.

Conclusion

We are still a long way from pinpointing the area of damage in the autistic brain, or even deciding which areas of functioning are awry. As indicated, the main problems centre round replication of findings, the specificity of the findings to autism, and the interpretation of those findings. It may be fair to conclude, however, with Bailey *et al.* (1996) that the biological research has revolutionised our concept of autism over the last 30 years and it is now accepted as a neurodevelopmental disorder where genetic factors have the prominent role in aetiology.

Further reading:

Bailey, A., *et al.* (1996) Autism: towards an integration of clinical, genetic, neuropsychological, and neuro-biological perspectives. *Journal of Child Psychology and Psychiatry Annual Research Review,* **37**, 89–126.

Bauman, M.L. and Kemper, T.L. (1994) *Neurobiology of Autism.* Baltimore: John Hopkins University Press.

Coleman, M. and Gillberg, C. (1985) *The Biology of the Autistic Syndromes.* New York: Praeger.

Schopler, E. and Mesibov, G.B. (eds) (1987) *Neurobiological Issues in Autism.* New York: Plenum Press.

Smalley, S.L. *et al.* (1988) 'Autism and genetics: A decade of research', *Archives of General Psychiatry,* **45**, 953–61.

Steffenburg, S. (1991) 'Neuropsychiatric assessment of children with autism: a population-based study', *Developmental Medicine and Child Neurology,* **33**, 495–511.

Chapter 5

Psychological Theories on the Nature of Autism

Introduction

As discussed in earlier sections, the level of explanation that is most useful for understanding autism from a treatment perspective is the psychological one. At this level we are dealing with theoretical constructs that help to make sense of observable behaviour, while fitting the constraints imposed by the little we know of the biological basis of that behaviour. Even within the psychological domain, some theories will be closer to biology (neuropsychological theories, for example), some closer to behaviour (learning theories, for example) and some purely abstract (such as information processing theories, based on a computer metaphor of brain functioning or psychodynamic theories based on myth or psychoanalytical theory).

Autism is a rich source of psychological theorising. At one level this arises because of the intriguing and bizarre behavioural manifestations of the disorder and the wide variation of behaviours displayed. This means that almost any theory can appear to explain, or at least describe, some of the features of autism and so can come to have face validity. At another level, autism involves a unique and early developmental disturbance that can throw light on the developmental process itself and offer insights into the role played by cognitive, affective (emotional), conative (motivational) and social factors in development. Theories of autism have a privileged status in developmental psychology, for that reason. For those attempting to live and work with people with autism, there is also the daily challenge that methods and approaches that work with all other groups do not seem to work with these individuals. There is, then, the need to understand what is going on, in order to devise better and more specific approaches. The number and variety of theoretical approaches reflect all of these interests and concerns.

Before tackling the theories, however, it is important to consider the role a theory should play in our understanding of autism and the features that would make it count as a useful theory. The first criterion is that it should account for all the behavioural features that distinguish autistic spectrum disorders from other conditions and from those with normal development: that is, the diagnostic criteria for autistic spectrum disorders. But in order to count as a theory, the explanation should not just be a reworking of a descriptive analysis, but should explain why and how the triad of impairments are related. Finally, to count as a scientific theory, and to be useful, it should give rise to testable hypotheses. This is not to say that a theory must account for autism through the operation of a single psychological mechanism. It is likely that several psychological mechanisms may be involved, but the theory would need to suggest ways in which these mechanisms worked together to produce autism, even if the biological details of that 'working together' are not spelt out.

Theory making, however, has its own pitfalls and this is particularly true when applied to autism. To begin with, it is not always clear exactly what the features are that require an explanation. Although there are set criteria for diagnosis, as we have seen, they describe a type of behaviour rather than an actual behaviour itself. There is no such thing as an 'autistic' behaviour, no behaviour that is characteristic of all and only those with autism. For example, one would look for disturbed social contact with others, but this 'disturbance' might take a variety of forms. At one extreme there could be extreme aloofness, whereby a child turns away from all social contact and retreats into a foetal position, flicking his or her fingers in front of his/her eyes. The other extreme might be a pattern of behaviour that Wing (1980) refers to as 'active but odd', whereby the child with autism will approach anyone and everyone, stand too close, stare unflinchingly into their eyes and talk at them for hours on a single topic. Topologically, the two kinds of behaviour have nothing in common, nor is either pattern found exclusively in autism. Their linkage, and the linkage of the triad of impairments, it might be argued, is already a kind of theory about the existence of the autistic syndrome.

Nor is it always clear which behaviours are primary, which are secondary and which are symptoms of a co-occurring disorder. Autism seldom occurs in a pure form and the history of theory making and testing in autism contains many examples of 'explanatory' concepts that turn out to apply only to children with autism who also have a co-occurring disorder or difficulty such as a low level of language ability. It also has to be remembered that with any developmental disorder one is not just seeing the results of that disorder manifest in the behaviour of the individual, but also the attempts the individual has made (with or without educational support) to compensate for any difficulty experienced. Apart from compensatory strategies that may have been developed, any difficulty in development will also have consequences on the person's self-confidence, level of frustration, motivation to succeed and so on.

Most attempts to develop theories have used experimental paradigms in an attempt to isolate the variable being studied and control for these contaminating factors. Even so, it is rare in real life situations with human subjects that the experimental test of an hypothesis derived from a theory will be so well constructed that its results are not open to alternative explanations. It is in the development of alternative theoretical models to 'explain' data from experimental tests of other theories that new theories of autism often arise. In relation to that particular experiment the new theory may offer a more convincing, parsimonious and elegant account of the data than the theory being tested. This then can be the first step in theory building, but it is important to realise that this kind of *post hoc* analysis of data is only an initial process. That theoretical account must then be formulated in such a way that it in turn can be subject to experimental test and analysis. The scientific process can rarely determine that a theory is correct, although it can sometimes show that it is incorrect. More commonly it is a question of selecting the theory that offers the 'best fit' for the data, or refining a theory to make a better fit, until it is replaced by a better theory.

Experimental investigations may be necessary to test theoretical accounts of autism but the weaknesses of the method should also be noted. Observational studies are not only useful in developing theoretical accounts but also in testing the validity of theoretical notions. It has to be remembered that a theoretical account of autism should account for the behaviour seen in real life situations, not just that produced in highly structured artificial ones. The latter may provide insights into functioning in these particular conditions that help determine underlying psychological strengths and weaknesses. However, unless it also gives insights into how that pattern of psychological functioning affects naturally occurring behaviour, it will not be a satisfying theory at the level of psychological understanding, nor a useful one at the level of translating theory into practice. There is sometimes a danger that theorists fall in love with their theories and begin to collect evidence, not to try to test or refine the theory, but to validate it. Another danger from this is that the collection of evidence becomes like applying a pastry cutter to the world; the bits that do not quite 'fit' are just lopped off!

The theoretical accounts of autism offered below are not exhaustive, nor entirely random. They have been chosen for analysis because they represent, in the author's view, important milestones in the thinking about autism. They are also heterogeneous. Some are carefully constructed scientific theories whereas others come from a qualitative tradition of research and do not concern themselves with the testing of hypotheses to determine validity. Some are well established and have given rise to a wide body of experimental investigation, others are just at the stage of *post hoc* analysis of the experimental investigations of other theories and have yet to formulate the theory in a testable form. Almost all, it seems to the author, have something to offer in terms of understanding the condition; a theory does not need to be right to be useful and even 'wrong' theories can lead to fresh insights in the attempts to test them.

A word of caution

The theories explored below have had to be summarised, as has the research surrounding them. This means that there may have been some author's distortion of the views expressed, but it also means that complex ideas are given very little space. The effect is to make the writing very dense and difficult to read at one sitting. Readers are advised to use the following accounts as introductions to the theories, so they develop awareness of what is being proposed and the significance it may have. If the reader is intrigued by a theory, the author suggests reading the original texts. Some of these are far from easy to read, but it may be easier to do so when readers have got the gist of the idea from the summary here. The author also found it impossible to eliminate all jargon without being too verbose. For that, she can only apologise.

As with the rest of the handbook, the reader, especially if unfamiliar with the theories outlined, is advised not to try to read them all at once. Rather, the text is intended as a reference point when the reader comes across these theories in his or her general reading.

Theory of mind theory

This theory proposes a cognitive deficit in autism linking possibly multiple neurological abnormalities to multiple behavioural manifestations and Frith (1991b) argues that it is the role of cognitive neuropsychology to identify the underlying cognitive process that gives rise to these 'surface' behaviours. In that sense, it is a genuine psychological theory of autism. The seminal work in this theoretical account was a study by Baron-Cohen *et al.* (1985) testing for understanding of false belief in autism, false belief being the mental state that best illustrates understanding of mental states *as* mental states that can be divorced from reality. In normally developing children the understanding that someone (including themselves) can believe something that is not in fact the case does not develop in this form until around four years of age (Astington and Gopnik 1991). Wellman (1990) referred to this understanding of the mental states of oneself and others as possessing a theory of mind on the basis that mental states are not visible and, therefore, have to be hypothesised.

Moore and Frye (1991) point out that a 'theory of mind' is predominantly a social tool, affecting the way the child understands and interacts with others. The common elements of mental state psychology such as belief, desire and intention are central to cooperative and competitive behaviour. Wellman and Estes (1986) demonstrated that three-year-olds know the difference between a mental image and reality and Wellman and Bartsch (1988) have shown that they can predict behaviour on the basis of desires. But neither this first level of representation of reality, nor the understanding of desires, requires an understanding of the nature of representations themselves, which is what this theory holds is needed for an understanding of false belief, and which does not appear in normally developing children until a year later. It is a problem with this stage in the development of a 'theory of mind' which is thought to underlie autism in this theoretical framework.

Empirical base

Baron-Cohen *et al.* (1985) tested 20 children with autism, and with mental ages well in excess of four years, on the now classic 'Sally-Ann' task. In this task two dolls (Sally and Ann) act out a scenario in front of the child in which Sally places a marble in her basket and then goes out (is taken away from the scene in front of the child). While she is out, Ann moves Sally's marble from the basket to her own box and then she too goes out. Sally then comes back in and the child is asked the test question. 'Where will Sally look for her marble?' They found that 80 per cent of the children with autism failed to understand Sally's false belief and said she would look in the box where they knew the marble to be. Yet 86 per cent of the control group of children with Down's syndrome (who did not have autism and had a slightly lower average mental age) and the normally developing four-year-olds, showed understanding of Sally's false belief, saying she would look in the basket where she had left it.

This finding has been replicated in numerous studies. Some of these responded to criticisms of the original study by using real people instead of toys, using a 'think' question instead of a 'look' question, inserting a 'true belief' question, and using a control group of children with specific language impairment. This latter control was for failure to understand the language used, as an alternative explanation of the findings (Leslie and Frith, 1988; Perner *et al.* 1989). Alternative tests of the ability to understand one's own false belief have also been derived (Perner *et al.* 1987; Happé 1989) and have shown a similar level of specific deficit in autism. Baron-Cohen *et al.* (1986b) compared the understanding of mechanical, behavioural and intentional understanding of picture stories in children with autism. They found that only those stories requiring understanding of mental states (the intentional stories) were differentially not understood by children with autism, compared to children with Down's syndrome and normally developing children.

Frith (1989b) has argued that difficulties in developing a theory of mind in autism can account for many of the characteristic behaviours shown; is a feature that is common to autistic spectrum disorders; and differentiates those with autism from other groups. She suggests that it succeeds in allowing researchers to make 'clean cuts' in what otherwise might appear to be similar behaviour, giving clues to the underlying mechanism at fault. Thus, Attwood *et al.* (1988) were able to show that it was only gestures that influence mental states (such as expressions of consolation, embarrassment and goodwill) that the group with autism did not display. Their production of other gestures (such as signals to come, be quiet or go away) was not significantly different from the control group of children with severe learning difficulties. In another study, Baron-Cohen (1989) found that children with autism were selectively impaired in protodeclarative pointing (pointing to establish joint attention) but not in protoimperative pointing (pointing to get needs met).

Tager-Flusberg (1989) also found, in her longitudinal study, that children with autism only developed communicative functions that affected the behaviour of others (such as 'request') and not those (such as 'comment') that affected mental states. Children with Down's syndrome, on the other hand, developed a wide range of communicative functions simultaneously, as do normally developing children. The author (Jordan 1993) supported this finding in her longitudinal study of the spontaneous signing of children with autism; the only spontaneous functional uses recorded were of request and refusal. Tager-Flusberg (1989) also found that children with autism did not use mental state verbs in their natural 'conversations' with others.

Development of theory of mind understanding, within this theory, is believed to continue beyond the four year watershed in normal development, when false beliefs are understood, and to have earlier precursors to this level of understanding. For example, normally developing children are said to go on to develop representations of other representations or 'second order theory of mind' understanding. As a precursor to 'false belief' understanding, Wellman (1991) has shown that three-year-olds can understand desire, but not belief. Within these knowledge-based (epistemic) mental states, of which belief is the prime example, there is also said to be a progression in understanding. Taylor (1988) reviews the evidence for normally developing children. He reports that they go from an early understanding that 'seeing equals knowing', through the four- to five-year-olds' understanding that access to relevant information leads to belief, and finally, to the six- to eight-year-olds' understanding that informational access interacts with preexisting knowledge to produce current knowledge.

If children with autism have difficulties with false belief, they may also have difficulties with the processes underlying that understanding. Oswald and Ollendick (1989) tested for understanding that 'seeing equals knowing' by using a penny hiding game with children with autism and they found an impaired capacity for deception which correlated with their performance on false belief tasks and measures of their social competence. Baron-Cohen (1992a) replicated those findings and used new analytical techniques (error analysis rather than simply pass/fail scoring) to discriminate the autistic group more clearly from the controls. The scoring allowed the construction of an index of simple deception (gives no clues) and complex deception (tries to deceive). He found that subjects with autism were able to appreciate the game at the level of occlusion (keeping things out of sight) but could not understand information occlusion (keeping things out of mind). This supports the idea that those with autism do not understand that 'seeing leads to knowing', although they may be able to act behaviourally to block sight of an object. Similarly, Sodian and Frith (1992) found that children with autism were able to sabotage the chances of an 'opponent' in a game (by blocking access to a desired object) but were not able to deceive (by misinforming the 'opponent'). However, there was a heavy linguistic factor involved in these studies.

Baron-Cohen (1991) examined the awareness of one's own mental states with test questions that were specific as to time, since this had been found to be a critical factor in normally developing children's understanding of their own prior beliefs (Lewis and Osborne, 1990). He found that children with autism showed a different developmental sequence in their understanding of mental state terms than the group with learning difficulties and normally developing control group. For the autistic group, the order of difficulty was first their own perception and desire, then imagination, then pretence, and finally belief. For the control groups, desire was more difficult than perception, imagination and pretence, although belief was also acquired last. Baron-Cohen *et al.* (1997) found that children with autism were no different from verbal age-matched control groups in telling where eyes are looking, or judging whether or not a person depicted in a photograph was looking at them. However, they were specifically impaired in not being able to 'read' eye points to judge intention or desire or thinking. Phillips (1994) argued that previous studies of intention in autism have confused desire with intention. He used a 'fortuitous success' paradigm (which divorced intention from desire) to overcome this problem. Judgement of intention itself was later to develop than false belief in all the groups studied and was specifically delayed in autism, although it is a non-epistemic mental state (that is, it does not depend on the actor's knowledge). This has relevance for Leslie's (1987, 1991) construction of the 'theory of mind theory'.

In general, the finding that individuals with autism have difficulties in understanding and using mental state terms, beyond any difficulties expected due to mental or verbal age, has been a robust one. Yet it was clear from the original study by Baron-Cohen *et al.* (1985), and it has been supported by other studies, that there is a proportion of individuals with autism who do pass the false belief tasks used. To see if more advanced development of a 'theory of mind' was affected in this group, Baron-Cohen (1989) gave those children with autism, and verbal age-matched controls, a test for their understanding of second order belief attribution. He used an adaptation of the 'ice-cream van' task developed by Perner and Wimmer (1985). In this task, the child has to predict the behaviour of a puppet protagonist acting on a false belief about the false belief of another protagonist in the story. All the children with autism who had passed first order false belief tasks, failed this second order false belief task whereas 90 per cent of the normally developing and 60 per cent of the Down's children passed. Baron-Cohen also got the subjects to give justifications for their responses and he found that those with autism used either first level theory of mind attributions to the protagonist or used physical state justifications for their responses.

Bowler (1992) made a particular study of theory of mind in Asperger's syndrome. He found no significant group differences comparing the Asperger's group to schizophrenic and normally developing subjects in first order theory of mind tasks. In fact, he found that the schizophrenic group performed least well on these tasks. With second order tasks no significant group differences were found and none of the groups referred to mental states as justification. Bowler then devised a different story to the ice cream van story and used one that allowed more focus on mental states and was more age-appropriate to the group being tested (the 'overcoat' story). In this story the event leading to the false belief was a non-intentional 'random' one. He found that this story led to a greater use of mental state justifications in all three groups. However, fewer normally developing and schizophrenic subjects passed with this story than with the ice-cream van one, whereas the number of Asperger's syndrome subjects passing second order belief questions was the same (73 per cent) in both stories. Yet the subjects with Asperger's syndrome who passed both second order theory of mind tasks did not perform any better in real life situations. Bowler suggests that high functioning people with autism may possess the ability to reason about others' mental states but are unable to apply that reasoning in demanding conditions, such as when there are time constraints, or no visual cues, or in social situations with competing multiple stimuli.

Happé (1994b) used an advanced test of theory of mind, using understanding of specially constructed stories, with able groups with autism, those with learning difficulties and normally developing children and adults. She found that performance on these story tasks mirrored the performance of the subjects on theory of mind tasks but revealed further difficulty in the group with autism with more naturalistic stories. Some stories involved third order 'theory of mind' understanding of the type 'he knows they think he will lie'. Happé suggests that some of those with Asperger's syndrome who pass second-order false belief tasks do so by non-mentalising means. She suggests that is so because they do not display knowledge of mentalising abilities in real life situations and give idiosyncratic responses to advanced theory of mind tasks, constructing an elaborate and unusual physical explanation for the scenarios, which bypasses the need for mentalising. The present author's problem with this study is that examples of physical state justifications that are given as illustrating the difficulty of individuals with autism with mental state justifications seem to include the recognition of intentions. For example, justifications such as, 'so he won't have to go to the dentist', 'so she won't get spanked', or 'in order to sell the kittens' may relate to the behaviour of the protagonists but they refer to the intentions behind the behaviour rather than the behaviour itself. The author can understand the argument that such statements could be given without an understanding of mental states (that is, with a simple awareness of the behavioural consequences of actions). However, they do not seem to be strong evidence that there is *not* an awareness of mental states, being pragmatically appropriate expressions of implied mental states.

Holroyd and Baron-Cohen (1993) have examined the development of theory of mind over time in autism. Seventeen children with autism (13 of whom had failed the first order theory of mind tests) were tested after a period of seven years. They found a mean of two years change in mental age, yet none of the subjects passed the ice-cream van test and only three passed the Sally-Ann test. These three successful subjects had a minimum verbal mental age (VMA) of 8;1, a minimum chronological age (CA) of 13;3 and a minimum non-verbal mental age (MA) of 8;6. The most interesting finding was that the three who passed at follow-up did not differ from the others in terms of CA, non-verbal or verbal MA. Of the 17 subjects in the study, four had passed the Sally-Ann test on original testing. Of those four, two passed on follow-up and two failed. Only one who had originally failed passed on retesting. Thus, there were no significant group changes in the number passing over time.

The 'puzzling out' of mental states, alluded to above by Bowler, is described very well in a personal account of her own cognitive and social difficulties by a high functioning adult with autism (Grandin 1995; Sacks 1995). Grandin (1995) claims'... In autistic people, the intellect is used to learn social skills' (p. 147) and again '...I use logic and intellect to guide my decisions rather than emotions'

(p. 149) Frith *et al.* (1991) also suggest that children who pass false belief tasks may do so by another route: by learning the surface form rather than learning about mental states. They suggest, for example, that successful passing of the Sally-Ann task may be due to learning rules such as 'choose the container where the ball is not found' or 'choose the container where Sally first put the ball' rather than by the attribution of mental states.

This view would be supported by the work of Ozonoff and Miller (1995) who gave social skills training and theory of mind tasks to individuals with autism. Over a four and a half month study, they found that training improved the performance of the treatment group, on theory of mind tasks and laboratory-based social skill responses, relative to controls. Yet there were no differences in the actual social skills exhibited by the two groups in real life situations, as rated by parents and teachers. The work of Starr (1993), teaching the appearance-reality distinction to children with autism, was in accord with this, showing no evidence of transfer of training to real life scenarios and no improvement in social behaviour from those who learnt appearance-reality distinctions (previous false perceptions). Swettenham (1996) devised a computer version of the Sally-Ann task and used it to teach false belief to children with autism, children with Down's syndrome and normally developing children. Initially all the children failed four false belief tasks. One was the doll's version of the Sally-Ann task (close transfer task) and there were three versions involving different scenarios (distant transfer tasks). Following teaching, all three groups were able to pass the Sally-Ann task but only the children with autism alone were unable to pass the distant transfer tasks. Swettenham suggests that the children with autism constructed a different strategy to pass the Sally-Ann task, supporting the view of Frith *et al.* (1991).

Reviewing her own and others' work on theory of mind and autism, Happé (1995a) concludes that children with autism require a far higher verbal mental age to pass false belief tasks than do those with learning difficulties, or normally developing children. She suggests a verbal MA of 9;2 rather than 4;0 is needed. Yet Tager-Flusberg and Sullivan (1994) studied a group of high functioning adolescents with autism and found they were not significantly different from a control group with learning difficulties in two short stories of deception involving second order theory of mind. The difference between this and earlier studies, however, was that these stories had low information processing demands, and the researchers suggest that this may have led to the failure to find autism-specific difficulties. Yimiya *et al.* (1992), working with high functioning children with autism, found that only in the autistic group was performance on empathy and conservation measures correlated with intelligence. Happé, (1993, 1994b) has shown that theory of mind performance is a good predictor of test performance in figurative language, and speaker's meaning across a range of utterances such as jokes and lies, but this does not prove a causal relationship, nor the direction of causation. Tager-Flusberg (1996) has suggested that high functioning individuals with autism with good structural language ability use that ability through their knowledge of the particular grammar of mental state verbs (to think/feel/want, etc.) to pass theory of mind tests.

Ozonoff *et al.* (1991a) have also studied theory of mind in Asperger's syndrome, comparing the performance of that group with those diagnosed as 'high functioning autistic'. They found differential responses in the two groups and claim that it was only the high functioning autistic group that were impaired on theory of mind tasks. They also replicated the study of Baron-Cohen *et al.* (1986b) with stories. As with the Baron-Cohen *et al.* study, they found the groups with autism and Asperger's syndrome performed better on the physical stories but both these groups and the control group performed poorly on the mental state stories. Thus they found no specific deficit in this, attributable to autism, once language ability was controlled. Perner *et al.* (1989), however, found no relationship between theory of mind ability and verbal mental age (VMA), chronological age (CA) or non-verbal mental age (NVMA).

Eisenmajer and Prior (1991) examined the cognitive and linguistic correlates of theory of mind ability in children with autism. Their sample of high functioning children with autism had a mean MA of 7;9 which was over two years in advance of that of the children in the Baron-Cohen *et al.* (1985) study and seven months in advance of the children in the Leslie and Frith (1988) study. In the first study they replicated the Sally-Ann task as presented by Baron-Cohen *et al.* (1985) but in the second condition they changed the critical question to 'Where will Sally look for her marble *first?*'. This was in deference to the concerns over the interpretation of the task voiced by Siegel and Beattie (1991). This change resulted in 50 per cent of those who failed under the original presentation passing, with this emphasis on the explicit intention of the question: that the child should say where Sally will look first, rather than where she would have to look to find it. Overall, the percentage passing was much higher than that reported by the earlier studies, being 60 per cent. The verbal mental age of all those with autism who passed was above 5;0 and the CA above 8;0, but there was not a complete correlation between verbal MA and ability to pass theory of mind tasks.

On the other hand, Sparrevohn and Howie (1995), although they found no relationship between performance on a series of theory of mind tasks and real life social skills, did find that verbal ability was a significant factor in success on these tasks. Siegal and Peterson (1994) and the work of Dunn (1988, 1991) showed that theory of mind abilities in normally developing children depended at least in part on the richness of their conversations with others (including siblings) in natural settings. Both Happé (1995a) and Yirmiya *et al.* (1999) show there is a strong association between level of language ability and passing theory of mind tests but, as Rutter (1999) remarks, this connection has not yet been elaborated. He also suggests that it is an insufficient explanation for the theory of mind problems found in autism.

Leslie's representation theory

Leslie (1987) has been largely responsible for developing the theory of a theory of mind deficit in autism. His model is an information processing one and he suggests that this includes an innately endowed Theory of Mind Module (TOMM). He suggests (Leslie, 1991) that understanding propositional attitudes (believing that p, desiring that p, pretending that p) underlies a theory of mind and that the key to this development is the capacity for pretence and 'metarepresentation' (sic). Leslie uses 'metarepresentation' in an idiosyncratic way and this has been the basis for some of the criticism of the theory. Leslie contends that what is represented in the pretend act is opaque in its meaning in the sense that it does not refer to reality but to someone's (oneself's or someone else's) attitude to that reality; in Leslie's jargon the representation has to be 'decoupled' from reality. As Leslie (1991; p. 64) points out, 'intentional behaviour is often understood in relation to counterfactual situations.' Thus, in order to take part in shared pretend acts the child must access in Leslie's terms a metarepresentational module. The present author would draw attention to the shared aspect of pretence which features in Leslie's account but does not appear crucial to it, whereas the author believes that it is this shared aspect that may be part of the difficulty in autism. In Leslie's view, however, it is this metarepresentational function that is claimed to be dysfunctional in autism.

In proposing a theory of mind deficit at the heart of autism, however, Leslie is not claiming that people with autism are like normally developing three-year-olds, stuck at that stage of development. He notes the reports and the research, pointing to an impairment and/or delay in 'pretend play' in autism (Ungerer and Sigman 1981; Libby *et al.* 1995). Unlike normally developing three-year-olds, individuals with autism may be impaired on true as well as false belief (Leslie 1991) and on the understanding of 'false' desire (unfulfilled desire) (Harris and Muncer 1988). Baron-Cohen (1992b) has also established that children with autism have difficulty distinguishing actual objects from thoughts about objects (or at least that they have difficulty with the vocabulary that establishes that distinction) whereas Wellman and Estes (1986) found this was no problem for normally developing three-year-olds. Leslie and his colleagues, therefore, are proposing a deficit in autism in which a failure to develop a theory of mind, as evidenced through false belief understanding, is central, but in which there are significant precursors.

Leslie (1991) specifies the theory thus: 'Autistic children are impaired and/or delayed in their capacity to form and/or process metarepresentations. This impairs (delays) their capacity to acquire a theory of mind' (p. 73). He also draws a parallel between intentional communication and pretence whereby in the former (following an account of the computation of relevance, as given by Sperber and Wilson 1986) a communicative gesture not only refers to something but also contains within it the display of that intention to communicate. But the intended message has to be inferred and Leslie claims that this inference involves metarepresentation. Both communicative acts and pretend acts, then, are exaggerated to provide a perceptual marker of their 'decoupling' from their normal function. Leslie further suggests that the capacity to perceive these intentional acts may be hardwired (genetically endowed) and the perceptual module that allows this provides essential input to the later developing TOMM.

Leslie (1987, 1994) and Leslie and Roth (1993) have developed this theory in greater detail. They use the term 'metarepresentation' to refer to a kind of data structure computed by the cognitive system, which may or may not be a conscious process. It provides an 'agent-centred' description of a situation. Thus it has a number of components with different functions, as follows:

- specification of the agent;
- specification of the information relationship between the agent and the other two components;
- a primary representation; and
- a 'decoupled' representation.

For example, mother (agent) PRETENDS the banana 'is a telephone' (proposition).

TOMM is said by Leslie to comprise two systems. System 1 develops in the first year of life and is signalled by gaze monitoring, request pointing and understanding of desire, and System 2 develops in the second year and involves M-representations, intentional communication, declarative pointing and showing and, later, pretence. It also has a 'decoupler' and one function of this has three parts:

1. The *expression raiser* – copies the primary representation into decoupling marks.
2. The *manipulator* – changes the copy of the primary representation within decoupling marks and represents this change to be used for pretence purposes.
3. The *interpreter* – coordinates the pretend representation with the primary representation to ensure execution of the pretend act.

Note that in Leslie's view, (and in those of the theorists who take this position), although the notion of 'agent' is raised, there is no privileged status to 'self-as-agent'. Thus the perception of mental states as mental states (and presumably the actions resulting from them, although the theory does not refer to actions) is meant to be the same, whether those mental states are one's own or belong to someone else. Russell (1996) offers cogent criticism of representational accounts such as this, which make no mention of action.

Criticism of this theory

Studies have been carried out on normally developing children's difficulties with theory of mind tasks suggesting factors that might affect performance, other than understanding other minds. One factor is the relationship between implicit and explicit knowledge. Clements and Perner (1994) found that monitoring the eye-gaze of normally developing 2;11 to 4;5 year-olds showed that 90 per cent pass the Sally-Ann false belief task if they are only required to look at the place where Sally will look when she enters but, when asked to respond to a question, only 45 per cent are able to answer the question explicitly. The researchers distinguish representing a fact from making a judgement about that fact. This time lag in development between implicit and explicit knowledge and understanding might be even more crucial in autism where difficulties in self-awareness and an inability to reflect on one's own thought processes might lead to an even greater developmental lag between the two.

Zaitchik (1990) has challenged Leslie's 'metarepresentational' explanation of theory of mind difficulties in three-year-olds. She showed that they experience even greater difficulty in understanding that instant photographs could depict a past reality, and suggests that this is not due to the metarepresentational nature of the photographs, but to the dominant saliency of the existing situation. Studies replicating Zaitchik's experiment (by this author and others), or adapting it slightly, with children with autism (Jordan and Powell, 1991; Leekam and Perner 1991) have shown that these children find 'false' photographs easier to understand than false belief (in contrast to normally developing children). Their greater understanding of photographs might reflect teaching conditions where photographs are well used and the greater chronological age of the children with autism tested. Jordan and Powell (1991) and Leekam and Perner (1991) both argue that it cannot, therefore, be a problem with metarepresentation that leads to theory of mind difficulties in autism, as Leslie (1991) had suggested, as false photographs involved the same degree of metarepresentation as false beliefs. Criticisms of these studies on the grounds that the photographs were not really 'false' led Parkin and Perner (1994) to conduct a similar experiment using instant photographs with an appearance-reality task to produce truly misleading photographs. The children with autism tested still found this task easier than the false belief task (unlike the normally developing children who found it of equal difficulty), although more difficult than the Zaitchik type photograph task. Leslie and Thaiss (1992) replicated the findings in relation to photographs and amended the theory to take account of them, making the theory of mind module specific to mental representations.

Variable performance on tasks designed to test the same kind of fundamental ability have also led to queries concerning the unitary nature of the phenomenon being considered. Parkin (1995) found a lack of correlation between false belief task performance and performance on appearance-reality distinction tasks in children with autism and also found a difference in the relations between the self and other conditions on the deceptive contents task for the autistic group only. Bowler *et al.* (1999) comment on the similarity of false belief tasks to Piagetian number conservation tasks and claim that they are open to the same criticisms as the latter. They cite the McGarrigle and Donaldson (1974) study with normally developing children, showing that failure in a number conservation task was due to the failure to understand the intentional structure of the interaction, not difficulties with conservation as such. Bowler *et al.* used a false drawing paradigm with normally developing children and found that significantly more children correctly identified the contents of the drawing when made and hidden by 'naughty snaky' than by the experimenter. Under these conditions the task became easier than a false belief task. Bowler *et al.* cite Fodor's argument (1992) that children have the capacity to understand false belief from birth but lack the computational resources to solve the problems set. They suggest that their study supports a performance model in terms of theory of mind difficulties both in normally developing young children and in those with autism, and a process of social learning in the acquisition of explicit knowledge of mental states.

Sodian and Frith's (1992) study which found children with autism competent at sabotage (locking the box to prevent a sweet being taken) but not at deception (saying the box was locked or pointing to an empty box), has also been given a performance interpretation by Hughes and Russell (1993). Using an adaptation of Sodian and Frith's procedure, whereby the child simply had to point to the clearly visible empty container to obtain the sweet, they found that children with autism could not refrain from pointing at the full container, regardless of whether or not there was a competitor. Thus, they suggest that the difficulties are not in deceiving, but in inhibiting actions. Control children with learning difficulties performed less well when there was no competitor, suggesting that they may have been affected by the abnormal pragmatics of the situation (i.e. pointing to an empty box for no reason) whereas this was not a factor in the responses by the autistic group.

An associated argument suggests that the nature of the language used (rather than just its complexity) may cause specific difficulty for children with autism. Lewis and Osborne (1990), working with normally developing three-year-olds, compared 'What did you think was in the box?' (the standard question in a task concerning recall of one's own past false belief), 'What did you think was in the box when the top was still on it?' (the 'when' question) and 'What did you think was in the box before I took the top off?' (the 'before' question). They found that three-year-olds were more able to answer false belief questions when the time was specified and they were then equally able to predict their own and others' beliefs. 'When' was more difficult than 'before'. This suggests that the standard question may rely on pragmatic implications for its interpretation and it may be this that causes the difficulty in autism. Wagstaff (1995) has suggested, following an experimental adaptation of the Sally-Ann task involving transparent and opaque requests for the item misplaced, that children with autism do not have a problem with referential opacity as such but with literality and a realist interpretation both of situations and the language used. Mitchell (1997) presents a strong case for the effects of a concrete representation of the original belief in normally developing children, and this may be of even greater significance in autism.

Processing complexity has been found to be a significant factor in success on theory of mind tasks in a number of different studies. Chandler *et al.* (1989) used a hide and seek board game with normally developing children. They showed that even children aged 2;6 were capable of successfully employing a range of deceptive strategies that trade upon an awareness of the possibility of false beliefs and presuppose some already operative theory of mind. The researchers pointed out that classic false belief tasks involve initial processing of a lengthy narrative about characters (fictional or dolls) and that difficulties may stem from topic maintenance problems. Draper and Bowler (1994) have suggested that it is a difficulty in understanding the structure and content of narratives that leads to characteristic errors in young children and children with autism.

There are several advantages of the procedure used in the Chandler *et al.* study over traditional false belief tasks. One advantage is that it clearly engages the subject's own self-interests in that it pits the person's interests against those of another real person. Furthermore, it requires only a modicum of verbal instruction, it is computationally more straightforward, and it does not depend on memorising a story narrative. Finally, it allows direct evidence in action rather than requiring the child to passively describe. Of course, what may be advantageous to normally developing young children may not be so to those with autism, but such manipulations do show that task demands can be a significant factor in theory of mind task results. Chandler *et al.* also suggest that there may be a difficulty in talking about mental states rather than the assumed difficulty in hypothesising about them.

Some attempts to reduce processing demands, however, have had little effect. Bowler *et al.* (1993) attempted to reduce memory demands in a standard false belief task by adding a photograph to remind the subject of the original location and providing a handkerchief of the protagonist left at the original location. For preschool normally developing children, neither condition improved performance. Bowler and Briskman (submitted) found the same negative effects when they used photographic cues in the Sally-Ann task. Yet when Bowler and Stromm (1998) used enhanced behavioural and emotional cues for the protagonist in the 'story' the children with autism (as well as some of the young normally developing children) were able to improve their performance. Mere repetition of the task without enhancement produced no effect. The control group with learning difficulties, on the other hand, did not benefit from the enhancement procedure.

In second order theory of mind tasks, offering a choice rather than a single judgement seemed to make it easier for children with autism in a study by Leekam and Prior (1994). Using a forced choice task, they found 50 per cent of children with autism were able to pass second order theory of mind tests and make correct social judgements about lies and jokes in the task story. Yet parents reported no incidences of lying, intentional jokes or irony in the group passing these tests. Again, it appears that artificiality is of benefit to those with autism but the reverse is the case for the normally developing child. Processing information in real life situations may simply be too complex when there is no accessible way to code social information, as might be the case in autism.

Roth and Leslie (1991) used a speaker-listener scenario in which a lie was told, and found that normally developing five-year-olds attribute this to the speaker's deceit, three-year-olds to the speaker's mistake and children with autism do not consider the mental states of the speaker at all. Happé and Frith (1995) suggest that it is only children with autism who have a specific problem with mental representations. They attribute success by people with autism on theory of mind tasks to the fact that it may be a delay rather than an absolute deficit and/or to the use of compensatory strategies, which do not have to rely on mental state understanding.

A fundamental critique of this theory has come from Perner (1993). His first criticism concerns Leslie's use of the term 'metarepresentation', but is too technical to include here. In examining whether children with autism can be said to be 'decoupling impaired', as suggested by Leslie (under Perner's reinterpretation), Perner points out that one is looking for autism specificity. That being the case, there needs to be an explanation of why only 75 per cent of bright people with autism (with MAs greater than four years) fail theory of mind tasks. Perner goes on to analyse the components of Leslie's TOMM in terms of the performance of individuals with autism on tasks requiring each of these components in turn. He claims that the evidence can only support a weak (performance, rather than competence) version of Leslie's theory.

Perner (1993), however, favours an explanation for autism in terms of a domain general deficit in dealing with metarepresentations in their true sense. He (1991) had argued that a new view of representation is acquired at four years – his notion of metarepresentation. He suggests further that we all start as situation theorists, and that this way of thinking persists into adulthood, but by four years of age we add the ability to be representation theorists. The situation theorist, then, would not differentiate representational media and content and cannot differentiate mental states such as dreaming or imagining from ones representing reality such as belief (that is, 'thinking *of*' versus 'thinking *that*'). He proposes that children with autism are limited to a situation theory, but with age they are more sophisticated in their knowledge of situations such as photos. Such a limitation might arise through problems in the knowledge base, perhaps in turn arising from problems with shifting attention (Courchesne 1991), which would limit engagement in social interactions in which continual monitoring is essential.

Spontaneous pretence also requires continuous monitoring of the real world against one's own pretend acts, and this may be a source of difficulty in autism. Lewis and Boucher (1988) and Boucher and Lewis (1990) suggest that children with autism are capable of elicited symbolic play and Baron-Cohen's data (1989) on elicited symbolic play shows this ability is correlated with passing first order theory of mind tasks. Yet even those who failed theory of mind tasks could perform symbolic acts when prompted, suggesting that it is the ease with which symbolic acts are effected that is a problem in autism, not the lack of symbolic acts as such. The performances on Zaitchik's task (outlined above) also suggest that individuals with autism have all the mechanisms of Leslie's proposed decoupler except perhaps for personalisation.

Leslie's answer to these criticisms is that the difficulty is domain specific and that there is a mechanism (TOMM) that deals with just those domain specific processes. Thus TOMM applies to agents only and yet it is a very passive form of agency as was pointed out earlier, in which agency is observed rather than experienced.

Adding to the criticisms of a theory of mind deficit as an explanation of autism have been those studies which show that other groups may share those difficulties. Peterson and Siegal (1995) showed that congenitally deaf children of hearing parents (who thus have no language with which to enter into conversational exchanges in their early years) show similar delay in theory of mind tasks (administered through sign language) to those with autism. Hobson (1995a) also showed that difficulties and delays in acquiring a theory of mind (or at least, in passing specially adapted false belief tasks) were characteristic of the congenitally blind. Although some blind children may share some of the features characteristic of autism in their development (especially in language), these children did not have autism, either defined clinically or through diagnostic criteria. Hughes *et al.* (1998) have even shown that subclinical groups of 'hard-to-manage' preschool children also show difficulties with false belief (and emotion understanding) tasks.

Those with severe learning difficulties (Ashcroft *et al.* 1999; Benson *et al.* 1993) may also share the same apparent 'deficits' in passing false belief tasks as children with autism. This may be puzzling, when considering that most experimental tests of false belief in children with autism have a control group of children with learning difficulties. However, it must be remembered that the term 'learning difficulties' is not a diagnostic term and covers a range of medical conditions. Children with Down's syndrome are often used as controls in such studies but we do not know whether these children (or any other group with learning difficulties) has an evenly delayed profile of skills. What if the Down's syndrome group were (as anecdotal evidence suggests) particularly advanced (compared to other skills) in social cognition? Comparison with such a group could not then be taken as indicative of a specific deficit in autism. Indeed, Yirmiya *et al.* (1996) conducted a study involving two comparison groups to the group with autism, one with Down's syndrome and one with non-specific general learning difficulties. They found a difference in performance across all three groups. On the other hand, Zelazo *et al.* (1996) showed that adults with Down's syndrome, who had more severe learning difficulties than those used as controls in other studies, also showed clear deficits in theory of mind tasks.

It is somewhat ironic that, just as there are increasing doubts about the theory of mind deficit account of autism, it seems to be gaining acceptance by practitioners. Of course, it may be helpful to those who have difficulty in understanding mental states to have specific teaching directed at this area of development. That will apply whether the individuals have severe learning difficulties (Ashcroft *et al.* 1999) or autism (Hadwin *et al.* 1996). It may even be helpful for the congenitally deaf or blind, although common sense suggests that access to a shared communication system with parents and others would be likely to be more broadly beneficial. What should be avoided is any implication that teaching about theory of mind, in contexts divorced from everyday processing demands, is necessarily going to be of general benefit to those with autism.

The doubts about the theory of mind theory of autism arise because neither condition for a satisfactory explanatory theory is met. It does not seem to apply to all those with autism (Baron-Cohen *et al.* 1985; Chandler *et al.* 1989; Draper and Bowler 1994; Leekam and Prior 1994; Perner 1993, Rutter 1999); nor does it appear to be limited to that condition (Ashcroft *et al.* 1999; Benson *et al.* 1993; Hobson, 1995a; Hughes *et al.* 1998; Peterson and Siegel 1995; Zelazo *et al.* 1996). The fact that passing false belief tasks also seems to be highly dependent on language ability suggests two things. Not only may language ability itself be a critical factor in determining success on theory of mind tasks, but the social difficulty experienced by children with autism may exclude them from the opportunities of learning about mental states. This may mean that they are then like the congenitally deaf child, deprived of hearing the vocabulary used in a context that would give it meaning. This is just the mechanism that Dunn (1988; 1991; 1994) proposes is necessary for understanding of mental states to develop. In other words, theory of mind difficulties may be a secondary rather than a primary disability in autism.

Evolutionary theory

The evolutionary theory is the latest development of the theory of mind theory (Baron-Cohen 1995), incorporating that theory and building precursors into it. In this theory, Baron-Cohen presents a four-stage model of acquisition of mindreading ability, set in an evolutionary context, and suggests that autism represents a specific case of 'mindblindness'. The theory builds on Humphrey's notion (1984) that 'human beings are born psychologists' (p. 3) and that this is the result of an evolutionary process. It also accepts Dennett's view (1987) of the 'intentional stance' which he defines as the ability to attribute a full set of intentional states (beliefs, desires, intentions, hopes, thoughts, memories, fears, promises, and so on) to others. Dennett claims that alternatives to understanding complex social systems, such as people, through other than the intentional stance, are:

1. The physical stance – in terms of their physical make-up (which depends on understanding the properties of the system, for example, knowing about the brain states involved; this is not yet known and is too slow and complex to be used in everyday settings) or
2. The design stance – in terms of their functions (which is used when the physical properties are not known but the functions of parts of the system are, and thus this makes predictions possible, but it relies on observable operational parts that are not true of much human functioning).

Therefore, Dennett concludes, the use of mindreading has emerged because it works at interpreting and predicting at speed.

Baron-Cohen proposes that humans have an innate 'mindreading instinct' (p. 10) which fills in gaps in communication that enable it to cohere, thus enabling normal communication to proceed on the basis of understanding what the speaker intends rather than a literal translation of what is said. He further suggests that there are four mechanisms, functioning as separate components of the human mindreading system, and that these mechanisms 'roughly reflect four properties of the world: volition, perception, shared attention and epistemic states' (p. 31).

ID (intentionality detector)

This first of the four mechanisms is a ' . . . perceptual device that interprets motion stimuli in terms of the primitive volitional mental states of goal and desire' (p. 32).

In other words, it enables the interpretation of approach and avoidance behaviour. It is activated by stimuli with self-propelled motion or non-random sound leading to the attribution of agent status to the source of that stimulation. This mechanism can operate within any modality so it is not destroyed by sensory loss short of total loss, although some sensory information (such as vision and sound) may be privileged. It is based on Premack's notion (1990) that goal detection is hardwired into the human brain (that it is a genetic endowment). The ID represents dyadic relations between an agent and an object or between an agent and self. It is not clear from Baron-Cohen's exposition whether it would also represent self as agent (using proprioceptive or kinaesthetic stimulation, perhaps). Baron-Cohen suggests that this mechanism is intact in autism. The evidence for this assertion comes from the use of volitional vocabulary by children with autism (Baron-Cohen *et al.*, 1986b; Tager-Flusberg 1989, 1993), from the fact that they are able to distinguish animacy (Baron-Cohen 1991) and understand that desires cause emotions (Baron-Cohen 1991; Phillips 1993; Tan & Harris 1991).

It appears from his exposition that Baron-Cohen (1995) intends to refer to a 'desire' detection device and the use of the term 'intentionality' detector is unfortunate, in view of Phillips' reservations (1994), mentioned above. As we have seen, people with autism may be able to understand about people wanting things, but they are likely to have much more difficulty in working out what they intend by their actions, which is why they have difficulties understanding that desires may be unfulfilled.

EDD (eye-direction detector)

This mechanism works only through vision. It has three functions:

1. To detect the presence of eyes or eye-like stimuli;
2. To compute whether the eyes are directed towards self or not; and
3. To infer from the individual's own case that eye direction equals seeing what they are directed at.

Mutual eye contact in humans and primates is associated with physiological arousal with positive affect. The regulation of eye contact is precocious in infants (Stern 1985) and infants strive to maintain an optimum level of stimulation (Maurer 1993). Baron-Cohen (1995) suggests that knowledge of seeing and not seeing, related to eye direction, is generalised to an agent by analogy with the self. This assumes that the notion of the self is primitive and Baron-Cohen offers no mechanism for its derivation. Russell (1996) has argued the case for such primacy, but it must be part of the theoretical account – not assumed.

The function of the EDD is to represent dyadic relations between an agent and an object or an agent and the self. Baron-Cohen maintains that during the early stages, when EDD is working alone, it is intact in autism. The evidence for this comes from several sources. There is the ability of individuals with autism to detect direction in photos (Baron-Cohen *et al.* 1997). There is also the fact people with

Autism use 'see' in speech (Tager-Flusberg 1993; Baron-Cohen *et al*, 1986b) and can work out another's eye direction (Hobson 1984; Baron-Cohen 1989, 1991; Tan and Harris 1991; Leekam *et al.* 1997; Leekam *et al.* 1998). However, this assertion fails to take account of the evidence (Leekam *et al.* 1997; Leekam *et al.* 1998; Loveland 1991) that gaze monitoring is not spontaneous in autism, but has to be cued or prompted. A failure to spontaneously activate a crucial, innate mechanism would seem to this author to be of significant developmental import.

SAM (shared attention mechanism)

This third mechanism is responsible for building the triadic representations that specify the relations between an agent, the self and a third object. It includes embedded knowledge that an agent and the self are attending to the same object, which accounts for the triadic nature of the representations. SAM receives information from the EDD as a privileged relationship but it can use information about perceptual states from other modalities. SAM also makes ID's output available to EDD so that eye direction is then read in terms of goals and desires. This also allows joint referencing so that eye gaze is interpreted as an intention to refer (a kind of pointing). Baron-Cohen suggests that this mechanism is specifically impaired in autism so that it does not function through any modality (vision, touch or audition). Thus, in autism, there is no output from SAM to trigger TOMM. The evidence of its failure to work in autism comes from joint attention studies (Baron-Cohen *et al.* 1995; Dawson and Fernald, 1987; Landry and Loveland 1988; Leekam *et al.* 1997; 1998; Loveland 1991; Mundy *et al.* 1986).

TOMM (theory-of-mind mechanism)

This part of Baron-Cohen's theory is derived directly from Leslie (1994). This fourth mechanism is the system for inferring the full range of mental states from behaviour. It represents the epistemic mental states (pretending, thinking, knowing, believing, imagining, dreaming, guessing and deceiving). Leslie calls the representations of propositional attitudes necessary for the representation of epistemic mental states 'M-representations'. TOMM receives input from ID and EDD via SAM. Thus, a further function is to convert triadic representations from SAM into M-representations.

The developmental sequence proposed for the operation of the full system proceeds in phases. During Phase 1 (from birth to nine months), the ID is present and so are the basic functions of EDD, all representations at this stage being dyadic. Trevarthen (1979) calls this the stage of 'primary intersubjectivity' (although not, of course, as part of this explanatory framework). During Phase 2 (from nine to 18 months) SAM is also present. Now there are triadic representations and the linking of ID and EDD. Trevarthen (1979) calls this the stage of 'secondary subjectivity'. During Phase 3 (from 18 to 48 months) TOMM begins to operate, triggered by SAM. This heralds the onset of pretend play and the building of M-representations. ID, EDD and SAM can only represent limited aspects of intentionality (aboutness and aspectuality) but TOMM can also represent misrepresentation. TOMM has 'referential opacity' (Perner 1991). Baron-Cohen maintains that TOMM is also impaired in autism, using the wealth of experimental studies as detailed in the section above to support his claim. Not all mental states are equally affected, however, not even all epistemic ones. Baron-Cohen states that, for example, 'knowing' is easier than 'believing' for both normally developing children and those with autism. There are also different levels of impairment, which will lead to different effects. According to this theory, TOMM is specifically impaired in autism, and it is not impaired in sensory disability (even in the deaf-blind), although failure to be able to use privileged routes (such as through EDD) may lead to developmental delays in its operation in these groups.

An overall 'test' of the theory has come from its application. As we saw in earlier sections, Baron-Cohen *et al.* (1992, 1996a); developed a screening device for autism based on this theory and piloted it among 'at risk' 18 months-olds with a diagnostic follow-up at 2;6 years. The 1992 report suggested there were five predictors of later autism at 18 months. The 1996 study reported that consistent failure in only three items from the checklist at 18 months. were accurate predictors of autism at a later date. The predictors were: protodeclarative pointing, gaze monitoring and pretend play; and failure in all three at 18 months carried an 83.3 per cent risk of autism at 2;6. The theory would include the first two of these as part of the functioning of SAM (although this author feels that gaze monitoring should more properly be seen as part of EDD) and pretend play as falling under TOMM. Other items on the checklist concerning social or cognitive development were not predictors of autism.

Humphrey's (1986; 1993) view is that mindreading is made possible through introspection on inner states and analogy. He is suggesting, in other words, that consciousness of self is primary. This begs some questions about the development of this sense of self and the basis for the analogous projection of mental states onto others, which will be dealt with below. Following Humphrey's exposition, Baron-Cohen (1995) suggests that the prime deficit in autism is damage to the OFC (orbito-frontal-cortex) – STS (superior temporal sulcus) – amygdala circuit in the brain.

The four mechanisms proposed in this theory are seen by Baron-Cohen as part of the 'social brain' or the 'social module' proposed by Brothers (1990) and Brothers and Ring (1992), not all of the social brain being damaged in autism. Thus, like the theory of mind theory, this is a cognitive view of autism, albeit that the cognitive mechanisms proposed all process social information.

In evaluating this theory, one also needs to consider its explanatory power. For example, there may be good evidence for suggesting that children with autism have specific difficulty with joint attention, say, but does locating control of that process in a separate cognitive module (SAM) add to the understanding of that phenomenon, or autism as a whole? The rationale for this information processing and modular approach, presumably, is that it allows the separation of certain functions into those that are predicted to be impaired (all those controlled by SAM and TOMM) and those that should remain intact (those controlled by ID and EDD). As indicated above, the evidence for this separation is not unequivocal and without that separation it is hard to see the theory as more than descriptive. The strength is that it is clearly formulated (apart from some ambiguity over behaviour such as gaze monitoring) and should thereby lead to testable predictions from which it can be modified, if necessary, or give rise to a better theory.

Baron-Cohen specifically excludes the role of emotion from his theorising on the grounds that not enough is known of normal emotional development to make this worthwhile. This is certainly showing justifiable caution, yet it remains a moot point whether a satisfactory account of autism can be given without considering it as a 'disturbance of affective contact' (Kanner 1943).

Intersubjectivity

The intersubjectivity theories of autism are in some respects the antithesis of the cognitive theories, yet, as will be demonstrated, their predictions and thus their empirical base have much in common with those cognitive theories. Hobson (1987; 1990a; 1990b; 1991; 1993a) has the longest established and best developed theory in this tradition, although the title of an 'intersubjectivity' theory is associated with Rogers and Pennington (1991) and 'intersubjectivity' was first used by Trevarthen (1979) in describing the early interactional stages between infants and their caregivers. This section will also include the author's views on at least one of the major difficulties in autism (Powell and Jordan 1993b) which constitutes a theoretical construct (an 'experiencing self'), if not a fully developed theory.

Hobson's Theory

Hobson (1990a; 1991) began to formulate his theory of autism in reaction to the cognitive 'metarepresentational' theory of Leslie. He suggested that it was misleading to interpret either normal development or the difficulties associated with autism as being concerned with a 'theory' about minds. He suggested that what children acquire is not a theory, but knowledge of people with minds, acquired through the experience of interpersonal relations. He felt that humans were social beings with a capacity for personal relatedness, which is partly innately determined. The innate component he saw as perceptual-affective sensibilities towards the bodily appearance and behaviour of others. His view of social sensibility is akin to that of Forrester (1993) who talks of innate responsiveness to the 'social affordances' of social interactions.

Both Forrester and Hobson have built on the ideas of Gibson (1979) in relation to physical perception and the notion of 'meaning sensitive' perceptual faculties. In this view, the social, cultural and emotional meanings of social interactions are made apparent to infants through interactions and the infant is innately programmed to recognise meanings in the form of these 'affordances'. Bretherton (1991) cites Baldwin (1884) that infants understand others only as 'projects', known through their behaviour and its effects. Through interaction, Bretherton claims, meanings are constructed since '...out of context messages are necessarily ambiguous. They acquire specific meaning only within an intersubjectively shared world.' (p. 51). There is some evidence that children with autism are not able to recognise and take advantage of these social affordances. Loveland (1991) has shown that, for example, eye direction fails to act as an orienting signal for children with autism.

Awareness of the self/non-self distinction needs to be distinguished from consciousness of the self's own mental states (Hobson 1990a). Hobson's view is that awareness of others as subjective persons is a precondition for self-reflection and self-consciousness, for indexical thought, and for an objective stance. This is in direct contrast to Russell's (1995) view that construction of the subjective self has to proceed in tandem with the construction of the other, but arises first (see below). In Hobson's view, the individual acquires a self-concept only in so far as he or she is able to be aware of other persons as centres of their own subjective experiences, so the concepts of 'self' and 'other' also develop in tandem, but with 'other' perception taking the lead.

There is evidence from normal development that young infants have the basis for making distinctions between people and things (Fagan 1972). Children with autism appear to distinguish themselves as beings who can act and other objects as things that can be acted upon, but this leaves out the 'I/thou' relationship altogether. They succeed in line of sight activities (Hobson 1984) and are able to react to their own mirror image but they do not show the typical coy reactions (Dawson and McKissick 1984; Spiker and Ricks 1984; Stefanik and Balazs 1995). Thus it appears that the capacity to act is there in autism but the behaviour does not occur spontaneously and the infant is not naturally cued by normally salient social signals. Nor is there the normal emotional overlay to 'social' actions, so that it is the circumstances and quality of the behaviour that is important in this view of autism, although attempts to validate or refute it do not always pay attention to this fact.

Hobson (1993a) has made much of the role of personal pronoun development as an expression of the development of this understanding of personal relatedness and the 'I/thou', 'I/it' distinctions. He sees these relationships as central both to the development of intersubjectivity and interpersonal relations and to the development of the personal pronoun system. He, therefore, sees the autistic difficulty with personal pronouns as indicative of a more fundamental problem, only loosely connected to any linguistic problems. Indeed, Hobson (1993b) suggests that '...autistic children's characteristic language abnormalities might reflect social incomprehension rather than more restrictively 'linguistic' deficits' (p. 205). Experience of '...reciprocal, affectively-patterned reactions with others' (Hobson 1993b, p. 205) is regarded as essential to building up knowledge and understanding of persons but that '...in order to become engaged in personal relations, an individual needs to perceive and react to the bodily appearances, expressions, and actions of others with ...'natural' reactions involving feeling' (p. 205). Furthermore he sees the development of a sense of self and other as intricately related and bound up with the understanding of minds. He points out that it is necessary to have a concept of another as a person like oneself, who might share the same kind of mental experiences *before* one could impute mental states to them, whether through analogy or through the development of some theory about minds. As Hobson says, '...to understand minds is also to understand the nature of selves who have minds' (p. 210).

Livoir-Petersen (1995) suggests that baby is well equipped to extract cues related to living beings and especially to intraspecific interactions (see also Stern 1977). Emotions contribute to the anchoring of mental processes: '...a baby's emotions are revealed to him mostly in relation to people who solicit them, mirror them, possibly moderate them and underline their cultural aspects' (Livoir-Petersen 1995, p. 45). Thus, 'anchoring' is the result of what Stern (1985) calls 'attunement'. The autistic baby is not equipped to use interactions as anchoring points in this way. The baby with autism will seek repetition as compensation. Emotional cues within the self are not matched to those of caregivers.

Hobson (1993b) also takes issue with the notion that mental states are 'invisible' and abstract entities the existence of which can only be imputed through the development of a theory. He suggests that the pattern of emotional engagement with others is characterised by actions and facial expressions that are innate triggers for coordinated reactions in the partners in the interchange and the control of this patterned exchange is effected through the emotions. In his view, facial expressions are as much a sign of a tendency to certain actions as they are to inner feelings. Expressions also have the power to evoke similar experiences in the minds of the observers. In social referencing, for example, where the infant's reactions to a strange situation are governed by checking the familiar adult's facial expression, the infant may not be conceiving of the adult having a propositional attitude (that is, thinking that...). Instead, the infant may be aware of the attitude expressed by the other in an emotional way and be aware that that emotion can give a new meaning to the thing related to in the environment.

In this way, the child then comes to distinguish an 'attitude' from a 'thing' and grasps how it is possible to confer new subjective meanings on reality as given. This also enables the adoption of an attitude to one's own experience and thus enables a sense of 'self' as a source of attitudes, feelings and points of view. Hobson (1990a) suggests that some degree of differentiation between 'I' and 'not-I' is present almost from birth (p. 168). From this initial sense of intersubjectivity comes joint attention, shared reference, and the understanding not only of emotions but also of epistemic mental states.

Hobson's theory about the primary disturbance in autism is firmly rooted in the emotions, but it is in no sense confined to them, although 'tests' of his position have tended to centre on this aspect of his theory. This is not surprising in that it has proved difficult to formulate testable predictions from this theory aside from the predictions related to a failure to engage emotionally with others. This is the only part of the theory that would lead to predictions distinct from those arising from the cognitive perspective. There is empirical support for the theory, which will be discussed below, but its nature is such that much is open to interpretation. The strength of the theory lies not in new data that 'prove' a derivable hypothesis, but in the depth and quality of the argument in tracing the ontogenesis of the symptoms of autism from an initial failure in interpersonal relatedness (Hobson 1993a).

Hobson (1993b) suggests that children with autism's lack of participation in intersubjective social experience has two results which are especially important, namely i) a relative failure to recognise people as people with their own feelings, thoughts, wishes, intentions and so on, and ii) a severe impairment in the capacity to 'abstract' and feel and think symbolically (p. 3). Thus the cognitive sequelae to this affective theory are similar to those from the metarepresentational or evolutionary theories. Nevertheless, although many of its predictions would be common to the cognitive theories, one distinctive prediction would be that autistic disturbance of affective relatedness to others should be present from birth. The cognitive theories, however, predict that the cognitive difficulties should not be apparent until at least the second year and the 'secondary' emotional difficulties should arise later than the cognitive problems from which they are assumed to originate.

However, autism is seldom diagnosed until the third year of life, and often later, so there is still little prospect of establishing empirical tests of this prediction. Much of the 'evidence' on this matter is retrospective and anecdotal, relying on the recollections of parents and other caregivers. The routine acquisition of video recording of babies is beginning to offer 'harder' evidence, as we saw in earlier sections, as does the checking of developmental records, but such recording is often unsystematic and not directly related to the evidence being sought.

Dunn (1994) has studied normally developing young children in home situations and concludes that the ability to interpret other minds is not a once and for all acquisition but depends on social interaction, what the child is trying to achieve and how what the other is doing is interpreted. Kanner (1943) suggests that this kind of social learning is disrupted from an early age in autism. He offers some conclusions from the case histories of the 11 children upon whom he based his new diagnosis: '...the outstanding, 'pathognomonic,' fundamental disorder is the children's *inability to relate themselves* (original emphasis) in the ordinary way to people and situations *from the beginning of life* (author's emphasis)' (p. 242). Fein *et al.* (1986) also conclude, from a review of studies, that '...the social/affective deficits in autism are primary and not secondary to deficits in traditionally defined cognitive functions' (p. 209).

Lord (1993) reviewed early social development in autism. She found that children with autism present many fewer opportunities to engage in interaction in infancy and the quality of those interactions are poorer, due to their poorer emotional engagement. In spite of the wealth of evidence, however, from parental reports or from extrapolation to infancy of later behaviour, there is some conflicting evidence of normal development in the early infancy of children with autism. Knobloch and Pasamanick (1975) found that children referred for abnormal social responsiveness in the first year of life did not develop autism (or any other disturbance of development) on later follow-up, but those who showed disturbance at two years were found to have autism on follow-up. Johnson *et al.* (1992) in a screening study, supported this finding. O'Connor and Hermelin (1967) questioned whether there was eye gaze avoidance in autism, although their findings are refuted by Richer and Cross (1976). From a study of developmental records, Frith *et al.* (1993) report that two thirds of mothers of children with autism (and without additional learning difficulties) were not disturbed by social abnormalities in the first year. Part of the problem, in interpreting all these results, lies in separating the effects of autism from the effects of co-occurring developmental disorders or in deciding if there are two kinds of autism, early and late onset, as some authors have suggested (Wing 1988).

Klin *et al.* (1992) have provided some empirical evidence in support of early social deficits in autism. They used the first 20 items from the socialisation scale of the Vineland Adaptive Behaviour Scales (Sparrow *et al.* 1984) on 29 children with autism with a mean CA of 4;3 and a mean MA of 1;8. The kind of behaviours, in this section of the checklist, normally appears before eight months. Compared with CA and MA matched controls, they found that significantly fewer of the children with autism showed nine of the 20 behaviours. The behavioural items that distinguished the groups included items such as 'shows anticipation of being picked up' and 'reaches for familiar person'. The researchers suggested that the fact that there are a few children with autism who passed on these items might indicate subgroups within the condition.

The evidence for specific emotion-related difficulties in autism is also conflicting. One source of this conflict, identified by Hobson, is that the very matching measures may contain emotion-related items that distort the matching process and thus the conclusions that can be drawn. Hobson and Lee (1989) worked with adults and adolescents with autism and BPVS (British Picture Vocabulary Scale) (Dunn *et al.* 1982) matched retarded controls and compared their performance on BPVS items of emotionality and high abstraction (judged by raters). The autistic group scored lower on emotion versus non-emotion items not related to social content (compared to controls) but similarly on abstract versus concrete items. The researchers conclude, therefore, that subjects with autism in an experimental paradigm, matched with controls on such measures, will perforce already have been selected for a greater ability in the area being investigated.

Hobson (1986a) studied mental age-matched children with autism, normal development and learning difficulties. He tested them on their ability to choose drawn and photographed facial expressions of emotion to go with a person videoed in gestures, vocalisations and contexts, indicative of the emotional states of 'happy', 'unhappy,' 'afraid', 'angry' and 'neutral'. All groups were able to match drawings of non-personal objects to videoed cues, but the children with autism were significantly worse than the controls in selecting appropriate emotional expressions. This ability in the children with autism related to mental age. Thus, this study showed no evidence of a general impairment in autism in semantic or perceptual categorisation in visual stimuli (static or involving movement) or in auditory modes, but there was a specific difficulty related to emotional stimuli. He also found in a further study (Hobson 1986b) that the group with autism was worse at matching age and gender related gestures, vocalisations and contexts. In a picture-sorting task, the group with autism was less likely to see emotional expressions as salient and chose to sort by other features such as hats.

Hobson *et al.* (1988) investigated both identity and emotion-recognition from schematised faces and found that only the group with autism was almost as good at identifying these features when the faces were upside down as when they were in the upright position. They suggested that children with autism may be perceiving faces as mere patterns, and not be looking for the automatic emotion-identifying pattern that normally developing children are. Hobson *et al.* (1989) in a further study of emotion recognition both in faces and in voice tone, found that children with autism were less able to do this than matched control groups of children with learning difficulties and normally developing children. It was not that they lacked emotional vocabulary terms, but that they applied them almost haphazardly to these stimuli – making far more errors than the control groups. In a study involving interpretation of a moving light display, Hobson (1995b) found that individuals with autism were able to perceive actions (when the light display depicted humans in action) but not attitudes, unlike mental age-matched controls.

Baron-Cohen (1991) studied the ability of children with autism verbal age-matched children with learning difficulties and normally developing children to describe a protagonist in a story as 'happy' or 'sad' in accordance with situations, desires and beliefs. The only significant difference between the groups found was on the belief tasks. Thus, the children with autism had no specific difficulty (compared to the other groups) in understanding the situations or desires as causes of emotion but did have significant difficulties in understanding which beliefs would lead to which emotion. Again, it is hard to see this as a test of specific predictions of the Hobson theory since beliefs would also be affected according to that theory and knowledge *about* which desires and situations lead to which of two very visible emotions could well result from learning.

In an attempt to avoid the effects of learned 'rote' responses, Blair (1994) measured the electrodermal (skin conductance) responses to distress cues, threatening cues and neutral stimuli in three verbal age-matched groups. He found no significant difference in the overall responsiveness of those with autism, those with moderate learning difficulties and normally developing children; all three groups were most responsive to the distress cues. However, it is not Hobson's contention that children with autism do not experience emotions in relation to emotional cues. His view is rather that they are unable to recognise and use emotions to regulate interactions with others, which is to do with the timing and control of emotions as well as with emotional expression.

Capps *et al.* (1992) studied children with autism without additional learning difficulties. They found that the children with autism did not differ from verbal age-matched control children in talking of emotions like 'pride', that only involves self-awareness, whereas they were significantly different from controls in talking about 'embarrassment' which requires a sense of social audience. This supports the cognitive view of the emotional difficulties in autism in that it is demonstrating a 'cognitive cut' in otherwise similar behaviour of talking about emotional states. However, this is to misrepresent the Hobson position, once again, since his theory would predict that emotional understanding would have to be learnt cognitively, as it were, and thus it would be expected that less complex emotions would be mastered first. The situations in which one could be said to be proud are more easily demonstrable than those where one would suffer embarrassment, since these would take account of one's reactions to the reactions of others to one's behaviour – a very indirect and recursive kind of understanding, therefore, being required.

Baron-Cohen (1988) has discussed the rival affective and cognitive theories as explanations for autism. He shows how affective theory makes better sense of results from emotion recognition tasks, and how cognitive theory is superior in that it predicts the particular pattern of impaired and unimpaired social skills in autism, as well as the pragmatic deficits. This view of Hobson's theory, however, does not recognise that the theory of mind difficulties that Baron-Cohen attributes to the predictions of a cognitive theory would also follow from Hobson's view of how such understandings arise in normal developmental 'emotionally-charged' interactions. It is important that studies look at quality, not just quantity, of any social or interactive measure studied. Langdell (1978), for example, showed that it is not total attention to faces that is important, but the style of that attention, and he found that individuals with autism paid more attention to the lower half of faces than to the eye region.

Serra *et al.* (1995) examined emotional role-taking abilities of children with a pervasive developmental disorder not otherwise specified. These were children who did not have classical autism but who fell within the autistic spectrum of disorders (Wing 1996). They found that these children showed a specific deficit, relative to verbal MA-matched controls, in using emotionally charged information to judge others' reactions and predict behaviour. They also had problems in judging the affective meaning of social situations. Of course, the existence of social and emotional difficulties in autism does not automatically imply that an 'intersubjectivity' deficit is at the heart of the condition. It may just be that social stimuli have particular properties that relate to a cognitive difficulty in processing. Klinger and Dawson (1992) adopt that line of reasoning in proposing that the specific social impairments in autism result from an inability to process social information because of its novel, unpredictable nature.

Children with autism certainly respond to cueing and structure in social and emotional behaviour in the same way as they do for more 'cognitive' tasks. They are also more socially aware and responsive when an adult initiates the interactions (Kasari *et al.* 1993). Yet, Sigman *et al.* (1995) suggest they are most deviant where social responsiveness involves social knowledge as in social referencing, but they suggest this is because 'early social referencing and joint attention seem to involve emotional as well as cognitive factors' (p. 161). They conducted a study of 18 high functioning individuals with autism with CAs of 9;3 to 16;10 and IQs of 75 to 136. The normally developing controls were matched for CA and IQ. In the first task they were presented with a list of seven emotional labels (proud, happy, embarrassed, satisfied, angry, sad and afraid) and asked to tell about a time when they had felt each emotion. Most were able to relate roughly appropriate experiences. Four in each group had problems. The researchers investigated 'happy', 'sad', 'proud' and 'embarrassed' in more depth. Although slow, the autistic group did well on labels but gave qualitatively different responses. Those with autism were the only ones to refer to food as a source of happiness, and never to talk of birthdays or birthday parties in that context. Four of the subjects with autism gave the same example for 'happy' and 'proud' whereas all those without autism distinguished the two. Two of the autistic examples of 'proud' were inappropriate ('proud of a dog', 'somebody gave me gold and silver'). There was some confusion in the autistic group between 'embarrassment' and 'sadness', reporting external-uncontrollable events for both (instead of just for sadness). The group with autism offered more examples of being hurt or teased for both emotions.

Parental reports also suggest more experiences for those with autism that make them hurt and sad (Capps *et al.* 1993). The ability of the autistic group to identify the affect of others from photographs with contextual cues in the Sigman *et al.* (1995) study was fairly good but significantly less accurate than the normal group. They were also slower and needed more prompts. In a videotape presentation of a child displaying different emotions, they were asked to describe the emotion of the protagonist and themselves as witness, using Feshbach's (1982) three components of empathy as a score (see below). They found significant group effects on all three. Again, the group with autism also took longer and needed more prompts '...the high-functioning children with autism appeared to be using their cognitive skills to figure out the right response, as if they were "solving math problems", according to one viewer' (p. 168). Only in the autistic group was IQ related to these scores.

In analysing the emotion of the viewers, Sigman *et al.* found the autistic subjects showed more concentration and more positive emotion. This behaviour contrasts with younger children with autism studied who showed no interest in adult expressions of emotion. They also found that in these older children, the autistic group showed more emotional expression than the normally functioning children, and suggest that may come from failure to learn the display rules used by the normal children. In other words, the other children had learnt to inhibit displays of emotion in public. It was also clear that the autistic group showed emotional reactions to videos that they were not always able to express verbally.

On tests of cognitive ability, the autistic group, in a perspective-taking task, were less able to take the visual perspective of another (by rotating a turntable to reproduce for the child the perspective seen by an adult). They were also less able to pass conservation tasks (2-D space, number, substance, continuous quantity, weight and discontinuous quantity). As many as 50 per cent of the children with autism did not conserve and their ability to do so related to IQ and empathy scores. This might have some relevance to Russell's views of agency (see below). However, there were no differences in a series of seriation tasks although, again, the autistic group was slower. The researchers suggest that the flow of human interaction is too fast for the slow processing of social cues by the autistic group, so they cannot always utilise their abilities in everyday life: 'In our view, the only children who achieve metarepresentation and social comprehension without recourse to the nearly automatic emotional understanding that most normal people possess are autistic children' (p. 174 Sigman *et al*. 1995).

Hermelin and O'Connor (1985) also conclude, from a review of experimental studies, that high functioning autistic individuals use logical processes in problem solving in the social and affective domain. This would suggest to the author that, far from lacking a theory of mind as a core deficit, children with autism are the only ones who need to approach understanding of minds through the construction of a theory. Given the complexity of such an undertaking, it is not surprising that only the most able succeed in doing so.

Davies *et al*. (1994) have conducted a careful study of face perception in two groups of subjects with autistic spectrum disorders (high-functioning autism or Asperger's syndrome: HFA&AS and low-functioning autism: A) and two groups of verbal age-matched controls. The study involved processing facial and non-facial stimuli for both facial expressions of emotion and individual recognition from a variety of orientations. The faces used varied orthogonally on three dimensions: incidental features, emotions and identity. Non-facial stimuli were coloured shapes varying also on a third dimension of border. They found no differences between the A group and its control group in that both groups were unable to perform the task, but the HFA&AS group was significantly worse than its control group on all the tests. Thus, this group showed a general perceptual deficit, not specific to faces or emotions and yet this was not found across the spectrum. The researchers conclude that such a perceptual difficulty must be a correlate of autism and Asperger's syndrome rather than a core symptom.

When looking at qualitative aspects of the results, however, there was evidence from the children's comments that those with autism matched the faces on, for example, mouth shape rather than emotion as such, and the same 'look' rather than the same identity. Accordingly, the researchers tried to eliminate these problems for interpretation by conducting a further experiment. In their second experiment they used four match-to-sample tests:

• matching face identity across orientation differences;
• matching face identity across emotional expressions;
• matching emotions across identities; and
• matching symbol pattern across different configurations.

The same results were found.

This supports the findings of Ozonoff *et al*. (1990) that, when matched on verbal age, there are no emotion-specific deficits. Yet this is still assuming that the intersubjectivity theory would predict specific matching emotion deficits, but is this true? As has been pointed out above, it is not so much the perception of emotion as a specific pattern that is difficult in autism, although that may be so at the start, but the lack of affectual directedness in that perception. In lower functioning groups it may be that those with learning difficulties rely on the richness of emotional cueing from multiple stimuli for emotion recognition and so the one-dimensional task in this experimental situation made it difficult for them. On the other hand, Hobson (1986a) has shown that children with autism find it particularly difficult to integrate multiple cues to emotions, so the one-dimensional task is easier for children with autism, especially if they can solve it through perceptual features. Those with a higher IQ and autism may still latch on to one feature, such as facial expression, but the control group does not now find the analytical task (isolating the crucial feature) difficult. This kind of analytical task is a problem for those with autism, however, regardless of the supposedly 'emotional' meaning of some of the stimuli. Frith (1989b) has shown that the perception of meaningful material by individuals with autism is impaired. Thus, this kind of experiment does nothing to validate Hobson's views, but nor is it strong evidence against them.

Indeed, Davies *et al.* (op cit.) cite Carey (1986) and Rhodes *et al.* (1989) showing that there is a developmental transition from attention to specific detailed features of a stimulus to a response to relational configural information. They suggest that this transition does not occur in autism so individuals with autism never become expert at face recognition nor emotion recognition, although this experiment really only tests one feature of emotion recognition. Sigman *et al.* (1992) have shown that young children with autism are relatively unresponsive to expressions of strong emotion in adults, and so the problem in autism may be in determining the meaning of emotions rather than in performing a matching task as here.

An interesting finding by Mundy *et al.* (1993), in their study of shared attention, communication and pretend play, was that, although the performance of the children with autism was poorer on all of these measures, some did show shared attention and a degree of communication and pretend play. Yet there was a qualitative difference in the performance of those who did score on these measures, compared to normally developing and learning disabled controls. The performance of the children with autisms on these items was marked by a lack of emotional expression and a seeming lack of engagement with the activities. It was as if they had learnt to do these things but they did not really see the point and could not be enthused by them.

If the key feature of autism is a lack of empathy and this is what is developed through intersubjectivity, as Hobson proposes, then all aspects of empathy might be affected. Feshbach (1982) has suggested that there are three components to empathy:

- the ability to recognise and discriminate among the affective states of others;
- the ability to assume the perspective and role of another; and
- an emotional response.

Most of the research has centred on the first component because of its testability, but the breakdown in autism might be in any or all of the three components.

Feshbach's definition of empathy is useful in considering Hobson's theory but it leaves out any sense of self and one's own mental states, which is also an important feature. Certainly there is evidence from the writings of those with autism (Grandin 1995; Sinclair 1992, for example) that introspection on feelings is difficult. Hurlburt *et al.* (1994) provided some empirical support for this in their study of three adults with Asperger's syndrome. They fitted their volunteer subjects with beepers, which sounded at intervals, and this was the signal for them to write down their current experiences at each beep. All three subjects reported thoughts, in the form of images, with no feelings, inner speech, or bodily sensations.

Rogers and Pennington's theory.

In many of its aspects, the 'intersubjectivity' theory of autism put forward by Rogers and Pennington in 1991 holds very similar tenets to Hobson's theory. Rogers and Pennington suggest that the core problem in autism is in the coordination of specific self-other representations leading to an impaired theory of mind, impaired emotion sharing and impaired imitation. Thus the significant difference to Hobson's views is the important role given to imitation within this theoretical position. The present author has only discovered one attempt to test the rival merits of this theory compared to Hobson's theory and the theory of mind. Brown and Whiten (1994) conducted an observational study of spontaneous imitation, social interaction, play and evidence of a theory of mind in children with autism and verbal MA-matched normally developing controls. They found a significant difference in the autistic performance in terms of social contact, evidence of theory of mind, and in imitation without echolalia. Quantity of play behaviour, and imitation, which included verbal imitation (that is, echolalia), were not significantly different between the two groups. In a qualitative analysis, however, there was much less symbolic play in the group with autism. As a corollary, there were more relational and manipulative play behaviours in the group with autism than other kinds of play. In the theory of mind evidence collected, joint attention was found to be the most significant discriminatory category between the groups.

There is evidence related to this theory from other sources. Meltzoff (1990) has shown that normally developing infants of 14 months are more responsive to an adult who imitates him or her. Meltzoff and Gopnik (1993) discuss the role of imitation in normal infant development and suggest that understanding of others, including mental states, is developed in the context of mutual imitation. They also relate mutual imitation (especially of facial expressions) to the sharing of emotion and suggest that this is an inbuilt mechanism that allows species-specific identification and thus provides the representational base for building a concept of self and others. This leads to the prediction that visually-impaired children would share some of these difficulties, since visually-mediated mutual imitation would not be available to them. There is no suggestion that all visually-impaired children have 'autistic-like' difficulties; however, they do share some of the early problems, especially in relation to personal pronoun development (Brown *et al.* 1997; Fraiberg and Adelson 1975).

DeMyer *et al.* (1972) found that body imitation was poorer than object imitation in a group with autism, although this is the opposite pattern to that found in normal development. Dawson and Adams (1984) reported that few children with autism reached stage 6 in imitation in the Uzgiris and Hunt (1975) scales. Most studies show that imitation is related to MA, but abstract gesture imitation may be particularly difficult.

Paradoxically, of course, verbal imitation of a persistent and non-mitigated kind has long been seen as a feature, and indeed, even as a problem, in autism. Kanner (1943; 1946) drew attention to this immediate or delayed echolalia in autism, which is a prominent feature of the early language, at least, of speaking children with autism; sometimes it is the only 'language' that is achieved (Fay and Schuler 1980). Boucher (1978) sees this as a manifestation of echoic memory capacity and in an experimental study matched children with autism and normally developing children on CA and digit span (a measure of short-term memory capacity). She found that both groups had similar echoic memory capacity for the immediate recall of words, but for the children with autism this ability was a peak compared to their other abilities and they were far worse at delayed recall. Boucher interprets this as showing that the good acoustic coding of children with autism did not compensate for their poorer semantic coding.

Given that delayed echolalia (even after years or decades) is also a prominent feature of autism, this cannot be the only explanation for poor delayed recall in this instance. Once again, the importance of the difference between spontaneous and cued actions in autism needs to be drawn. It may be that echolalia (immediate or delayed) is involuntary and does not reflect the same cognitive processes necessary for conscious imitation, often tapped in experimental investigations.

Sigman *et al.* (1995) also report that children with autism are less able to imitate gestures or engage in imaginary play. Hermelin and O'Connor (1970) show that compared to MA matched controls, children with autism have superior recall of random word strings and an inferior recall of sentences. This adds weight to the idea that they have difficulty with the later stages of imitation where cognition plays a part but they can imitate meaningless stimuli, especially in the auditory domain. It is not limited to the auditory domain, however, since Carr (1982) and Jordan (1993) also report 'echopraxia' in autism, where there is a similar meaningless echoing of actions, often associated with the teaching of a sign language.

Lord (1991) reports evidence from parent recollections that early imitation in autism is present in the same children who fail to score on later tests of imitative ability. Where there are difficulties in imitation, then, they seem to be in those aspects that require the adoption of alternative 'roles' in a 'dialogue' (as would be pertinent to Rogers and Pennington's position) or where normal social signals such as a smile fail to elicit a corresponding action (Park 1986). It seems to the author that the latter difficulty is better attributed to a failure to recognise, and be triggered by, normal social signals, rather than a difficulty in imitation as such. Or it may be, as Happé (1994a) suggests, that neonatal imitation may be subserved by different mechanisms to later childhood imitation. Difficulties in later imitation that requires social and cognitive role-taking may also be explained within the context of the demands of that role-taking situation, rather than attributing the difficulty to imitation.

An 'experiencing self'

In 1993, the author and a colleague (Powell and Jordan, 1993b) put forward the idea that one of the fundamental difficulties of those who have autism might lie in establishing an 'experiencing self'. Jordan and Powell (1995a) developed this idea further, showing how it might relate to the range of difficulties found in autistic spectrum disorders. Their idea arose from the identification of problems in 'personal episodic memory' specific to those with autism (Jordan and Powell 1992). Dritschel *et al.* (1992) had suggested that the development of personal episodic memory depends on the existence of such an 'experiencing self' (Brewer 1986), which codes events as part of a personal dimension. Without this, events would be coded 'from the outside' as it were, and the individual with autism would experience events in a non-subjective way. It is interesting that Russell (1996) also relies on Brewer's analysis in his depiction of the way agency contributes to a developing sense of self, but theories diverge over the role of emotion in this process. The mechanism for developing this sense of self has not been identified by Jordan and Powell, but it might well relate to disturbance in the affectual colouring of events, due to abnormalities in emotion regulation. Lazarus (1991) has shown how emotions allow a personal appraisal of situations, so that they are perceived in terms of their personal meaning, that is, subjectively. Iversen (1996) has also identified disturbances in the relay of emotional messages to the cortical (thinking) areas of the brain in schizophrenia, which might also apply to autism.

There has been no systematic direct 'test' of this idea to date, although Millward *et al.* (in press) offer some confirmatory evidence. They found that children with autism (as compared to normally developing, verbal-age and chronological-age matched controls) found it easier to spontaneously recall events they had witnessed happening to others than events they had participated in themselves. Boucher (1981), in an experimental investigation, showed that children with autism had an impaired ability to recall a recent event in which they had participated and a difficulty in deliberately evoking memories. These would be direct predictions of a failure in establishing an 'experiencing self'. Russell (1996, p. 255) also reports results from experimental investigations of memory with Jarrold in which the children with autism found it easier to remember the actions of the experimenter or puppets (whether self or other administered) than their own. Of course, this is also consistent with Russell's own theory (below) and it may prove difficult to distinguish between the two in any definitive way.

Boucher and Lewis (1989) have also shown that children with autism only show a deficit with spontaneous rather than cued recall and that it is personal episodic memory (although they do not themselves make this distinction) that is impaired in autism. Given Dritschel *et al*.'s (1992) delineation of the role of an 'experiencing self' in the spontaneous recall of personal episodic memories, this provides a rationale for the idea. However, Minshew and Goldstein (1993) report an experimental study that does not support a relative deficiency in cued as opposed to spontaneous recall ability in autism, so this needs further investigation.

Anecdotal support for the difficulties of experiencing events subjectively in autism comes from the reflections of the most able about their own ways of perceiving and thinking. Sacks (1995) cites Grandin, for example, describing her way of processing the world as being like a video recorder which she can replay at will to try to work out how and why people behave as they do. She also describes this very explicitly in her own writing: 'When I access my own memory, I see many different "videos"' (Grandin 1995, p. 142).

The differentiation of this theoretical idea from the view of Hobson or Russell is difficult, except in terms of derivation. Inasmuch as all the 'intersubjectivity' views of the autistic deficit would involve problems in developing a sense of self, they would all lead to similar predictions. The one advantage of this view is that it does distinguish ideas of the self 'from the outside' from an 'experiencing' sense of self, in a way that is not done by Hobson (1993b) or Rogers and Pennington (1991). Russell (1996) does make this distinction and here, as indicated earlier, the differentiation lies in the role of intersubjectivity as opposed to agency alone in the ontogenesis. Most theorising on the self-concept and its development (such as Burns 1979) do not make this distinction either, although the model proposed by Damon and Hart (1982) is an exception to this.

Central Coherence

Frith (1989b) first postulated the theory that a weak drive for central coherence could account for the difficulties in autism not accounted for by the theory of mind theory. She saw these as those findings about autism which were not encapsulated in the 'triad of impairments'. Some of these findings were her own work (Frith 1970; Hermelin and Frith 1971) showing that semantic meaning was not as helpful to children with autism as it was to control groups in a memorisation task. There was also her work with Shah (Shah and Frith 1983, cited, 1993) on the superior performance of children with autism on an embedded figures test and on both a regular and an amended version of the Block Design Test. She also cites the work of Hermelin and O'Connor (1970) who concluded that, although general perceptual and cognitive functioning was unimpaired in autism (unless there are additional difficulties), perception of meaning is always impaired.

The study by Shah and Frith (1983, cited 1993), examining performance on the Children's Embedded Figures Test, showed that children with autism scored above average for their mental age, and high scores on such tests have been taken to show 'field independence' as a cognitive style (Witkin and Goodenough 1981). Frith suggested that the good performance of children with autism on this test did not, as it might with others, represent the 'overcoming' of a tendency to see the whole meaningful picture as one, in order to analyse out the shape contained within it. Rather, it represented a failure to perceive the 'whole' in the first place. She attributed this 'extreme analytical style' to a weak or even missing 'search for meaning' in autistic thinking and perceiving. She proposed that this would lead to social as well as intellectual detachment. Joliffe and Baron-Cohen (1997) have confirmed the superiority of individuals with autism on the embedded figures task, this time with high functioning adults with autism.

The amended Block Design Test built on the fact that children with autism peak on this subtest when it is included in intelligence tests. Frith postulated that good performance on block design might be determined by resisting (or lacking, in the case of autism) a central cohesive force for the overall pattern to be produced. If this was so, then the performance of young normally developing children and children with learning difficulties should be enhanced by cueing (by means of dotted lines or physical separation) the division of the overall shape into its component 'block-sized' pieces. The performance of those with autism, on the other hand, should be unaffected by this procedure. Shah and Frith found that this was indeed the case.

Frith and Snowling (1983) also demonstrated that children with autism are less able than dyslexic and normally developing controls to use the overall meaning of the sentence being read to disambiguate the pronunciation of a homograph. Frith went on to explore how other well documented reports of 'autistic' behaviour, such as their greater ability to do jigsaws with the picture side face down than with the picture visible, could be 'explained' by such a theory.

Shah and Frith (1993) and Frith and Happé (1994) have expanded on this theory and developed it to account for the need, as they see it, to go beyond a theory of mind explanation for autism. Happé (1994b) had examined the Wechsler IQ profile and theory of mind tests in a wide range of individuals with autism. She found that comprehension scores on language subtests correlated with passing theory of mind tests in autism, so that verbal ability seemed to be at least a part determiner of possession of a theory of mind. Happé, however, does not necessarily make this interpretation of her findings, suggesting that the causal direction might be the reverse, so that theory of mind ability would be a necessary precursor to developing a certain level of comprehension of language. In support of the central coherence theory, she found that a high score on the block design subtest was true of the full range of individuals with autism, regardless of language ability.

Yet Happé also cites her own PhD thesis (Happé 1991) that failed to support the prediction from the central cohesion theory that performance on mentalising tasks should be related to performance on a measure of central cohesion. She suggests that this might indicate that weak central coherence in autism is additional to, and separate from, impairments in mentalising. Happé (1995a) examined these same issues further and reached similar conclusions.

Cognitive style and autism

In a report of current research in this area, Happé (1995a) examined the particular strengths and weaknesses of theory of mind research findings in autism and suggested once more that there was a need to go beyond this to the idea that people with autism have weak 'central coherence'. She cites the clinical and research evidence for an attention to detail, rather than the whole, in autism, in all modalities. She suggests we should '...think of this balance (between preference for parts versus wholes) as akin to a cognitive style' (p. 125). She makes the specific suggestion that people with autism process the most local level available in open-ended tasks.

Mottron *et al.* (1999) contrast two models to explain the 'non-triadic' difficulties (after Frith and Happé 1994) of autism. The first of these is Frith's central coherence theory and the second is that of Mottron and Bellville (1993; 1995) who postulated a hierarchisation deficit, leading to a modification of the parts/wholes relationships. Mottron *et al.* studied 11 high functioning individuals with autism compared with a group matched by gender, IQ, CA and hand function laterality. In their first experiment, they used a hierarchical stimulus task (large letters composed of small letters) with varying morphological similarity. Central coherence theory predicts that those with autism should be better at local level processing whereas hierarchisation theory predicts an equivalent speed for local and global processing but a decrease in the interference effect for local rather than global letters. The results showed no differences in the interference effects between the groups.

In a further mental synthesis task both theories would predict an absence of 'goodness' effect (that is, one favouring the synthesis of parts that fit well together over those that are badly fitting) in autism. Also, both predict faster processing times for those with autism and that they will be better able to respond to the embedded figure element in the task. In fact there were similar reaction times for the two groups in the 'good' task although the group with autism was slower in both conditions. Thus, the predictions were confounded; there was no 'hidden figure' effect found in autism. Overall, the results showed a global bias in the individuals with autism, not predicted by either of the two theories.

Mottron *et al.* point out that their results support the findings of Ozonoff *et al.* (1994) who found no evidence of a global disadvantage (finding, in fact a global advantage) in the processing of high functioning individuals with autism. Mottron *et al.* suggest possible reasons for this difference in results to those obtained in the figures embedded and block design tasks, residing in the nature of the tasks used. Each of the tasks where a global deficit (or a local advantage) has been found have been ones involving processing time of minutes, whereas the tasks used by Ozonoff and her colleagues and Mottron *et al.* used processing times of less than a second. Mottron *et al.* further suggest that these different processing times reflect higher-order processing (in the longer times) and precategorical processing in the shorter times. Thus, precategorical processing may show no global deficit in autism but there may be problems with later higher-order forms of categorising. However, this is not then a matter of a difference in *cognitive* style (typically tapping pre-categorical processing) but it may reflect an important difference in *learning* style.

One criticism of the empirical base for central coherence theory that might be made comes from the work of Riding and Pearson (1994). They have shown how tests such as the Children's Embedded Figures Test are strongly related to intelligence and cannot, therefore, be considered as an independent measure of cognitive style. Riding and Cheema (1991) have grouped the different classifications of cognitive style into two principal cognitive style dimensions: the Wholistic–Analytic and the Verbal–Imagery dimensions. Riding (1991) has developed a computer-based version of tasks to assess these two dimensions. Riding and Cheema have demonstrated that the computer-based cognitive style analysis produces reliable and valid (measured against predicted school subject performance patterns) results in normally developing children and adults.

Jordan and Riding (1995) tested directly for cognitive style, using this computer presented test for the dimension of 'wholistic' versus 'analytic'. In contrast to the predictions of central coherence theory, the children and adults with autism tested were overwhelmingly found to process information 'wholistically'. The authors suggest a reason for these findings being different to those reported for the Children's Embedded Figures Test. The computer presented tasks involved abstract shapes, without social meaning, whereas the Children's Embedded Figures Test uses 'real' objects such as prams in which the shape (e.g. the triangle) is embedded. It is also very likely that the same factors affected the results as Mottron *et al.* discussed, since here too the processing times were less than a second.

Happé (1996) studied relative susceptibility to visual illusions in people with autism, and found them to be less susceptible. She interprets this as supporting the notion of weak central coherence in autism. To date there has been little else published that is a direct attempt to test central coherence theory.

However, there are contrary views of the cognitive processing style of individuals with autism, mostly developed in relation to language processing. Paul (1987), for example, in his review of communication, makes a strong case for a gestalt (holistic) type of language processing in autism. Baltaxe and Simmons (1977) analysed an autistic eight-year-old's bedtime soliloquies, which consisted largely of delayed echolalia. They suggest that: 'autistic echolalia could be seen, then, as an extreme reliance on a gestalt type of processing' (p. 68).

Prizant (1983) also developed the idea of 'gestalt' processing of language in autism leading to delayed echolalia and argued that this applies to other areas of cognitive functioning leading to rote memory, recognition of melodic patterns, and the reconstruction of visual-spatial arrays. He suggests that

a gestalt mode must be viewed in contrast to an analytic mode in which experiences or events are analysed and segmented into meaningful components based upon prior experience. In an analytic mode, irrelevancies or redundancies are given little attention while new or significant information is abstracted. (p. 300).

This is clearly the reverse of the predictions of the central coherence theory.

Wetherby (1984) also discusses this explanation for linguistic problems in autism, suggesting that a failure of emotional vocalisations to come under cortical control may result in rigid automatic language learning and a gestalt information-processing style. Finally, in another, more recent review of communication in preschool children with autism, Prizant and Wetherby (1993) again refer to a gestalt learning style to explain the phenomenon of echolalia: 'a rote memorisation strategy rather than a semantic-based strategy' (p. 98).

Of course these are views, based on experience, but not subject to experimental testing. At present, it would be fair to say that there is little evidence to support an analytical cognitive style in autism and what evidence there is suggests in fact that there may be a preference for global processing, at least at a preconceptual level. That leaves us with some unexplained data from experiments and experiences related to learning style and categorical processing. Even here, it is a mistake to think that people with autism are *analysing* information into its constituent details, as Frith (1989a) pointed out. The early (and perhaps continuing) preference for global processing may in fact result in a failure to categorise with the result that irrelevant features (i.e. those outside a categorical frame) are as likely to be noticed as relevant ones. After all, it is not the effect of the total context that needs to be resisted by the perceiver of the triangle in the embedded figures task, but the effect of the pram. The issue of levels and time of processing will be considered again in the context of the theory of an executive function deficit (below).

Executive Function

Ozonoff and her colleagues are most closely associated with the idea that a disorder of executive control functions might be responsible for the fundamental disorders of autism (Ozonoff *et al.* 1991b). In an experimental study investigating the distinctiveness of Asperger's syndrome from 'high functioning autism', Ozonoff *et al.* (1991a) found that only the latter group was impaired on theory of mind and verbal memory tasks but both groups were impaired in tasks designed to tap executive functioning. The theory of mind tasks used in this study were a replication of Baron-Cohen *et al.*'s (1986) study with the ordering of different kinds of picture stories. Like the original study, they found that the group with autism performed better on mechanical causation stories but both the autistic and the control groups performed poorly on the mental state stories; in other words, they found no specific deficit in autism.

Neuropsychological evidence

Ozonoff (1995) describes executive function as a cognitive construct for behaviours that are mediated by the frontal lobes. It is defined as the ability to maintain an appropriate problem-solving set for the attainment of a future goal (Luria 1966) and thus includes planning, impulse control, inhibition of prepotent but incorrect responses, set maintenance, organised search, and flexibility of thought and action. It also involves the ability to disengage from control by the external context and to guide behaviour by mental models or internal representations (plans, goals or scripts: Dennis 1991). Ozonoff points out that the frontal cortex is involved in executive functions, the regulation of social behaviour, emotional reactions and social discourse.

Goldman-Rakic (1987) proposes that the function of the prefrontal cortex is to guide behaviour by mental representations or 'inner models of reality' (p. 378).

The orbital cortex is thought to guide behaviour using representations of affective and social information and failure in this system would result in dependence on external cueing. This fits the problems found in autism in spontaneous, compared to cued, behaviour of all kinds. Frontal impairment is offered as an explanation of autism by Damasio and Maurer (1978), Gedye (1991) and Reichler and Lee (1987). It is also espoused by Russell (1995; 1996), but his particular account of autism is given in a separate section below.

Bishop (1993) has produced a review article using Damasio and Maurer's neurological model (1978) as the basis of exploring the executive functioning theory of autism. The Damasio and Maurer model is based on a disturbance in the mesolimbic cortex that controls movement, posture and intentional goal-directed behaviour. They point out that motor disturbance is often found in autism, although it only features in one of the current diagnostic systems for Asperger's syndrome (DSM-IV: APA 1994). They suggest that there are signs of dysfunction in the basal ganglia (for example, persistent maintenance of posture due to exaggerated muscle tone in the feet, and hands and stereotyped movements suggesting chorea, athetosis or both) and parallels with the mutism found in recovery from mesal frontal lobe lesions. Goal-directed activity in autism is also like that found in patients with known frontal cortical damage. The mesolimbic system is important in marking the significance of a stimulus in relation to the goals and emotional state of the individual and this has clear parallels with the motivational and intentional problems found in autism.

Rumsey (1985) used the Wisconsin Card Sorting Test (WCST: Grant and Berg 1948), which is used to identify perseverative responding in a concept-learning task with high functioning men with autism, and found significantly more perseveration than age, sex and IQ matched controls. Rumsey and Hamburger (1988) examined further the WCST performance of this same group and found that the group with autism had a lower number of categories achieved and poorer completion of a planned search task. The same distinctions were found when their performance was compared to that of a dyslexic group (Rumsey and Hamburger 1990). McEvoy *et al.* (1993) examined executive functioning in very young children with autism (three to seven years) and found significant differences from control groups on spatial reversal measures; the group with autism had significantly greater difficulty in shifting set and produced more perseverative errors. They found there was a significant relationship between ability in joint attention and executive functioning.

Executive function deficits have been offered as alternative explanations for many of the experimental findings in autism. Bishop comments on the fact that Frith and Frith (1991) have proposed that second order representations (in Leslie's terms) are controlled in the frontal cortex, and she suggests that this could be the explanatory base for theory of mind findings. Perner (1991) notes that second order representations are involved in planning or hypothesising; yet children with autism can perform false photograph tasks (Jordan and Powell 1991; Leekam and Perner 1991; Leslie and Thaiss 1992) that also involve second order representations, albeit of a non-mentalistic kind.

Green *et al.* (1995), in an examination of cognitive functioning in autism, point out that executive function tasks are all impaired and prone to perseverative errors, which suggests prefrontal cortex damage. In language, also, children with autism rely on perseveration of grammatical structures as alternatives to repair and recoding strategies (Waterhouse and Fein 1982). Grandin (1995) supports the executive control explanation in her vivid description of her own difficulties in cognitive processing: 'I cannot hold one piece of information in my mind while I manipulate the next step in the sequence' (p. 145).

Russell and Jarrold (1995) explain theory of mind failure as not residing in mental representations themselves but in an inability to disengage from the environment and use an internal representation. Mistakes in emotion recognition tasks (such as Ozonoff *et al.*'s (1991b) finding that individuals with autism confused 'fear' and 'surprise' because of the shared perceptual feature of an open mouth) is consistent with a deficit in an ability to hold a schema of a prototypical affective expression 'online'. Hammes and Langdell (1981), similarly, account for imitation failures in terms of the lack of a mental model to copy. Harris (1993) suggests pretend play deficits can be explained as a deficiency in internal versus external cueing of behaviour. The ability to guide behaviour by internal representations appears at around the same time as behaviours associated with characteristic delay or deviance in autism such as joint attention, gaze monitoring, eye contact and referential pointing (Diamond and Goldman-Rakic 1985).

Prior and Hoffman (1990) tested for frontal lobe function and found significant effects in autism compared to controls. The children they tested with autism were no worse at copying figures but approached it in a more piecemeal way. Turner (1999) also offers executive functioning disorders as a convincing explanation of her findings of a fluency disorder in the generation of novel ideas in autism. Her study was interesting in finding a difference in the medium of the ideas. On tasks involving word fluency, the deficit in performance seemed to be related to an inability to self-cue by categories. On the ideational fluency tasks, both groups with autism (high and low functioning) were considerably poorer than their matched controls, with the high functioning individuals with autism scoring as poorly as the low functioning group with autism and considerably worse than the low-functioning controls. In the design fluency tasks, however, the groups with autism did not produce fewer designs than the control groups but their designs were often repetitive of previous ones i.e. they showed perseveration. Some of the high functioning individuals with autism were aware of this perseveration and were disappointed that they were performing in this way (showing that they had understood the rules), but they were still unable to prevent it happening.

Executive function tasks are also often found to be best at discriminating those individuals with autism who can pass theory of mind tests and those who cannot. Jarrold *et al.* (1993) review studies of symbolic play in autism and do not find a specific deficit in symbolic play that would fit with Leslie and Happé's (1989) 'metarepresentational' deficit but rather find that both spontaneous functional and symbolic play are impaired in autism. They conclude that the problem in autism may be due to a performance rather than a competence deficit, given that symbolic play can be obtained in autism in elicited conditions. Ozonoff *et al* (1991b) suggest that theory of mind tasks involve the use of stored information to govern behaviour and this might be the crucial impairment, rather than any inability to mentalise or 'metarepresent' in Leslie's terms.

Yet the picture is not one of an exact account of the specific symptoms of autism. For example, Sodian and Frith (1992) found children with autism were able to sabotage but not to deceive, although Russell *et al.* (1991) explain this by suggesting that the key problem may be an inability to inhibit habitual responses to salient objects. They tested this with a 'windows' task where the task was one of inhibiting a prepotent response to the sight of a bar of chocolate in a transparent-sided box, while pointing to a clearly empty box, in order to actually get the chocolate. Children with autism were significantly impaired in this, compared to control groups.

Yet other studies (for example, Baron-Cohen 1989; 1991) are not easily explained as a failure in inhibition; nor do all prefrontally damaged patients have autism, so an executive functioning deficit may be a necessary but not a sufficient condition for autism. Prior and Hoffmann (1990) suggest that additional subcortical abnormalities must exist. In addition, executive functioning deficits would lead to the prediction that object permanence would be affected but this is not always found to be so in autism (Morgan *et al.* 1989).

Ozonoff (1995) suggests that it may not be an absolute deficit but a function of the salience and familiarity of external cues, the nature and complexity of the mental representations and the number of competing response alternatives. It might also relate to the imaging possibilities of the representation, given the importance that 'concrete' visualisation appears to have in the thinking of those with autism (Grandin 1995). Photographs would provide a singular representation to hold in mind, for example, whereas belief has no ready-made image. Overall, Bishop (1993) concludes that the executive function deficits that have been found in autism have also been found in other groups and cannot, therefore, be a satisfactory explanation of the specific problems of autism. As an example of this, Baron-Cohen *et al.* (1994) found difficulties in children with Gilles de la Tourette syndrome in editing their intentions, although a recent study of his (Baron-Cohen *et al.* 1999) suggests a heretofore unexpectedly large overlap between the two conditions. Pre-frontal cognitive dysfunction has also been found in attention deficit disorder (Cheune *et al.*, 1986), conduct disorder (Leuger and Gill 1990) and early-treated phenylketonuria

(Welsh *et al.* 1980). It may be the prior disability that leads to executive function deficit in autism that needs to be addressed, in the search for an autism-specific deficit. Executive function theory, then, seems well able to meet the criterion of being present in all those with autism, but less able to meet the criterion of specificity.

As was argued for Baron-Cohen's (1995) evolutionary theory above, executive functioning theory also needs to be questioned in terms of its explanatory power. It is undoubtedly the case that many of the processes that are presumed to originate in the frontal areas of the brain can be shown to be disturbed in autism. But does it increase our understanding of this to say, for example, that the difficulties people with autism experience in perseveration of incorrect responses lie in an executive control disorder which leads to perseveration? Such an analysis appears at best somewhat circular and descriptive. What is needed is some exposition of how these effects relate to one another (other than by presumed processing in a particular area of the brain), how they normally develop, and how that process is disrupted in autism. This kind of exposition is addressed by Russell (1996), below, in his analysis of the role of agency in autism.

Piagetian theory

Russell (1996) has put together a theoretical model of the basic disorder in autism based on the notion of agency and its relationship with mental development. It has clear links to the intersubjectivity theories (especially the idea of an 'experiencing self'), but offers a distinct cognitive analysis based on neo-Piagetian theory (what Russell prefers to refer to as 'piagetian' with a lower case 'p' to distinguish it from traditional Piagetian constructs). He suggests that mental development can be thought of as the process of forging a division between an objective reality and a subjective one and he argues for a link between this division and agency. He points out that only agents can make this division because only agents can cause changes in perceptual input by their own actions (for example, by head or eye turning). He cites von Holst and Mittelstaedt's identification (1950) of a primitive mechanism for recording self-induced changes in perception, which they called 'efference copying'. Russell says:

> '...if an organism cannot determine whether it is it or the world that is responsible for a change in perceptual input it cannot take the first step towards achieving self-world dualism. *Action monitoring* (original emphasis), as I shall call it, is one way of ensuring that this distinction is made'. (p. 77).

This 'monitoring', however, is at the subpersonal level and does not mean that actions are overseen or reflected on as part of this process; Russell is talking of very early and very basic responses. Another characteristic of actions, rather than reactions, is that they should be instigated by the individual, and not by the environment. In other words, they should have temporal sequences, independent of sequences of events in the world. The agent can move head and eyes, or merely shift attention, so that items or events appear in perception in an order that is self-determined i.e. at will.

Here there is a departure from the intersubjectivity theories that ally themselves with Gibson's 'ecological view' (1979). Gibson makes the assumption that percepts of the objective world carry all the information about their own nature (movement and so on) so that their 'meaning' is directly perceived through the 'affordances' that interdepend with the proprioceptive information of the individual. The Gibson view is that there is no inner-outer distinction to information. Yet, as Russell points out, acts of intention depend on action monitoring and reversibility and they have a degree of independence from physical events and a mental component which makes them subjective. Gibson's view could specify that what is seen is a particular point of view but it cannot specify that it is a particular *person's* point of view.

Piagetians distinguish between the 'representation permanence' of objects and 'externality'. 'Representation permanence' depends on representing occluded data during an occluded period, as is assessed through many tests of developing object permanence (for example, Uzgiris and Hunt 1975) but 'externality' means that this representation must include a conception of the object as external to the self. Russell argues that search includes not just knowledge of how the world is configured but how that configuration relates to us. Since object permanence is relational knowledge, then, knowledge of the self must develop in parallel.

He does, however, distinguish two phases in this development. At the first stage there is only subpersonal processing that enables the computation of a subjective sense in owning both one's actions and one's perceptions. But at this stage, that is not sufficient for self-awareness, a true sense of self. This second sense of self is at the reflective level and enables one to have what Russell (after Evans 1992) refers to as 'I-thoughts' and 'I-actions': what the author would see as the 'experiencing self'. It is Russell's contention that the second true sense of self develops from the first and cannot, therefore, develop without it. The development of this second stage of mind includes awareness of others as agents but the argument for how this happens is not well developed. Russell relies on the representational innate views of Leslie and Happé (1989), for example, to suggest ways in which behavioural observations are translated into understanding others as agents. He differs from them, though, in claiming that this is not possible without the prior understanding and experience of the self as an agent.

Russell views autism as a case where executive function difficulties lead to difficulties in developing the initial state of agency. Without that sense of agency, the second stage of self-awareness and a subjective self cannot develop and neither can the ability to understand the agency of others. Without understanding other people's agency, one cannot 'read' their mental states, and hence the failures in theory of mind tasks.

Theories of theories of minds

In making his case, Russell reviews theories of how knowledge of other minds might develop. He divides the theories into two kinds. In the Cartesian view, first person knowledge of the mind is immediate and secure and knowledge of other minds is gained through projection such as inference and hypothesis. In the 'theory-theory' (Morton 1980) mental categories are regarded as theoretical constructs and knowledge of minds, including our own, is regarded as being theoretical. He says that piagetians agree with the first view, in that some aspects of mind must be subjective and they distinguish mind itself from theories about it. On the other hand, piagetians also agree with some aspects of the second view, to the extent that they take the language of mental life to be a theoretical structure which children accommodate as they develop. This would accord with all the data, reviewed above, that relates language ability to theory of mind task performance, where that performance depends on understanding and using mental state terms.

Yet Russell acknowledges that there are problems with the notion of ascribing predicates to oneself alone, which would be implied by the first view. He argues instead that there is a first person phenomenology (immediate sensory awareness) in, for example, pains and feelings of comfort but this is not conceptualised as such by the subject. That is, the infant experiences the pain but does not necessarily know that there is a 'self' that is experiencing it. He also points out that there are some mental states (such as belief) that have no phenomenology (citing Dennett 1978). The piagetian theory espoused by Russell proposes that the experience of agency is necessary but not sufficient to ground a concept of agency which can be applied to the self and then to others. The early sense of agency is immediate and does not involve ascribing predicates to oneself (i.e. 'I am doing this'), only experiencing the doing immediately. A later full conception of mind, however, depends on this ability to ascribe agency predicates (as is involved with a concept of beliefs).

As we have seen, this theory accepts some of the aspects of the cognitive theories in accepting that there are innate modular input systems for computing mental predicates (although this is most plausibly seen as part of the linguistic system). However, it claims that it is only through action (even if only at the level of attention-switching) that one can exercise agency and, through that, gain a sense of the self acting on the world (as well as of the world to be acted upon).

A sense of agency

Russell's view is that the construction of physical knowledge occurs through a sense of agency. This begins through the efferent copying of actions and it develops through further exercise of that agency in establishing the externality of the world (i.e. that it has its own properties that are independent of the agent's will). In discussing the role of imitation in early interactions (p. 202) Russell appears to accept some social and emotional contributions to this conception of the self, although he couches this in cognitive terms. He appears to recognise the existence of an innate propensity to engage with others, especially in his earlier work (Russell 1995) and to perceive desires and dispositions, but he would not necessarily identify this with what Hobson (1989) has called 'affective resonance'.

His position on accepting that the construction of self-awareness might be effected through social agency, exercised in social interactions, remains ambiguous.

Russell has consistently opposed notions from Vygotsky (1962) that early interactions represent a process of social transmission or internalisation. His view is constructivist, in that knowledge of the physical world is gained through self-generated perceptual sequences producing spontaneous actions, inhibiting prepotent but incorrect responses, and exhibiting planned monitored behaviour. Yet social knowledge could also be considered to be constructivist, gained through the instigation of actions within social interactions and the inhibition, planning and monitoring of these social acts, just as with physical knowledge. As Russell would insist, it is the ability to improvise (the mark of the agent) that is crucial to this. Russell does imply, as indicated above, that social interaction would be necessary to construct the externality of other agents and to impute agency to them, but the nature of this imputation is vague, compared to the detailed and careful analysis of how externality arises.

The role and nature of agency, in Russell's theory, is closely akin to the role of executive functioning. The differences between subpersonal and reflecting systems, for example, could be seen as the distinction between routine action 'scripts' and the 'Supervisory Attentional System' (Norman and Shallice 1986), which functions as an executive overseer taking charge in novel situations. Russell suggests that this might explain why autism represents a condition with a co-occurrence of difficulties with executive functioning and with mental states.

In relating this to autism, Russell refers to the work of C. Frith (1992) in suggesting a cognitive explanation for two of the symptoms of schizophrenia (auditory hallucinations and the sense of alien control of behaviour) being rooted in a neurological deficit in the efferent copying of willed actions. Frith and Frith (1991) have already explored the commonalities of autism and schizophrenia at a cognitive level, but they offer their own cognitive explanation in terms of a metarepresentational deficit. Russell proposes that this mechanism (efferent copying) for self-monitoring may be absent from an early age in autism (rather than occur as a result of biochemical breakdown after the development of the personality, as in schizophrenia). This would mean that the individual with autism would lack this first step in an awareness of self. If this early stage were not impaired, there might be difficulties with later stages in building externality and thus a true sense of self and other.

Russell's theory has not long been published, so it has not attracted a great deal of empirical testing or critical scrutiny. Its strength lies in its developmental detail and the way it accounts for a range of experimental and clinical findings in relation to autism. In particular, it suggests that there are executive functioning deficits but it makes these specific to autism by tying them into subjective experience and the development of a sense of self, which has resonance with all of the intersubjectivity views of autism. It also accounts for the development in understanding in mental states from a subjective viewpoint through to propositional understanding (where he is prepared to accept some kind of innately endowed mechanism – rather like TOMM – for the propositional content of mental state knowledge, albeit tied into the linguistic system). Thus he accepts that some aspects of the cognitive architecture that bring about such mental development may be both propositional and modular as the cognitivists have claimed.

However, the very breadth of its explanatory power makes it problematic as a scientific theory open to experimental validation or refutation. It would predict a strong autism-specific association between a lack of spontaneous actions and difficulties in developing a sense of self and, in particular, a weak sense of agency. It is difficult, however, to derive a test of the theory that would exclude alternative explanations.

In spite of the lack of direct empirical support, Russell's views do help to make sense of some aspects of clinical and empirical findings that other theories do not. Thus, Butera and Haywood (1995) draw attention to the lack of purposeful search behaviour, which has been attributed to arousal deficits. This might be reconceptualised (according to the Russell theory) as showing a lack of efferent copying and a consequent inability to mark their own effects on the world, as distinct from being a passive recipient of externally derived events. In the present author's views, the theoretical framework offered by Russell provides the first opportunity she is aware of to make sense of some of the particular fascinations of people with autism. In the past, the author has noted the common property of the fascination with spinning objects, rotating drums, flickering light, falling water and flames as being that all these experiences involve movement in the visual field without the need to alter head or eye movement to perceive these effects. She had suggested that this might arise through difficulties in computing head and/or eye position and movement in relation to the visual field and had tied this in with the other well-attested phenomenon in autism of a failure to become giddy from continual twirling and spinning of the self. Russell's theory offers a theoretical framework for these speculations.

As indicated, Russell's theory also has a lot in common with the author's own theory of difficulties with an 'experiencing self' in autism. The difference between the two concepts (of a full sense of agency and an experiencing self) seems to lie more in the presumed derivation of these states than in their nature. It is hard for the author to claim an objective view in this, but she feels that Russell's sense of self through agency gives a much fuller and more satisfactory account of the difficulties people with autism have in acting effectively in the world. However, she thinks it offers less, when it comes to considering how the world is perceived by the person with autism. In that case, she believes the notion of a difficulty with an experiencing sense of self allows more insight into the 'video-like' perceptions that have been described by people with autism (c.f. Grandin 1995; Gerland 1997).

Nor can the author accept Russell's (1996) dismissal of the role of emotional and social factors. There is the argument used above, in relation to a critique of Baron-Cohen's (1995) evolutionary theory, that an account of autism that ignores these aspects appears to have little face validity. What is happening in all that early interaction, all that sharing of affect, comodulation of levels of arousal, coordination of movements, innately triggered imitation, if it has nothing to add to the story of how a sense of self develops? What of people with autism who seem well able to operate in the world upon objects (and have a fine appreciation of their properties in relation to those of themselves as agents acting on those objects) yet cannot appreciate nor exercise a role of social agency? Why should people with autism become attached to objects (and see Morgan 1996 for good examples of attachment and loss of objects in relation to adults with autism) rather than people, if there is nothing social about their difficulties? And why should emotional engagement make such a difference to learning in both people with autism and normally developing individuals if it has no real role in our interactions with the world? For that matter, why should it be easy for people with autism to become emotionally involved with pursuits that are not so engaging for the rest of us, yet so difficult to become emotionally engaged in social interactions? It appears to the author that Russell offers a good account of how the 'I–it' relationship (Hobson 1993) develops, but is not so convincing when it comes to 'I–thou'.

It may be that some of the questions raised above are rhetorical, and it is certainly difficult to see how they could have empirically derived answers. Nevertheless, they are questions that arise from long experience of working with and thinking about people with autism. They are questions that the author feels need to be addressed by theories.

Narrative

The last theory to be considered in this review of psychological theories relates to an awareness that the interactional difficulties in autism inevitably lead to relative failure in socialisation, and in becoming part of a culture. Grandin is well aware of this when she refers to herself, in relation to her attempts to understand others, as being like an 'anthropologist on Mars' (Sacks 1995). Others have also been aware of the way in which people with autism stand outside the culture in which they are raised and individuals with autism have been described as having an alien culture (Mesibov 1993) or being 'acultural' (Baron-Cohen 1993; Jordan and Powell 1995a). The studies of Leekam *et al.* (1997) showing no spontaneous gaze monitoring in autism help to elucidate the mechanism that could in part account for a failure to learn from others since, if there is no shared attention, there can be no common topics for elaboration. It is ironical that a disorder that so clearly affects the social environment of the child should, until recently, not have attracted an explanation in terms of this culturalisation process.

Bruner and Feldman (1993) have offered such an explanation for autism in terms of an impaired ability to carry on social interactions due in part to an inability '…to be able to represent culturally canonical forms of human action and interaction by the vehicle of narrative encoding' (p. 267). They draw on the literature for normal infant development to show that a child, through mutual imitation, can recognise a connection between its own subjective intention, its bodily expression and that expression in another. Bruner and Feldman suggest that a child's understanding of other minds comes gradually through transactions with others and that the first transactional process is one of reciprocal attribution, the joint attribution of intention, of agency. This theory differs from Russell's view of the role of agency in autism, not just in the derivation of agency but in proposing that the characteristic shape of the 'formats' in which these transactions take place is a narrative one. A narrative format is identified as one involving a canonical (conforming to a norm) steady state, then a precipitating event, then a restoration and finally a coda marking the end. An example would be a game of peek-a-boo:

- Canonical state – mutual eye gaze
- Precipitating event – mother hides face
- Restoration – cloth is removed revealing face again
- Coda – Boo!

The authors suggest that experience of this 'cultural framing' of events allows the child to generalise to other situations. In such a way, the child is enabled to build canonical representations of how the world works.

Evidence for a failure in narrative ability

In autism, this theory takes as its starting point the fact that two elements of productive language are missing; in the first place, individuals with autism cannot extend another's comment (that is, they do not seem to know where it is going) and secondly, they cannot make a story. In normal development, Bruner and Feldman suggest, patterns of narration scaffold the metacognition of intentions upon which a theory of mind depends. '...narratives are exercises in canonical encoding, and, specifically, in the making of non-idiosyncratic or culture-embodying meanings' (p275).

In a study with adolescents with autism and severe learning difficulties, they found that 91 per cent of the utterances produced were socially accommodating, 84 per cent maintained the adult's topic, and the study group was most successful at this in response to declaratives. But only 6 per cent went beyond topic maintenance to make a comment. Thus, the authors suggest, it is not the 'asociability' of the language of people with autism that is marked, but a specific deficit in relation to topic/comment structure. In a further study, with high functioning adolescents with autism, they found a good deal of topic initiation. This group was also able to speak about intentions (in answer to probes) and even showed metacognition, but individuals were seldom able to go beyond one rote comment even when they were talking on their own topic. The attempts made were so far removed from the canonical set of possible comments that they seemed like a change of topic.

Bruner and Feldman cite an unpublished study of Scopinsky (1986) using a story-telling task in which pictures were added in a line one at a time. The standard prompts were 'And what happens next?' etc. The subjects were then asked what the whole story was about, 'putting them all together'. Subjects with autism gave shorter and more grammatically simpler stories than MA-matched normally developing controls, and neither group talked about intentional states. The subjects with autism attributed less intentionality to the actions described and did not link actions to the purpose in performing them. Virtually no narrative markers were used by the autistic group, neither causal, temporal nor intentional, nor did they produce different genres for interviews and story telling, although the former contained more first and second pronouns and the latter more descriptive modes.

Bruner and Feldman used four folk-tales with high functioning autistic 15-year-olds, and read the stories to them with interjected queries, asking what was going to happen and why they thought that. Then the children were asked to tell the story in their own words. The results showed that they did understand what the stories were about, the deceptions involved in the stories, and their likely effects. But, when telling the story back in their own words, there was either no mention of the deception or, if it was mentioned, it was as incidental to the plot. They could produce the events in the correct sequence but with no weighting given to those events. The authors suggest that, without a narrative bent, children with autism do not organise experience into the canonical forms by which people regulate their sociality; in the authors' words, they lack a semiotic for organising narratives.

The role of narrative in the construction of self, as well as in the participation in culturally important interactions, has been studied in normal development. Miller *et al.* (1992) conducted an observational study of co-narrated personal experiences occurring in the spontaneous talk of children with others in a family setting. The children were 2;5 year olds and five-year-olds. Ten naturally occurring stories of personal experience were collected for each child. They found that children at both ages portrayed themselves through interpersonal experiences, and this increased with age. They compared self with others on dimensions of actions, emotions and possessions. Peterson and McCabe (1992) also studied personal narration in a longitudinal study of mother/child dyads. They studied two contrasting dyads and collected three sets of data: mothers' elicitations, children's spontaneous contextual orientation in narratives elicited by the experimenter (at 27-44 months) and the overall narrative structure at 44 months. They found the child's narrative development reflected the eliciting style of the mother and suggest that parents scaffold narratives. Peterson and McCabe cite Grimes (1975; 1978) in proposing that personal experience narratives are universal across cultures, supporting Bruner and Feldman's notion of inbuilt canonical forms to narrative that may be based, as they suggest, in even earlier interactive 'formats'.

Taylor and Cameron (1987) argue that intersubjectivity cannot be 'real' but must arise through the unarticulated agreement to adopt narratives of individuation and internal state personhood and to incorporate a 'working agreement' that all selves are fundamentally the same. This brings together the intersubjectivity theories of autism with this narrative theory of Bruner and Feldman, suggesting that narration is the encoding of the developing intersubjectivity.

Forrester (personal communication) suggests that narrative ability lies at the heart of socialisation and learning to be part of a culture. He suggests that if the child is unfamiliar with narratives, through a lack of participation in the social situation in which they are constructed, or a lack of knowledge of the social practices in which they are embedded, then it is increasingly impossible for the child to understand that narrative structure. It then becomes impossible to follow these structures and they are seen as incoherent, unintelligible, unutterably alien.

If Bruner and Feldman are correct about the original failure of infants with autism to participate in narrative construction through preverbal transactional formats, then it is likely that this will lead to further incomprehension and further withdrawal from communicative contexts. This would mean that the linguistic problems in autism would be primarily pragmatic, and related to discourse (including narratives), and this is indeed the case (Baron-Cohen 1988; Tager-Flusberg 1993). Tager-Flusberg (1993) also proposes that there may be in autism an impaired ability to communicate novel information. This could be evidence in support of Russell's theory, or of an executive function deficit, or it could support the notion that individuals with autism are unable to comment, because of an inability to recognise and use a narrative structure.

There has been only been one direct attempt (to the author's knowledge) to test Bruner and Feldman's theory of autism, although there have been studies investigating narrative ability in autism in the context of the cohesive role of anaphoric pronouns (Jordan, in preparation). Draper and Bowler (1994) have studied narrative ability and its relationship to theory of mind problems in the normally developing young child and in autism. They conclude that a failure in narrative understanding may indeed be a better explanation of theory of mind problems, especially when false belief tasks are used with a long and complex narrative structure. As has been noted in the previous subsections, children with autism perform better on theory of mind tasks when this narrative element is simplified (Bowler 1992; Tager-Flusberg 1993).

Of course, even if there are problems with narrative forms in autism (and the author has a paper in preparation that suggests that there are), that may not be direct support for the theory. It would not offer direct evidence, for example, that such difficulties are at the heart of autism or that they arise in the way suggested by Bruner and Feldman.

Relation to practice

The psychological theories presented in this section can be seen to have elements in common, as well as significant differences. In general they can be said to accept the same 'data' on autistic functioning, but to offer alternative analyses for the interpretation of that data. It has seldom proved possible to design experimental tests of hypotheses derived from the theories that will give unequivocal support to a particular theory or refute another. The reader may, therefore, be bemused by the complexity of the theories, and the conflicting evidence, of their validity. There is not space in this handbook to develop an argument for the 'best' of these theories. In any case, research is still in progress and it is for the reader to make his or her own judgement.

However, it is encouraging for the practitioner to note that the practical implications may be the same in many of these cases, even when the theories seem to occupy completely contrary positions. Much of the notion of conflicting practice arises because of a confusion between what is proposed as a difficulty or a defect in autism and what can be used as a teaching approach. One should remember that the best approach is not necessarily one that teaches to the deficit, or tries to remedy it directly, but rather, one that builds on strengths. When that is considered, then the identification of a problem, in early interaction and the sharing of emotion, for example, does not mean that this has to be the focus of teaching. For the same reason, Leslie's position does not suggest that teaching about propositions, and how to make triadic representations, will be the best approach. In fact, it might suggest the opposite.

Cognitive teaching about mental states and attitudinal stances, for example, might just as easily follow from Hobson's viewpoint as it might from Leslie's. Both theories suggest that interpersonal development will not occur spontaneously in autism and will need to be taught, and each suggests that a cognitive route would be the most accessible to the child with autism. The difference would be that Leslie's approach would attach a ceiling beyond which the child could not follow, whereas Hobson's theory may not. It would suggest earlier intervention, using emotional involvement as part of the cognitive process, and allowing for the possibility that, if emotional engagement could be taught at a sufficiently early stage, the prognosis would be significantly better. Neither theory would suggest an approach that could lead to a cure, but the straight cognitive approach leads more naturally to compensatory approaches and the building of prosthetic learning environments, whereas intersubjective approaches are more open to the possibility of remediation and tackling the autism itself.

It is important that new methods and ideas are not adopted without a well-developed rationale, nor should a particular method or theoretical line be followed slavishly. Yet it is also important that new knowledge about autism is incorporated into practice. The ideal approach then might be:

- principled (that is, there is a reason for what is done and how it is done and this takes account of current research);
- eclectic (taking ideas from different sources and adapting them to fit the particular situation); and
- innovative (in that new ideas are welcomed and incorporated as long as they fit the principle and do not counter already good practice).

The author's view of a principled approach to the education and care of individuals with autism would be one that recognised that:

1. Normal intuitive routes to learning and understanding are absent or disturbed; and

2. Compensatory routes, using intact general cognitive abilities (more problematic, of course, in those with additional learning difficulties) must be developed.

In addition, the author is convinced (but this may not be a conviction the reader would share) from a number of theoretical accounts, including her own, that a remedial approach in which there are attempts to build a sense of self (and consequently of social agency) is also important.

Conclusion

There is as yet no one commanding theory to explain the cause of autism that can offer an explanation for all the characteristic symptoms, that applies to all with autistic spectrum conditions, and is exclusive to that group. Most have something to offer our understanding of the condition, even if they are not entirely satisfactory as full explanations. Theory of mind theories have offered us the valuable insight that many of the difficulties experienced by people with autism result from their difficulty in understanding their own, and other, mental states. Baron-Cohen's (1995) elaboration of SAM has shown the futility of simply teaching people with autism to 'look' in a behavioural way (whether at an addressee or at an object) when what is required is an awareness that we are looking. The intersubjective theories have given substance to our everyday awareness of the crucial difficulties with emotional understanding and engagement in autism and have reaffirmed the importance of emotional engagement for meaningful learning.

There is a wealth of practical implications from executive function theory. Perhaps the most important is the implication for behaviour management. It seems very clear from the research, and from clinical experience, that we cannot rely on people with autism being able to inhibit responses that are triggered either by powerful environmental stimuli or from past actions (habits); still less should we punish them for this disability. We need to alter the triggering stimuli or we need to actively teach the competing response that is needed. There is, thus, a clear rationale for the many structured approaches to teaching and care, which practical experience has already vindicated.

Russell (1996) sees his work as being within the executive function area but the author would see the implications of his work and her own (on an 'experiencing self') as lying in possible programmes for enhancing this sense of self, as well as compensating for its lack. Thus transportable cues will need to be incorporated into the learning process if learnt behaviour is to generalise. Agency can be specifically taught (although there is no evidence of the effectiveness of doing so) either through cognitive means (Jordan and Powell 1990) or (not supported by Russell's views) through emotional engagement.

Central coherence is not so helpful in giving fresh insights (it was, after all, developed as a theory to 'explain' features of autism that were very apparent) and was never intended as a full explanatory theory of autism. However, the work around this theory does show the importance of paying attention to learning style and to what is actually being perceived (rather than assuming this). Narrative theory is also rather short of empirical data and perhaps also was never intended to be a full explanatory theory. It is, however, useful as another reminder of the developmental nature of autism and how initial social difficulties may exclude the child with autism from the very learning situations that are vital for his/her later development.

It is both interesting, and encouraging, that the same good practice implications (in terms of teaching content and approach) can be derived from a number of contrasting theoretical understandings. Thus, facilitating interactive routines can be seen as deriving from:

- intersubjective accounts of autism (Hobson 1993a) but also from
- an appreciation of the role of SAM (Baron-Cohen 1995) or from
- the need to establish a sense of social agency (Russell 1996) or
- narrative structure (Bruner & Feldman 1993).

Equally, periods of reflection after activities (Jordan and Powell 1995a) might be derived from:

- this same notion of a failure to appreciate narrative structure
- the motivation to facilitate the development of an 'experiencing self' or a sense of agency.

However, as Rutter (1999) has pointed out, practitioners are not just the recipients of research information about autism, but can also contribute to it. In autism, there is often a disparity between what is shown in structured research situations and the everyday experience of living and working with individuals with autism. We need to bring these understandings together if we are to advance to a full understanding of the condition.

Further reading

Baron-Cohen, S. (1995) *Mindblindness: an Essay on Autism and Theory of Mind*, London: MIT Press.

Baron-Cohen, S. *et al.* (1993) *Understanding Other Minds: Perspectives from Autism.* Oxford: Oxford University Press.

Frith, U. and Happé, F.G.E. (1994) 'Autism: beyond theory of mind', *Cognition,* **50**, 115–32.

Hobson, R.P. (1993a) *Autism and the Development of Mind.* London: Erlbaum.

Jordan, R.R., *et al.* (1995) 'Theories of Mind: Why do they matter?' *School Psychology International,* **16**, 291–302.

Mitchell, P (1997) *Introduction to Theory of Mind: children, autism and apes.* London: Arnold.

Ozonoff, S. (1995) 'Executive functions in autism' in Schopler, E. and Mesibov, G.B. (eds) *Learning and Cognition in Autism,* New York: Plenum Press.

Powell, S.D. and Jordan, R.R. (1993b) 'Being subjective about autistic thinking and learning to learn' *Educational Psychology, 13,* 359–70

Russell, J. (1996) *Agency: its Role in Mental Development,* Hove, Erlbaum.

Chapter 6

The Individual with an Autistic Spectrum Disorder

Introduction

As indicated in earlier sections, the manifestations of autism vary between individuals and even in a single individual over time, while retaining aspects of the triad of impairments from which autism is defined. When attempting to diagnose in later childhood or adulthood, therefore, it is important to take a developmental history, to reach some understanding of where that individual's difficulties lie. It may be that the more able person with milder autism (although the two do not always go together in this way; it is the more able who develop better social skills, as pointed out earlier) may appear to be very sociable as an adult. Carers might then doubt the diagnosis, or assume the person has somehow overcome their autism. If the case history shows, however, that there have been significant social problems in the past, it is likely that that person has only been able to acquire such skills through extreme and constant effort. This means the behaviour is vulnerable to break down under conditions of stress and that maintaining the behaviour may leave the individual with little 'spare' capacity to learn new skills or cope with other changes in the environment. Once one knows that someone has autism, however good their current level of functioning, carers should look for the areas of vulnerability and provide appropriate support.

Equally, if one meets someone for the first time in extreme conditions, a history will help one decide whether this is part of a cyclical pattern of behaviour or whether the person is undergoing some form of regression, if skills are being lost and behaviour is deteriorating. It will also help carers to select appropriate strategies if they are aware of what has been tried before and what did or did not work.

Each person's development will be individualistic, depending on the interaction between their abilities and disabilities, the environments they are in and the education and training they receive. Autism does produce characteristic patterns of behaviour, and parents will be relieved and delighted when first meeting other parents of children with autism to find their children have a lot in common in terms of behaviour and mannerisms. Yet it is far from true that all people with autism behave in the same way or have the same reactions to things. They will still have their own overall personality which will both shine through, and interact with, their autism. And in a curious way, it can be argued that they may be more individualistic than other people. This is especially true of adults and of the more able. When they are young, there do seem to be some things that appeal to most of them, like Thomas the Tank Engine videos, or switching lights on and off. But they are less socialised into a particular social and family culture, so their interests can become more unique and idiosyncratic, and they are less inclined than others to share interests with others. That is why well-meaning attempts to organise club activities for able adults with autism seldom work (unless there is a particular focus on developing social or vocational skills, or 'counselling') because they are each only interested in their own particular hobby or pastime.

Sigman (1998) uses data from a longitudinal study of children with autism to comment on the stability of behavioural characteristics over time. She found that there was continuity in what might be considered 'core' difficulties (in joint attention, representational play and responsiveness to the emotions of others) but that, naturally, the ways these were expressed differed over time and between children.

Recognising needs arising from autism

Autism, as we have seen, appears in a great range of manifestations. It is perhaps easiest to recognise in individuals with low to average levels of general ability. Cases at either extreme of intelligence present a problem for diagnosis. In those with profound learning difficulties, it may be hard to diagnose autism because the individual's social, communication and adaptive skills may be very poor and it is hard to make the judgement that they are out of keeping with the individual's mental age. It may be even more difficult, when the individual's apparently 'antisocial' behaviour makes it difficult to approach them or make a proper assessment. And yet, that kind of behaviour can of itself be a strong indicator that the person is on the autistic spectrum and needs help in learning to accept people and to receive the care he or she needs.

The question sometimes arises in such cases, especially regarding the provision of services, of whether it makes any difference in terms of education or care whether a diagnosis is made or not. Certainly, one must recognise that progress is likely to be poor even with a diagnosis simply because the individual will find it difficult to learn through the cognitive route and will not be able to compensate for the lack of a spontaneous intuitive route to social development. Yet many of the advantages of a diagnosis apply whatever the general level of functioning. A diagnosis puts parents in touch with a support network, it gives access to literature that may help make sense of the behaviour, and it focuses teaching and behaviour management in ways that are likely to be more effective and more enhancing of the quality of life. It may not mean that specialist services are required, but it should mean that the service in question can then identify that person's needs and (with specialist input or training) work towards meeting those needs. As argued earlier in the handbook, this is the group who will always need people to care for them and so it is imperative that they have their autism addressed.

At higher levels of intelligence, people with autism may have devised coping strategies which disguise their real problems and so their residual difficulties are misunderstood. They may attract more potentially harmful labels such as 'lazy', 'rude' or even 'aggressive'. Bewildered by the hostility and lack of support they receive, they may lose their carefully constructed coping behaviours and could end up excluded from the service. Undiagnosed pupils often end in schools for children with emotional and behavioural difficulties, which (unless the school has made special provision) are unlikely to be suitable. Undiagnosed adults with autism may end up on the streets or even in prison because their behaviour is misunderstood and they are vulnerable to manipulation by others.

The social impairments

Problems in education and management

This section outlines the kinds of behaviour that are associated with social impairments. Difficulties in this area of development clearly have profound and complex effects on all other areas of development and they present particular difficulties in education and management. Education and training are largely social activities and rely on the role of a 'teacher' as a facilitator or mediator of learning. It is helpful to have someone to guide and assist learning for most people but for individuals with autism the very presence of another person may be stressful and counterproductive to learning.

The same problems arise when trying to get people to work together in groups; the person with autism may learn faster (although he/she will not learn about interaction, which will need to be taught separately) if they are able to learn by themselves, through computer assisted learning, for example. All this also has implications for integration if that is to be a real process rather than simply a matter of placing the person in a mainstream location. The individual with autism will need to be taught how to interact with others if he/she is to get anything from the interaction. The 'receiving group' will also need guidance on how to interact with the person with autism and an explanation of possible behaviour which they might otherwise find offputting or even frightening.

Particular social difficulties

Individuals with autism may not be globally impaired in social functioning. For example, they often seem to show attachment behaviours, which are not different on certain quantitative measures from those of other (non-autistic) individuals with severe learning difficulties (of the same mental age). People with autism actually may show mental age appropriate attachment in infancy (Dissanayake and Crossley 1996; Sigman and Ungerer 1984; Sigman and Mundy 1989; Shapiro *et al.*

1987), and later in life may show preferences for, and even 'crushes' on, certain people (e.g. Tantam 1991). What is striking is the lack of understanding of the two-way nature of relationships.

The kinds of objective measures used in such studies measure attachment by overt behaviours such as amount of eye-gaze, distress at parting, and physical proximity. Such 'findings' do not square with parental reports of 'being treated like objects' or with the observations of professionals where homesickness is extremely rare and individuals with autism may relate as happily to a stranger as to a parent or key worker. Of course individuals with severe learning difficulties may be extremely delayed in showing these kinds of bonding behaviours as well but, unless they also have autism, they do develop special attachments whereas individuals with autism may show these behaviours regardless of level of intelligence.

Perhaps even more importantly, one should recognise that certain behaviours may appear the same but the individuals concerned may have reached those behaviours by a different developmental route, and thus the behaviours may be qualitatively different in their meaning. A normally developing child (or an individual without autism) may be attached to a caregiver as a result of the normal processes of emotional bonding that arise through early interactions. An individual with autism may appear to show similar attachment behaviour, but this time it has the same quality (and serves the same purpose) as an attachment to familiar or obsessional objects. Thus a parent learns to be consistent with the child with autism who then finds this rewarding and comforting compared to others who are not so predictable. The difference often emerges when the object of attachment is lost. Typically, individuals with autism transfer their affections wholeheartedly (and often swiftly and abruptly) to a new person who acts in a similar way to the previously attached person. Yet loss of an attached object is not so easily assuaged. This is not to demean the feelings of those with autism; it is meant just to point out that mere behavioural observations may be misleading, if we do not put the behaviour we observe into its developmental context, and recognise that the same apparent behaviour may arise in different ways and serve different purposes for the individual.

A further difference in the attachment and bonding process can be seen as a child with autism develops into an adult with autism. The early bonding of the non-autistic individual provides a framework for future bonding with others, in friendship and love relationships; the more secure the initial attachment, the more successful these later bondings are likely to be. But in autism this is not the case. Early, apparently strong, attachment to a parent may remain and fail to extend into a capacity to form relationships with others, leading to the typical friendless but dependent adult with autism. This is because that early apparent attachment did not 'engage' the child at the level of interpersonal development (Hobson 1993a) and so did not provide the framework for later development.

Similarly, children with autism know about their physical identity in the sense that they can recognise themselves in a mirror at the normal mental age (Dawson and McKissick 1984). They are also as good as controls, of the same verbal ability, at recognising the faces of others (Ozonoff 1990; Smalley and Asarnow 1990). However, their 'knowing' of themselves may only be at this level of knowing *about* themselves; they may not experience a sense *of* themselves (Powell and Jordan 1993b; Russell 1996). One boy with autism appeared to identify himself with his favourite storybook character of Peter Rabbit and insisted that this was his name. This was accepted in his mainstream school at infant level but he was told firmly at seven that he must stop calling himself Peter Rabbit but become John Smith (his name). To everyone's surprise he accepted this without demur as if one name was the same as another – without any personal resonance for him.

Equally people with autism may rely on different cues in recognising and distinguishing between others (Langdell 1978). Nevertheless, people with autism are able to respond differentially to different people and to different types of approach (Clark and Rutter 1981). Many children with autism are not pervasively aloof, and do show proximity-seeking behaviours and vocalisations for social attention (Sigman and Mundy 1989; Sigman *et al.* 1986). It is the *quality* of social interactions that is different, not the *quantity*.

Against this backdrop of generally mental-age appropriate social behaviours, individuals with autism show a specific pattern of impairments in social understanding. There is some disagreement as to the age at which these difficulties first emerge since as yet autism is rarely reliably diagnosed before three years of age. There is little experimental work on the behaviour of the infant with autism, as was seen in earlier sections. As a result, social behaviours which are shown by the normally developing infant, have not been explored extensively in infants with autism – rather, these abilities have been examined in older children, or even adults, with autism.

The following account of the early development of individuals with autism is based on Lord (1993) who categorised autistic social difficulties as follows:

MOTIVATION TOWARDS PEOPLE

In laboratory studies children with autism look at people for as long as they look at objects (Dawson *et al.* 1990; Sigman and Mundy 1989; Wetherby and Prutting 1984) but the duration of gaze is shorter for both people and objects (Hermelin and O'Connor 1970). Three factors are found to discriminate autistic children's attention to other people: they avoid direct eye gaze or auditory input (Kubicek 1980), they rarely attract another's attention (Dawson and Galpert 1986) and they show specific deficits in joint attention (Kasari *et al.* 1990; Loveland and Landry 1986). Lord also reports that they are *'less likely to follow another's gaze'* (p. 63) which, as we have seen, has important implications for theory. As Lord suggests, there may also be some active avoidance of contacts with others. She reports avoidance of eye contact in infants with autism (Kubicek 1980; Massie and Rosenthal 1984) and avoiding behaviours and skills that are associated with social interactions.

IMITATION

Spontaneous imitation is less frequent and a more limited range of behaviours are copied (DeMyer *et al.* 1972; Dawson and Adams 1984). Children with autism have also been found to be less able to imitate gestures or actions (Bartak *et al.* 1975; Curcio 1978; Stone *et al.* 1990). Again, the question of whether difficulties in imitation are specific to autism was seen to have some theoretical significance. Stone and Lemanek (1990) also report poorer imitation skills in children with autism than in matched controls with severe learning difficulties.

SOCIAL KNOWLEDGE

Lord draws attention to the work exploring the difficulty in recognising sex and age (Hobson 1986a; 1986b; Weeks and Hobson 1987). She also cites work showing that people with autism are as able as mental age-matched normally developing or mentally handicapped peers to recognise themselves in a mirror (Dawson and McKissick 1984; Ferrari and Mathews 1983; Spiker and Ricks 1984). However, as Mundy *et al.* (1993) found for other activities, they behave differently (Neuman and Hill 1978), showing far less emotional engagement with their own image and making no attempt to play with it. This would be predicted from Hobson's (1993b) view, among others.

ATTACHMENT

Although, as suggested above, there appear to be no quantitative differences in attachment as measured in separation studies (Shapiro *et al.* 1987; Sigman and Mundy 1989; Sigman and Ungerer 1984) there are qualitative differences. Parents certainly report poor attachment (Le Couteur *et al.* 1989; Ohta 1987). Wing (1976) has reported that parents often feel that they are being treated like objects or wind-up toys that can be made to meet the demands of the individual with autism. It is also the author's experience that parents feel like this, although some children with autism at least do become attached, even if it is only at the level of attachment to the familiar and predictable. Stone and Lemanek (1990), however, discuss parental reports of social behaviours in autistic preschoolers showing no differences between children with autism and matched children with severe learning difficulties in parental reports of early relating behaviours such as responding to praise and attention and games such as pat-a-cake and peek-a-boo. If this finding were substantiated, it would be evidence against Bruner and Feldman's (1993) position.

UNDERSTANDING AND EXPRESSING EMOTIONS

Many children with autism do appear to have difficulty in responding naturally to a smile with one of their own (Dawson *et al.* 1990), although they can learn to do so as Park (1986) has testified. Lord reports that systematic studies show that children with autism develop a social smile later than others of an equivalent developmental age and they show a narrower range of appropriate facial expressions and more inappropriate ones.

Observations show fewer facial expressions, more negative than positive ones, and all of them less socially-directed (Kubicek 1980; Massie and Rosenthal 1984; Snow *et al.* 1987). Ricks (1972) showed that even their early vocal expressions for pleasant surprise, demand, greeting and frustration (which in normally developing babies show a common recognisable form across languages) were idiosyncratic and not recognisable except by those who had 'learnt' their meaning. Lord suggests that the autistic difficulty is not so much in labelling pictures of emotions (a common test of emotional understanding in studies) but in coordinating the nonverbal and verbal behaviour involved in real life situations (Hobson 1990a). Sigman *et al.* (1988) report problems differentiating facial expressions in a visual preference task and in matching facial expressions of emotion to gesture or emotional vocalisation. They cite Cohen (1980) who comments on *'(the) child's inability to form a stable, internal representation of the connectedness between his own inner states or a sense of himself as the locus of the organisation of initiative, feelings and thoughts'* (p. 360) in relation to autism.

Cognitive impairments

Green *et al.* (1995) have reviewed cognitive functioning in autism. Although people with autism may present problems in testing, the test situation with its clear structure and one-to-one attention is often an optimum environment for them, and the main problems for practitioners is that test performance may not be reflected in real life functioning. Nevertheless, Green *et al.* cite the work of Freeman *et al.* (1991) in showing that IQ is stable over time. Minshew *et al.* (1992) have demonstrated relative strengths in attention, associative memory and rule-learned abstractions but deficits in abstraction involving cognitive flexibility, verbal reasoning, complex memory and complex language. At all levels there appear to be deficits in conceptual problem-solving, metarepresentational ability, pragmatic aspects of communication, joint attention, symbolic play, and the recognition of emotions.

It is not clear from the literature whether repetitive stereotyped behaviour reflects a truly cognitive difficulty in expressing spontaneous creative behaviour or whether it represents a form of 'displacement' behaviour in the face of overwhelming social, emotional or cognitive overload. Individuals with autism, such as Williams (1992), will themselves, often report that they engage in repetitive activities as a way of coping with their inability to prepare for new situations.

In an earlier review of cognition in autism, Sigman *et al.* (1988) concluded that autism is not associated with pervasive deficits in discrimination, difficulties in reversal and non-reversal shifts, global memory deficits, or object permanence. Particular difficulties were, however, found in temporal sequencing, spontaneous imitation, cognitive processing and stored knowledge (primarily in the verbal domain). There were no differences between those with autism and control groups in sorting by shape or colour or in classification categories but there were significant deficits in joint attention, especially at an early age. An inability to reflect on their own thinking as well as a failure to appreciate the thinking of others may mean that they do not learn principles and are unaware of the strategies they have for problem solving. Learning tends, therefore, to be very context-bound and they have difficulty generalising to other contexts. They learn set sequences of behaviours for particular situations and even with these they may become very dependent on being 'cued' to go on to the next step or even to get started.

Courchesne *et al.* (1994) have shown impairments in the ability to shift attention between modalities and a selective impairment in shifting spatial attention. Executive function tasks are all impaired and prone to perseverative errors (Ozonoff *et al.* 1991). In memory, Boucher and Warrington (1976) have shown that cued memory is far better than free recall, but Minshew and Goldstein (1993) do not support this. In general, as Powell and Jordan (1993b) have pointed out, memory research has failed to take account of autobiographical memory and, in particular, personal episodic memory, and these authors suggest that this might be a crucial distinction in autism.

The fundamental difficulty (as seen by Frith 1989b at any rate) is a difficulty in extracting meaning from experiences, especially social or cultural meaning. The child with autism may interact with people and objects at a very primitive level of sensory stimulation – sniffing, touching, and licking – and may even be sensitive to underlying moods and tensions as revealed through people's changes in body chemistry. Because they do not perceive wider social or cognitive meanings, individuals with autism may have a low tolerance for changes in behaviour or routine and so may seek to make their life predictable by an insistence on sameness and a reliance on routine and ritual. These may also, of course, be the direct result of executive function deficits.

Stress may be caused by all manner of features of the environment. This may include people, language they do not understand, loud noises – or ones that appear loud to them – pressure to tackle a task whose outcome they cannot visualise and where they have no notion of themselves as being able to tackle that task, and so on. The wild outbursts that may be seen as so characteristic of the behaviour of people with autism, as well as some of the more compulsive routines they engage in, are not so abnormal, if we view them as manifestations of someone under severe stress, with very few alternative ways of expressing that. What is abnormal, of course, and difficult to comprehend, is the myriad commonplace occurrences that are likely to cause such severe stress in the individual with autism.

Problems in education and care come from behavioural management concerns and the need to create a structured learning environment that reduces stress and enables learning. This is partly in conflict with the other need to teach in the context of use, and clearly these two issues need to be carefully balanced. While structure and a positive approach to direct teaching (rather than allowing the person with autism to retreat into autistic behaviour or 'act out' feelings) are found to be very beneficial for people with autism, this should not be confused with a strictly behavioural approach. Skill learning can clearly benefit from methods of task analysis and teaching in graded steps, but there are aspects of learning where the person needs to learn to take the initiative and show understanding of the situation, rather than relying on set routines. Complete dependence on behavioural techniques is liable to exacerbate problems in generalising or coping with any change in the sequence learnt, or indeed in carrying out any task independently.

Play

In those with additional learning difficulties, play is likely to be restricted to immediate sensory stimulation. It may become functional, especially if this is taught, but pretend or symbolic play is extremely delayed and, even when it does develop, is restricted in scope and imagination. However, there have been recent encouraging examples of teaching pretend play to children with autism and additional severe learning difficulties (Sherratt, submitted). Play is found to be less appropriate and less functional in unstructured situations (Mundy *et al.* 1986; Sigman and Ungerer 1984, Stone *et al.* 1990). Even in structured situations children with autism show less symbolic play than others of a comparable mental or verbal age (DeMyer *et al.* 1967; Mundy *et al.* 1986). Sigman *et al.* (1988) report specific deficits in play behaviour, including poverty of symbolic play and fewer play sequences. There are great difficulties in reciprocal play even in the most able (Harris 1989; Leslie 1987). Some early studies did not distinguish between functional and symbolic play in their designation of a 'symbolic' play deficit in autism. Current studies suggest there are problems in both functional and symbolic play (Libby *et al.* 1996) although the studies have tended to be experimental ones that do not examine or try to develop social or reciprocal play. Jordan and Libby (1997) review the area of play in autism and offer some practical examples of how it might be developed. It is notable that Sherratt's successful technique was part of a daily programme and used highly emotionally engaging techniques to elicit the play.

Adaptive behaviour and flexibility

Adaptive responses, such as self-help skills, on the other hand, tend to be better than in age matched children with severe learning difficulties and sometimes they may be in advance of those in normally developing peers, although communication difficulties can have an effect here. Most disruptive to adaptive behaviours, however, is the extreme inflexibility of the learning and the fact that there is no 'common sense' applied to everyday life. Thus all behaviour is learned behaviour and is performed in the same way in response to the same cues. This makes it difficult for the person to tolerate changes in routines unless these are well prepared, to know how to behave in any new or different situation, to develop their own ways of solving problems and to take account of the views of others. Additional learning difficulties will exacerbate these problems.

Another feature of autism, which arises from the context-dependent learning style, is the lack of generalisation. For example, children with autism may show very great discrepancies between their behaviour in school and their behaviour at home. This poses special problems for teachers, and may require that specific behaviours are taught for specific situations. Rincover and Koegel (1975) found, for example, that a group of children with autism taught a response to a situation, actually took, as cues to the behaviour, very idiosyncratic and irrelevant features of the learning situation – for example the teacher's dress, the table, the room they were in. Their learning was significantly hampered because they would produce the response only in the presence of that cue. This also highlights the apparently bizarre focus of attention of individuals with autism – in looking at a picture-book an individual with autism may zoom in on some irrelevant and minor feature of the picture (e.g. a button) rather than responding to the salient and overall meaning (e.g. a policeman). In order to help the individual to focus on the relevant feature of a stimulus, and thus improve the chances of appropriate generalisation, it may be helpful to cut out excessive and irrelevant stimuli. Jordan and Powell (1990) suggest some other cognitive difficulties and ways of overcoming them.

A reliance on routine and a lack of understanding of others also means that everyday life is difficult and stressful for people with autism. Behavioural difficulties may arise from many causes, but prime among them may be reactions to this stress. Environments that are successful in reducing stress allow the individual to see (and it is often a matter of directly seeing, in the form of visual arrangements or pictorial representations) what they are supposed to be doing, where, when, how, and for how long (Peeters 1997). Such environments do not do anything in themselves to help people with autism overcome or deal with their particular difficulties, but they do give them the space and freedom to learn. They are what was referred to in an earlier section as 'prosthetic' environments for autism and the evidence is that people with autism can function well in such situations (Schopler *et al.* 1981).

Communication

The range of communicative ability in the autistic spectrum is very striking. At one extreme is the totally mute individual with autism who does not even use gesture to communicate. Then there may be the echolalic individual who may parrot whole sentences, or the individual who will use single words inflexibly as requests. At the other extreme is the fluently speaking but pragmatically bizarre individual with Asperger's syndrome. A great deal of research has been conducted into this range of manifestations of the autistic communication impairment. In spite of obvious language abnormalities associated with autism, it has been found to be a problem in communication, not in the structural aspect of language (see Frith 1989b, for a review; Jordan 1993; 1996; Schopler and Mesibov 1985; Paul 1987; Tager-Flusberg 1981).

Some more able individuals with autism, especially those diagnosed as having Asperger's syndrome, may have particular strengths in language learning.

However, language difficulties often accompany autism, as do other general learning difficulties. Difficulties in acquiring spoken language do exist, but it is true to say that autism alone does not lead to an individual failing to speak. This is more likely to be due to associated specific language impairment (especially in the cases of more able individuals with autism who remain mute) and/or additional severe learning difficulties which make the conceptual basis of language difficult to acquire. Autism will increase these difficulties in acquiring language by robbing it of its communicative framework. Children do not acquire a language and then learn to communicate with it; they learn language as part of the process of communicating. Individuals with autism do not understand about communication and so they cannot use this understanding to help them master the complexities of language. This applies to all languages including sign (Jordan 1993), although some will have aspects that make them easier to teach than spoken language.

Communication difficulties in autism are sometimes difficult to detect because they are subtle and because they may be masked by good or at least adequate language ability. Of course, additional learning difficulties, and sometimes additional language difficulties, mean that the majority of children with autism do have general language problems as well as those that arise directly from autism. There are still a significant proportion of individuals with autism who remain without usable spoken language, and delay in language acquisition occurs for all but the most able. Having a good grasp of language structure, however, does not mean that one necessarily knows how to use that language in communication or that one understands it in communicative situations. Normally developing children, and even those with learning difficulties apart from autism, come to understand all about communication before they ever acquire a language with which to communicate, but this does not happen with autism.

When there is language there are always some pragmatic difficulties – problems in understanding how language is used and understood in context – no matter how well the person apparently speaks. Early language development in autism is characterised by immediate and delayed echolalia and, for many, language development remains at this stage of learnt set phrases which they may or may not learn to generalise or adapt to fit to new situations. This applies to both spoken and signed language. Thus, although signing can be very helpful in giving the person something to work with in establishing communication, it is not a panacea for the communication problems of autism (Jordan 1985). Signing individuals with autism may show 'echopraxia' (the exact imitation of signs and gestures) in just the same way as their speaking counterparts show echolalia.

Where there is language understanding it tends to be pedantic and literal with great anxiety over linguistically based jokes and a difficulty in understanding idioms, metaphor, irony or sarcasm. Prosodic features are poor, either being monotonous or showing inappropriate singsong variations. People with autism can perceive intonational stress but they do not seem to understand how it can affect meaning. Their production also mirrors these difficulties with pedantic use of language and poor conversational skills. Their understanding of written language may often be better than their understanding of spoken language, since in the former the meanings are more explicit and less subject to interpersonal interpretation. They may even show 'hyperlexia' where they can 'read' far in advance of their understanding of what they are reading.

Alongside all the above difficulties with language are problems in nonverbal communication, with particular difficulties in understanding facial expressions or gestures that express, or involve an understanding of, how others are feeling or what they are thinking. Thus they may be able to point to indicate what they want (although this is slow to develop) but they do not point to show things to others, for information or simply to share an experience. They may have difficulty understanding how close to stand to people when interacting with them or even in realising that you need someone else's presence in order to have a conversation at all!

Language obviously plays a key role in any practical educational or care situation, and so any difficulty in this area is bound to have many consequences. There are problems, in that language is most commonly used as the medium of instruction and practitioners may need to think of more visual ways of getting the same points across. There are also difficulties arising from the fact that the language used in education is of a particular type and serves its own educational purposes. This may be to get the student to look at language itself, or to enable the student to use language more effectively in thinking, or to help the teacher judge the student's knowledge and understanding. This would all be fine except that it rests on the assumption (true for all, except those with autism) that communicative uses of language come first. If the person with autism does not have this communicative understanding, and is trying to learn how to communicate from the kind of language experience found in education, he/she is liable to end up with very peculiar notions of this process. These will include, for example, asking questions to which you already know the answer and having to take a turn in a 'conversation' even when you have nothing to say. In the latter case, this may happen even though the student has signalled clearly (by looking away and fidgeting) that s/he is not interested in the topic and positively does not wish to participate. People with autism are also liable to be misunderstood by others – peers and teachers alike – as being rude, when they simply do not understand how to have a conversation or to attend to the contributions of others.

In general, the teacher/carer needs to select a system of communication that the person with autism can use and understand. Where there is already good spoken language skills, clearly this is best. Even here, however, there is the danger that good speech will hide the fact that the person does not always understand. Neither may they know how to have a conversation, or how to use the language for a range of purposes other than getting needs met or talking at people about a few set topics. All these skills will need to be taught directly. For those without usable speech, visual methods are usually best, although sign can be used successfully if it is used in genuinely communicative ways and is supported by symbols. For others, symbols, pictures or even objects of reference will be needed. It should also be remembered that people with autism (even where there are additional severe learning difficulties) may well find it easier to read than to speak or to understand speech, and written language may be a way into spoken language rather than vice versa as is the normal case. Further ideas are given in the course materials or can be read in Jordan and Powell (1995a) or Jordan (1996).

Needs arising from the biology of autism

Although it is likely that many of the psychological difficulties that are found in autism (although not unique to it) are the direct result of some biological factor, few of these pathways have been confirmed. However, there have been some research studies (although without adequate controls) on the effects of particular diets in individuals with autism, following research showing certain biochemical abnormalities (Reichelt *et al.* 1981; Whiteley *et al.* 1999). It is unlikely that such abnormalities (and therefore the need for such treatment) will be found to be present in all individuals with autism but research can alert professionals to avenues worth exploring.

Since autism is associated with a range of other disorders, children with autism often have medical needs not directly due to their autism. Epilepsy is common in autism, and neuroleptic drugs may be prescribed to control seizures. Gillberg (1992) has stressed that a full medical and neurological 'work-up' or examination is of great value in all cases of autism – to identify any remediable medical conditions, and to make plain to parents, teachers and other professionals the biological (rather than, for example, psychogenic) basis of that child's problems. Rutter (1999), however, questions that necessity.

The work that Courchesne and his colleagues have done (Courchesne 1989) in relating known biological difficulties to brain function is very useful. For example, if the work, showing that people with autism have a severe attention-switching problem, is supported, it has important implications for teaching situations. It may mean, for example, that the person with autism may not 'hear' a message or an instruction until it is halfway through. This is because they have taken that time to change from attending to whatever they were doing before (even if we characterise that as 'twiddling' or 'doing nothing') to attending to the speaker. If this happens continually in a group situation, then the beginnings of all sentences will be lost. The beginnings tell you the topic of the sentence, so the person with autism will just hear a succession of comments without a linking topic. The result will be incoherence and no help to someone who (if Bruner and Feldman 1993 are right) might already be struggling to differentiate the topic comment structure of narratives. A succession of comments without a linking topic would be indistinguishable from a succession of new topics. The need, then, is for interactions to be slowed down, and for the 'teacher' to ensure the attention of the person before beginning to address them.

Autism as a developmental disorder

Autism is a developmental disorder, and lasts throughout life. The adolescent and adult with autism face special problems, and teachers and carers have to cope with issues such as sexuality, independent living, and employment. In some cases, secondary psychiatric problems may arise. For example, depression may occur in an individual with autism who has some insight into their own social problems – and this is not always easy to recognise in people with autism who may have rather wooden or unusual facial expression in general, and be unable to communicate their distress. The carer needs to look for changes in the 'normal' behaviour of the individual. That is another reason why in-depth knowledge of the person, as well as the disability, is so important. It may be true that many people with autism prefer to spend their time alone and can be characterised as 'aloof', but if someone you know has been more sociable and starts to withdraw, this may be a sign that something else is wrong. Someone should not be denied appropriate medical treatment or psychological help just because they already have a diagnosed disability. Nor is there anything in autism that protects the individual from developing other illnesses, including mental ones.

In a more optimistic vein, adults with autism often settle into a more productive and peaceful existence once the traumas of adolescence have passed, and all are capable of acquiring new skills and reaching new understanding well into adulthood. Thus, adult provision should always see education, not just care as part of its function.

Principles for provision in autism

The National Autistic Society (NAS) in the UK has been a world pioneer in establishing services for those with autism. Their work has been taken up by other local societies and charities and, increasingly, by statutory authorities. The NAS is currently concerned with monitoring the quality and effectiveness of these services and as a first step has set up an autism-specific quality monitoring system, based on peer review, for both adult and child services, under independent committees that award or defer accreditation (Reynolds and Druce 1996). The principles, which guide the provision of services in the NAS, can be seen in their mission statement, below.

National Autistic Society mission statement

The National Autistic Society aims to ensure that, by the year 2012 – the Society's 50th Anniversary – all those in the United Kingdom whose lives are affected by autism, or a related condition, receive services appropriate to their needs. The NAS works to achieve this through:

- raising professional and public awareness of the needs of people with autism and their families;

- directly providing services for people with autism and their families;
- working with statutory and other bodies to help and encourage them to provide services;
- providing information to lobby legislators and funding bodies to ensure that adequate funding is available to support the required services; and
- encouraging research into the causes and the effective management and treatment of autism.

Autism Europe's Charter of Rights

Autism Europe has developed a charter of rights for persons with autism and has had this accepted by the European Commission. It now remains for each member country to incorporate that charter into its own framework of legislation; the lobbying for this to happen, continues. Pat and Nula Mathews from the Irish Society for Autism had a key role in developing the charter and have been responsible for its first adoption, in the Republic of Ireland. Autism Europe (through the DAPHNE initiative) has also produced a European code for the prevention of violence and abuse against people with autism (Autisme Europe 1999). The Charter of Rights is reproduced below.

THE EUROPEAN PARLIAMENT WRITTEN DECLARATION ON THE RIGHTS OF PEOPLE WITH AUTISM

At least 1,000,000 citizens within the EU are affected by autism which is a mental disability. People with autism can have impairments in communication, social contact and emotions which can affect all senses including touch, smell and sight.

The European Parliament, bearing in mind its resolution on the human rights of disabled people, the rights of people with mental handicap, the Disabled People's Parliament, the UN Declaration on the Rights of People with Mental Handicap 1971 and 1975, the European Union's third action programme on disability and Charter for Persons with programme on disability and the Charter for Persons with Autism, calls on the European Institutions and member states to recognise and implement the rights of people with autism.

People with autism should have the same rights enjoyed by all EU citizens (where such are appropriate and in the best interests of the person with autism). These should be enhanced and enforced by appropriate legislation in each member state and include:

1. The right to live independently;
2. The right to representation and involvement as far as possible in decisions affecting their future;
3. The right to accessible and appropriate education, housing, assistance, and support services and to a sufficient income; and
4. The right to freedom from fear, threat and from abusive treatment.

This written declaration on the rights of people with autism tabled by Mary Banotti, Irish member of the European Parliament, was adopted by the European Parliament on Thursday 9th May 1996.

CHARTER FOR PERSONS WITH AUTISM

People with autism should share the same rights and privileges enjoyed by all of the European population where such are appropriate and in the best interests of the person with autism.

These rights should be enhanced, protected, and enforced by appropriate legislation in each state.

The United Nations declaration on the Rights of Mentally Retarded Persons (1971) and the Rights of Handicapped Persons (1975) and other relevant declarations on human rights should be considered and in particular, for people with autism the following should be included:

1. THE RIGHT of people with autism to live independent and full lives to the limit of their potential.

2. THE RIGHT of people with autism to an accessible, unbiased and accurate clinical diagnosis and assessment.

3. THE RIGHT of people with autism to accessible and appropriate education.

4. THE RIGHT of people with autism (and their representatives) to be involved in all decisions affecting their future; the wishes of the individual must be, as far as possible, ascertained and respected.

5. THE RIGHT of people with autism to accessible and suitable housing.

6. THE RIGHT of people with autism to the equipment, assistance and support services necessary to live a fully productive life with dignity and independence.

7. THE RIGHT of people with autism to an income or wage sufficient to provide adequate food, clothing, accommodation and the other necessities of life.

8. THE RIGHT of people with autism to participate, as far as possible, in the development and management of services provided for their well being.

9. THE RIGHT of people with autism to appropriate counselling and care for their physical, mental and spiritual health; this includes the provision of appropriate treatment and medication administered in the best interest of the individual with all protective measures taken.

10. THE RIGHT of people with autism to meaningful employment and vocational training without discrimination or stereotype; training and employment should have regard to the ability and choice of the individual.

11. THE RIGHT of people with autism to accessible transport and freedom of movement.

12. THE RIGHT of people with autism to participate in and benefit from culture, entertainment, recreation and sport.

13. THE RIGHT of people with autism of equal access to and use of all facilities, services and activities in the community.

14. THE RIGHT of people with autism to sexual and other relationships, including marriage, without exploitation of coercion.

15. THE RIGHT of people with autism (and their representatives) to legal representation and assistance and to the full protection of all legal rights.

16. THE RIGHT of people with autism to freedom from fear or threat of unwarranted incarceration in psychiatric hospitals or any other restrictive institution.

17. THE RIGHT of people with autism to freedom from abusive physical treatment or neglect.

18. THE RIGHT of people with autism to freedom from pharmacological abuse or misuse.

19. THE RIGHT of access of people with autism (and their representatives) to all information contained in their personal, medical, psychological, psychiatric and educational records.

Presented at the 4th Autism-Europe Congress
Den Haag, May 10th, 1992

World Autism Organisation

In 1998, Autism Europe also took the initiative in establishing the first genuinely international organisation for autism – the World Autism Organisation. This started with a preliminary code of practice and an initial elected board. Finalisation of both will be at the Autism Europe conference in Glasgow in 2000.

Further Reading

Autisme-Europe (1999) *The European Code of Good Practice for the Prevention of Violence and Abuse against People with Autism.* Brussels: DAPHNE/Autisme-Europe.

Courchesne, E. (1989) 'Neuroanatomical subsystems involved in infantile autism: the implications of cerebellar abnormalities'. in Dawson, G. (ed.) *Autism: Nature, Diagnosis, and Treatment.* New York: Guilford Press.

Howlin, P. (1997) *Autism: Preparing for Adulthood.* London: Routledge.

Jordan, R. and Powell, S. (1990) *The Special Curricular Needs of Autistic Children: learning and thinking skills.* London: The Association of Heads and Teachers of Children and Adults with Autism.

Jordan, R. and Powell, S. (1995a) *Understanding and Teaching Children with Autism.* Chichester: John Wiley & Sons.

Morgan, H. (1996) *Adults with Autism.* Cambridge: Cambridge University Press.

Peeters, T. (1997) *Autism: From Theoretical Understanding to Educational Intervention.* London: Whurr.

Sigman, M. (1998) 'Change and continuity in the development of children with autism' *Journal of Child Psychology and Psychiatry,* **39**, 817–27.

Appendix 1

ICD-10 diagnostic criteria for childhood autism and Asperger's syndrome

Diagnostic criteria for F84.0 childhood autism

A   Abnormal or impaired development is evident before the age of three years in at least one of the following areas:

1. receptive or expressive language as used in social communication;
2. the development of selective social attachments or of reciprocal social interaction;
3. functional or symbolic play.

B   A total of at least six symptoms from 1, 2, and 3 must be present, with at least two from 1 and at least one from each of 2 and 3:

1. Qualitative abnormalities in reciprocal social interaction are manifest in at least two of the following areas:
    (a) failure adequately to use eye-to-eye gaze, facial expression, body posture and gesture to regulate social interaction;
    (b) failure to develop (in a manner appropriate to mental age and despite ample opportunities) peer relationships that involve a mutual sharing of interests, activities and emotions;
    (c) lack of socioemotional reciprocity as shown by an impaired or deviant response to other people's emotions; or lack of modulation of behaviour according to social context; or a weak integration of social, emotional and communicative behaviours;
    (d) lack of spontaneous seeking to share enjoyment, interests or achievements with other people (e.g. a lack of showing, bringing or pointing out to other people objects of interest to the individual).

2. Qualitative abnormalities in communication are manifest in at least one of the following areas:

    (a) a delay in, or total lack of, development of spoken language that is not accompanied by an attempt to compensate through the use of gesture or mime as an alternative mode of communication (often preceded by a lack of communicative babbling);

    (b) relative failure to initiate or sustain conversational interchange (at whatever level of language skills is present), in which there is reciprocal responsiveness to the communications of the other person;

    (c) stereotyped and repetitive use of language or idiosyncratic use of words or phrases;

    (d) lack of varied spontaneous make-believe or (when young) social imitative play.

3. Restricted, repetitive and stereotyped patterns of behaviour, interests and activities are manifest in at least one of the following areas:

    (a) an encompassing preoccupation with one or more stereotyped and restricted patterns of interest that are abnormal in content or focus; or one or more interests that are abnormal in their intensity and circumscribed nature though not in their content or focus;

    (b) apparently compulsive adherence to specific, nonfunctional routines or rituals;

    (c) stereotyped and repetitive motor mannerisms that involve either hand or finger flapping or twisting, or complex whole body movements;

    (d) preoccupations with part-objects or nonfunctional elements of play materials (such as their odour, the feel of their surface, or the noise or vibration that they generate).

C   The clinical picture is not attributable to the other varieties of pervasive developmental disorder: specific developmental disorder of receptive language (F80.2) with secondary socioemotional problems; reactive attachment disorder (F94. 1) or disinhibited attachment disorder (F94.2); mental retardation (F70—F72) with some associated emotional or behavioural disorder; schizophrenia (F20.—) of unusually early onset; and Rett's syndrome (F84.2).

Diagnostic criteria for F84.5 Asperger's syndrome

A   There is no clinically significant general delay in spoken or receptive language or cognitive development. Diagnosis requires that single words should have developed by two years of age or earlier and that communicative phrases be used by three years of age or earlier. Self-help skills, adaptive behaviour and curiosity about the environment during the first three years should be at a level consistent with normal intellectual development. However, motor milestones may be somewhat delayed and motor clumsiness is usual (although not a necessary diagnostic feature). Isolated special skills, often related to abnormal preoccupations, are common, but are not required for diagnosis.

B   There are qualitative abnormalities in reciprocal social interaction (criteria as for autism).

C   The individual exhibits an unusually intense, circumscribed interest or restricted, repetitive and stereotyped patterns of behaviour, interests and activities (criteria as for autism; however it would be less usual for these to include either motor mannerisms or preoccupations with part-objects or nonfunctional elements of play materials).

D   The disorder is not attributable to the other varieties of pervasive developmental disorder: simple schizophrenia (F20.6); schizotypal disorder (F21); obsessive-compulsive disorder (F42.-); anankastic personality disorder (F60.5); reactive and disinhibited attachment disorders of childhood (F94. 1 and F94. 2 respectively).

Reprinted with permission from World Health Organisation (1993)
Mental Disorders: A glossary and guide to their classification in accordance with the 10th revision of the International Classification of Diseases (ICD–10).
Geneva: World Health Organisation.

Appendix 2

DSM-IV: Diagnostic categories

299.00 Autistic disorder

Individuals with this disorder have abnormal functioning in at least one of the following areas, with onset before three years of age 1) social interaction, 2) language as used in social communication, or 3) symbolic or imaginative play. The diagnosis also requires:

A. A total of six (or more) items from (1), (2), and (3), with at least two from (1), and one each from (2) and (3):

1. qualitative impairment in social interaction, as manifested by at least two of the following:

    (a) marked impairment in the use of multiple nonverbal behaviours such as eye-to-eye gaze, facial expression, body postures, and gestures to regulate social interaction;

    (b) failure to develop peer relationships appropriate to developmental level;

    (c) a lack of spontaneous seeking to share enjoyment, interests, or achievements with other people (e.g., by a lack of showing, bringing, or pointing out objects of interest);

    (d) lack of social or emotional reciprocity.

2. qualitative impairments in communication as manifested by at least one of the following:

    (a) delay in, or total lack of, the development of spoken language (not accompanied by an attempt to compensate through alternative modes of communication such as gesture or mime);

    (b) in individuals with adequate speech, marked impairment in the ability to initiate or sustain a conversation with others;

(c) stereotyped and repetitive use of language or idiosyncratic language;

(d) lack of varied, spontaneous make-believe play or social imitative play appropriate to developmental level.

3. restricted repetitive and stereotyped patterns of behaviour, interests, and activities. as manifested by at least one of the following:

(a) encompassing preoccupation with one or more stereotyped and restricted patterns of interest that is abnormal either in intensity or focus;

(b) apparently inflexible adherence to specific, nonfunctional routines or rituals;

(c) stereotyped and repetitive motor mannerisms (e.g. hand or finger flapping or twisting or complex whole body movements);

(d) persistent preoccupation with parts of objects.

George was the third of three children born to a professional couple after an uneventful pregnancy and delivery. His development appeared normal for the first few months. He turned over, sat up, and crawled at appropriate times during his first year. However, his mother became concerned about other aspects of his development. A few weeks after he was born she noticed that he seemed different than his brother had at the same age. George rarely made eye contact with her and could not be soothed by being held when he was upset. His lack of interest in other people continued during his first two years. He did not interact with his parents or siblings when they were around or follow them when they left the room. Instead, he became extremely attached to a large plastic serving spoon that he played with endlessly, spinning it round and round in his hands.

In the middle of his second year George's parents became increasingly concerned because he had not started to speak. Initially they thought that he might have difficulty hearing because he did not respond when his name was called or members of the family spoke to him. However, they noticed that he did respond to the sound of the washing machine and cars honking their horns in the street outside the house. When they mentioned their concerns to the family paediatrician, they were told, 'George is probably a late talker. Don't worry, some kids take longer.' However, George's lack of social interaction and communication with the people around him continued. His play was also unusual. He appeared unable to grasp the concept of various toys. He examined them in detail, but could not use them appropriately.

At the beginning of his third year George was referred for a developmental evaluation. The tests showed that his motor skills were near normal, his nonverbal skills were mild to moderately impaired, and his language and social skills were severely impaired. George began receiving remedial education, and gradually his social skills and language began to improve. He developed some recognition of his parents and appeared able to differentiate between them. His speech was clearly abnormal and sounded stilted and artificial. He was able to communicate concrete needs but unable to engage in a social conversation.

Subsequent testing when George was aged nine years showed that he was mildly mentally retarded with an IQ of 53. George continued to receive special education through adolescence. At age 15 he developed a seizure disorder. Despite this he began to gain some self-sufficiency and a limited ability to relate to other people.

299.80 Rett's disorder

Individuals with this disorder develop normally for the first five months of life, followed by a deceleration of head growth (between five and 48 months), loss of previously acquired purposeful hand movement (between five and 30 months), loss of social engagement, development of poorly coordinated gait or trunk movements, and severely impaired expressive and receptive language development with severe psychomotor retardation.

299.10 Childhood disintegrative disorder

Individuals with this disorder develop normally for the first two years and then demonstrate a significant loss of previously acquired skills in two of the following areas: expressive or receptive language, social skills, bowel or bladder control, play, or motor skills. They also have abnormalities of functioning in two of the following: social interaction; communication; and restricted, repetitive, and stereotyped patterns of behaviour, interests, and activities such as those described in the criteria for autistic disorder.

299.80 Asperger's disorder

Individuals with this disorder fulfil criteria A and B below but lack any clinically significant delay in language or cognitive development.
A. Qualitative impairment in social interaction, as manifested by at least two of the following:

 1. marked impairment in the use of multiple nonverbal behaviours such as eye-to-eye gaze, facial expression, body postures, and gestures to regulate social interaction

 2. failure to develop peer relationships appropriate to developmental level

 3. a lack of spontaneous seeking to share enjoyment, interests, or achievements with other people (e.g. by a lack of showing, bringing, or pointing out objects of interest to other people)

 4. lack of social or emotional reciprocity

B. Restricted repetitive and stereotyped patterns of behaviour, interests, and activities, as manifested by at least one of the following:

 1. encompassing preoccupation with one or more stereotyped and restricted patterns of interest that is abnormal either in intensity or focus

2. apparently inflexible adherence to specific, nonfunctional routines or rituals

3. stereotyped and repetitive motor mannerisms (e.g. hand or finger flapping or twisting, or complex whole-body movements)

5. persistent preoccupation with parts of objects

299.80 Pervasive developmental disorder not otherwise specified.

Individuals with this disorder may have severe and pervasive impairments in reciprocal social interactions and communication skills or may develop stereotyped behaviour, interests, or activities, but the criteria for a specific pervasive developmental disorder are not met.

Reprinted with permission from The Diagnostic and Statistical Manual of Mental Disorders, Fourth Edition. Copyright 1994 American Psychiatric Association

References

Adams, C. and Bishop, D.V.M. (1989) 'Conversational characteristics of children with semantic-pragmatic disorder I: Exchange structure turntaking repairs and cohesion', *British Journal of Disorders of Communication,* **24,** 211–39.

Adrien, J.L. *et al.* (1991) 'Autism and family home movies: preliminary findings,' *Journal of Autism and developmental Disorders,* **21**, 43–9.

Adrien, J.L. *et al.* (1992) 'Validity and reliability in the Infant Behavioural Summarised Evaluation (IBSE): a rating scale for the assessment of young children with autism and developmental disorders', *Journal of Autism and Developmental Disorders,* **22**, 375–94.

American Psychiatric Association (1987) *Diagnostic and Statistical Manual of Mental Disorders,* 3rd edn. (DSM-III-R). Washington DC: American Psychiatric Association.

American Psychiatric Association (1994) *Diagnostic and Statistical Manual of Mental Disorders* 4th edn. (DSM-IV). Washington DC: American Psychiatric Association.

Ashcroft, A. *et al.* (1999) 'A theory of mind (TOM) and people with learning disabilities: the effects of a training package', *Journal of Applied Research in Intellectual Disabilities,* **12**, 69–76.

Asperger, H. (1944) 'Die 'autistichen Psychopathen' im Kindesalter', *Archiv fur Psychiatrie und Nervenkrankheiten* **117**, 76–136.

Astington, J.W. and Gopnik, A. (1991) 'Theoretical explanations of children's understanding of the mind', *British Journal of Developmental Psychology* **9**, 7–31.

Attwood, A.H. *et al.* (1988) 'The understanding and use of interpersonal gestures by autistic and Down's syndrome children', *Journal of Autism and Developmental Disorders* **18**, 241–57.

August, G.J. *et al.* (1981) 'The incidence of psychological disabilities in the siblings of autistic children' *British Journal of Psychiatry* **138**, 416–22.

Autisme-Europe (1999) *The European Code of Good Practice for the Prevention of Violence and Abuse against People with Autism.* Brussels: DAPHNE/Autisme- Europe.

Bailey, A., *et al.* (1993) 'Prevalence of fragile X phenomena amongst autistic twins and singletons', *Journal of Child Psychology and Psychiatry* **34**, 673–88.

Bailey, S. *et al.* (1995) 'Autism/Asperger syndrome: a strongly genetic disorder: evidence from a British twin study', *Psychological Medecine* **25**, 63–77.

Bailey, A. *et al.* (1996) 'Autism: towards an integration of clinical, genetic, neuropsychological and neurobiological perpectives', *Journal of Child Psychology and Psychiatry* **37**, 89–126.

Bailey, A. *et al.* (1998) 'A clinico-pathological study of autism', *Brain* **121**, 889–905.

Baltaxe, C.A.M. and Simmons, J.Q. (1977) 'Bedtime soliloquies and linguistic competence in autism', *Journal of Speech and Hearing Disorders* **42**, 376–93.

Baron-Cohen, S. (1988) 'Social and pragmatic deficits in autism: Psychological or affective?', *Journal of Autism and Developmental Disorders* **18**, 379–402.

Baron-Cohen, S. (1989a) 'Perceptual role taking and protodeclarative pointing in autism', *British Journal of Developmental Psychology* **7**, 113–27.

Baron-Cohen, S. (1989b) 'Are autistic chidren 'behaviourists'? An examination of their mental-physical and appearance-reality distinctions', *Journal of Autism and Developmental Disorders* **19**, 579–600.

Baron-Cohen, S. (1991) 'The development of a theory of mind in autism: deviance and delay?', *Psychiatric Clinics of North America* **14**, 33–51.

Baron-Cohen, S. (1992) 'Out of sight or out of mind? Another look at deception in autism', *Journal of Child Psychology and Psychiatry* **33**, 1141–55.

Baron-Cohen, S. (1993) 'Are children with autism acultural?', *Behavioral and Brain Sciences* **16**, 512–3.

Baron-Cohen, S. (1995) *Mindblindness: an Essay on Autism and Theory of Mind.* London: MIT Press.

Baron-Cohen, S. *et al.* (1985) 'Does the autistic child have a theory of mind?', *Cognition* **21**, 37–46.

Baron-Cohen, S. *et al.* (1986) 'Mechanical behavioural and intentional understanding of picture stories in autistic children', *British Journal of Developmental Psychology* **4**, 113–25.

Baron-Cohen, S. *et al.* (1992) 'Can autism be detected at 18 months? The needle the haystack and the CHAT', *British Journal of Psychiatry* **161**, 839–43.

Baron-Cohen, *et al.* (1993) Editorial in Baron-Cohen, S. *et al.* (eds) *Understanding Other Minds: perspectives from autism.* Oxford: Oxford University Press.

Baron-Cohen, S. *et al.* (1994) 'Can children with Gilles de la Tourette syndrome edit their intentions?', *Psychological Medicine* **24**, 29–40.

Baron-Cohen, S. *et al.* (1995) 'Are children with autism blind to the mentalistic significance of the eyes?', *British Journal of Developmental Psychology* **13**, 379–98.

Baron-Cohen, S. *et al.* (1996) 'Psychological markers in the detection of autism in infancy in a large population', *British Journal of Psychiatry* **168**, 158–63.

Baron-Cohen, S., *et al.* (1997) 'Is there a link between engineering and autism?', *Autism: The International Journal of Research and Practice* **1**, 101–9.

Baron-Cohen, S, *et al.* (1999) 'The prevalence of Gilles de la Tourette's syndrome in children and adolescents with autism', *Journal of Child Psychology & Psychiatry* **40**, 213–18.

Baron-Cohen, S. and Bolton, P. (1993) *Autism: The Facts.* Oxford: Oxford University Press.

Bartak, L. *et al.* (1975) 'A comparative study of infantile autism and specific developmental receptive disorders: 1. The children', *British Journal of Psychiatry* **126**, 127–45.

Barthelemy, C. *et al.* (1989) 'Exchange and development therapies (EDT) for children with autism: a treatment programme from Tours, France', in Gillberg C. (ed.) *Autism: The State of the Art.* New York: Elsevier.

Bauman, M.L. and Kemper, T.L. (1994) N*eurobiology of Autism.* Baltimore: John Hopkins University Press.

Benson, G. *et al.* (1993) 'Development of a theory of mind in individuals with mental retardation', *American Journal of Mental Retardation* **98**, 427–33.

Bernabei, P. (1998) 'An evaluation of early development in children with autism and pervasive developmental disorders from home movies: preliminary findings', *Autism: the International journal of research and Practice* **2**, 243–58.

Bettelheim, B. (1956) 'Childhood schizophrenia as a reaction to extreme situations', *Journal of Orthopsychiatry* **26**, 507–18.

Bettelheim, B. (1967) *The Empty Fortress: Infantile autism and the birth of the self.* New York: The Free Press.

Biklen, D. (1990) 'Communication unbound: autism and praxis', *Harvard Educational Review* **60**, 291–314.

Bishop, D.V.M. (1989) 'Autism, Asperger's syndrome and semantic-pragmatic disorder: Where are the boundaries?', *British Journal of Disorders of Communication* **24**, 107–21.

Bishop, D.V.M. (1993) 'Autism, executive functions and theory of mind: a neuropsychological perspective', *Journal of Child Psychology and Psychiatry* **34**, 79–293.

Bishop, D.V.M. and Adams, C. (1989) 'Conversational characteristics of children with semantic-pragmatic disorder II: What features lead to a judgement of inappropriacy?', *British Journal of Disorders of Communication* **24**, 241–63.

Blair, R.J.R. (1994) 'Vicarious emotional responding in the autistic child', *Paper to 1994 Meeting of the British Psychological Society Developmental Section.*

Bleuler, E. (1987) 'The prognosis of dementia praecox: The group of schizophrenias', English translation in Cutting, J. and Sheperd, J. (eds) *The Clinical Roots of the Schizophrenia Concept.* Cambridge: Cambridge University Press.

Blomquist, H.K. *et al.* (1985) 'Frequency of the fragile-X syndrome in infantile autism: A Swedish multicentre study', *Clinical Genetics* **27**, 113–17.

Bolton, P., *et al.* (1994) 'A case-control family history study of autism', *Journal of Child Psychology and Psychiatry* **35**, 877–900.

Bolton, P. and Rutter, M. (1990) 'Genetic influences in autism', *International Review of Psychiatry* **2**, 67–80.

Booth, T. (1983) 'Integrating special education; Introduction,' in Booth T. and Potts, P. *Integrating Special Education.* Oxford: Blackwells.

Booth, T. (1991) 'A perspective on inclusion from England', *Cambridge Journal of Education* **26**, 87–99.

Boucher, J. (1978) 'Echoic memory capacity in autistic children', *Journal of Child Psychology and Psychiatry* **19**, 161–6.

Boucher, J. (1981) 'Memory for recent events in autistic children', *Journal of Autism and Developmental Disorders* **11**, 293–302.

Boucher, J. and Lewis, V. (1989) 'Memory impairments and communications in relatively able autistic children' *Journal of Child Psychology and Psychiatry* **30**, 99–122.

Boucher, J. and Lewis, V. (1990) 'Guessing or creating? A reply to Baron-Cohen', B*ritish Journal of Developmental Psychology* **8**, 205–6.

Boucher, J. and Warrington, E.K. (1976) 'Memory deficits in early infantile autism: some similarities to the amnesic syndrome', *British Journal of Psychology* **69**, 73–87.

Bowlby, J. (1969) *Attachment and Loss Volume 1: Attachment.* London: Hogarth.

Bowler, D.M. (1992) 'Theory of mind in Asperger's syndrome', *Journal of Child Psychology and Psychiatry* **33**, 877–93.

Bowler, D.M. *et al.* (1993) 'The effects of additional cues on children's understanding of false belief', Paper presented to the IVth European Conference on Developmental Psychology, Bonn, August 1993.

Bowler, D.M. *et al.* (in press) 'Experimenter effects in children's understanding of false drawings and false beliefs', *Journal of Genetic Psychology.*

Bowler, D. M. and Briskman, J. A. (submitted) 'Photographic cues do not always facilitate performance on false belief tasks in children with autism', submitted to *Journal of Autism and Developmental Disorders.*

Bowler, D.M. and Stromm, E. (1998) 'Elicitation of first order theory of mind in children with autism', *Autism: the International Journal of Research and Practice* **2**, 33–44.

Bretherton, I. (1991) 'Intentional communication and the development of an understanding of mind', in Frye D. and Moore C. (eds) *Children's Theories of Mind.* New Jersey: Erlbaum.

Brewer, W.F. (1986) 'What is autobiographical memory?', in Rubin D.C. (ed.) *Autobiographical Memory.* Cambridge: Cambridge University Press.

Brothers, L. (1990) 'The social brain: a project for integrating primate behaviour and neurophysiology in a new domain', *Concepts in Neuroscience* **1**, 27–51.

Brothers, L. and Ring, B. (1992) 'A neuroethological famework for the representation of minds', *Journal of Cognitive Neuroscience* **4**, 107–18.

Brown, R. *et al.* (1997) 'Are there autistic-like features in congenitally blind children?' *Journal of child psychology and Psychiatry* **38**, 693–704.

Brown, J.D. and Whiten, A. (1994) 'An observational study of spontaneous imitation, social interaction, play and evidence of theory of mind in autistic and non-autistic children', *Proceedings of the British Psychological Society* **2,** 17.

Bruner, J. and Feldman, C. (1993) 'Theories of mind and the problem of autism', in Baron-Cohen, S. *et al.* (eds) *Understanding Other Minds: Perspectives from Autism.* Oxford: Oxford University Press.

Bryson, S.E. *et al.* (1988) 'First report of a Canadian epidemiological study of autistic syndromes', *Journal of Child Psychology and Psychiatry* **29**, 433–45.

Burd, L. and Kerbeshian, J. (1987) 'Asperger's syndrome', *British Journal of Psychiatry* **151**, 417.

Burns, R.B. (1979) *The Self Concept: Theory, Measurement, Development and Behaviour.* London: Longman.

Butera, G. and Haywood, H.C. (1995) 'Cognitive education of young children with autism: an application of Bright Start', in Schopler, E. and Mesibov, G.B. (eds) *Learning and Cognition in Autism.* New York: Plenum Press.

Capps, *et al.* (1992) 'Understanding of simple and complex emotions in non-retarded children with autism', *Journal of Child Psychology and Psychiatry* **33**, 1169–82.

Capps, L. *et al.* (1993) 'Parental perceptions of emotional expressiveness in children with autism', *Journal of Consulting and Clinical Psychology* **61**, 475–84.

Carr, E.G. (1982) 'Sign language', in Koegel, R.L. *et al.* (eds) *Educating and Understanding Autistic Children.* New York: College Hill Press.

Chandler, M. *et al.* (1989) 'Small scale deceit: deception as a marker of two-, three- and four-year-olds' early theories of mind', *Child Development* **60**, 1263–77.

Cheune, G. J., Ferguson, W., Koon, R. and Dickey, T.O. (1986) Frontal lobe disinhibition in attention deficit disorder, *Child Psychiatry and Human Development* **16**, 221–32.

Ciadella, P. and Mamelle, N. (1989) 'An epidemiological study of infantile autism in a French department (Rhone): a research note', *Journal of Child Psychology and Psychiatry* **30**, 165–75.

Clarke, A.M. and Clarke, A.D.B. (1976) 'Formerly isolated children', in Clarke, A.M. and Clarke, A.D.B. (eds) *Early Experience: Myth and evidence.* London: Open Books.

Clarke, P. and Rutter, M. (1981) 'Autistic children's responses to structure and interpersonal demands', *Journal of Autism and Developmental Disorders* **11**, 201–17.

Clements, W.A. and Perner, J. (1994) 'Implicit understanding of belief', *Cognitive Development* **9**, 377–95.

Cohen, K. *et al.* (1989) 'Parent-child dyadic gaze patterns in Fragile X males and non Fragile X males with autistic disorder', *Journal of Child Psychology and Psychiatry*, **30**, 845–56.

Coleman, M. and Gillberg, C. (1985) *The Biology of the Autistic Syndromes.* New York: Praeger.

Cook, E.H. (1990) 'A review of neurochemical investigations', *Synapse* **6**, 292–308.

Cook, E.H. *et al.* (1997) 'Evidence of linkage between the serotonin transporter and autistic disorder', *Molecular Psychiatry* **2**, 247–50.

Courchesne, E. (1989) 'Neuroanatomical subsystems involved in infantile autism: the implications of cerebellar abnormalities', in Dawson, G. (ed.) *Autism: Nature, Diagnosis, and Treatment.* New York: Guilford Press.

Courchesne, E. (1991) 'A new model of brain and behaviour', *Proceedings of the Autism Society of America.* **25**, New York: ASA.

Courchesne, E, *et al.* (1994) 'Cerebellar hypoplasia and hyperplasia in infantile autism', *The Lancet 1st Jan 1994* **343**, 63–4.

Courchesne, E. *et al.* (1995) 'Neurodevelopmental principles guide research on developmental psychopathologies', in Cichetti, D. and Cohen D.J. (eds) *Manual of Developmental Psychopathology.* New York: John Wiley and Sons.

Creak, M. (1964) 'Schizophrenic syndrome in childhood: further progress report of a working party' *Developmental Medicine and Child Neurology* **6,** 530–5.

Curcio, F. (1978) 'Sensorimotor functioning and communication in male autistic children', *Journal of Autism and Childhood Schizophrenia* **3**, 281–92.

Curtiss, S. (1977) *Genie: A Psychological Study of a Modern-day 'Wild Child'.* New York: Academic Press.

Damasio, A.R. and Maurer, R.G. (1978) 'A neurological model for childhood autism', *Archives of Neurology* **35**, 777–86.

Damon, W. and Hart, D. (1982) *Self Understanding in Childhood and Adolescence.* Cambridge: Cambridge University Press.

Davies, S. *et al.* (1994) 'Face perception in children with autism and Asperger's syndrome', *Journal of Child Psychology and Psychiatry* **35**, 1033–57.

Dawson,G. *et al.* (1990) 'Affective exchanges between young children and their mothers', *Journal of Abnormal Child Psychology* **18,** 335–45.

Dawson, G. and Adams, A. (1984) 'Imitation and social responsiveness in autistic children', *Journal of Abnormal Child Psychology* **12**, 209–26.

Dawson, G. and Fernald, M. (1987) 'Perspective-taking ability and its relationship to the social behaviour of autistic children', *Journal of Autism and Developmental Disorders* **17**, 487–98.

Dawson, G and Galpert, L. (1986) 'A developmental model for facilitating the social behaviour of autistic children', in Schopler, E. and Mesibov, G. (eds) *Social Problems in Autism.* New York: Plenum Press.

Dawson, G. and McKissick, F.C. (1984) 'Self-recognition in autistic children', *Journal of Autism and Developmental Disorders* **14**, 383–94.

DeGelder, B. (1987) 'On not having a theory of mind', *Cognition* **27**, 285–90.

DeLeon, M.J. *et al.* (1986) 'Is there a right hemisphere dysfunction in Asperger's syndrome?', *British Journal of Psychiatry* **148**, 745–6.

DeMyer, M.K. *et al.* (1967) 'Toy-play behaviour and use of body by autistic and normal children as reported by mothers', *Psychological reports* **21**, 973–81.

DeMyer, M.K. *et al.* (1972) 'Imitation in autistic, early schizophrenic, and non-psychotic subnormal children', *Journal of Autism and Childhood Schizophrenia* **5**, 109–28.

Dennett, D.C. (1978) 'Beliefs about beliefs', *The Behavioral and Brain Sciences* **4**, 568–70.

Dennett, D.C. (1987) *The Intentional Stance*. London: MIT Press.

Dennis, M. (1991) Frontier lobe function in childhood and adolescence: a heuristic for assessing attention regulation, executive control and the intentional states important for social discourse, *Developmental Neuropsychology* **7**, 327–58.

Diamond, A. and Goldman-Rakic, P.S. (1985) 'Evidence that maturation of the frontal cortex of the brain underlies behavioural changes during the first year of life: The A not B test', *Paper to Society for Research in Child Development*, Toronto.

DiLavore, P.C. *et al.* (1995) 'The pre-linguistic autism diagnostic observation schedule', *Journal of Autism and Developmental Disorders* **25**, 355–79.

Dissanayake, C. and Crossley, S.A. (1996) 'Proximity and social behaviours in autism: evidence for attachment', *Journal of child Psychology and Psychiatry* **37**, 149–56.

Donnellan, A. and Leary, M. (1994) *Movement Disturbances and Diversity in Autism and Mental Retardation*. Wisconsin: D.R. Press.

Draper, L. and Bowler, D. (1994) 'The false belief task: a problem of narrative comprehension?', *Paper to BPS London conference*, 1994.

Dritschel, B.H. *et al.* (1992) Autobiographical fluency: a method for the study of personal memory', *Memory and Cognition* **20**, 133–40.

Dunn, J. (1988) *The Beginnings of Social Understanding*. Oxford: Blackwell Science.

Dunn, J. (1991) 'Young children's understanding of other people: evidence from observations within the family', in Frye, D. and Moore, C. (eds) *Children's Theories of Mind*. New Jersey: Erlbaum.

Dunn, J. (1994) 'Changing minds and changing relationships', in Lewis, C. and Mitchell, P. (eds) *Children's Early Understanding of mind: origins and development*. Hove: Erlbaum.

Dunn, L.M. *et al.* (1982) *British Picture Vocabulary Scale: Manual for long and short forms*. Windsor: NFER/Nelson.

Ehlers, S. and Gillberg, C. (1993) 'The epidemiology of Asperger's syndrome: a total population study', *Journal of Child Psychology and Psychiatry* **34**, 1327–50.

Eisenberg, L. and Kanner, L. (1956) 'Early infantile autism' *American Journal of Orthopsychiatry* **26**, 556–66.

Eisenmajer, R. and Prior, M. (1991) 'Psychological linguistic correlates of theory of mind ability in autistic children', *British Journal of Developmental Psychology* **9**, 351–64.

Fagan, J.F. (1972) 'Infants' recognition memory for faces', *Journal of Experimental Child Psychology* **14**, 453–76.

Fay, W.H. and Schuler, A.L. (1980) *Emerging Language in Autistic Children*. London: Edward Arnold.

Fein, D. *et al.* (1986) 'Toward a neuropsychological model of infantile autism: are social deficits primary?', *Journal of the American Academy of Child Psychiatry* **25**, 198–212.

Fein, G.G. (1981) 'Pretend play: An integrative review', *Psychological Development* **52**, 1095–118.

Feshbach, N.D. (1982) 'Sex differences in empathy and social behavior in children', in Eisenberg, N. (ed.) *The Development of Pro-social Behavior*. New York: Academic Press.

Folstein, S. and Rutter, M. (1977) 'Infantile autism: A genetic study of 21 twin pairs', *Journal of Child Psychology and Psychiatry* **18**, 297–321.

Forrester, M.A. (1993) 'Affording social-cognitive skills in young children: the overhearing context', in Messer, D.J. and Turner, G.J. (eds) *Critical Influences on Child Language Acquisition and Development*. London: Macmillan.

Fraiberg, S. (1977) *Insights from the blind*. New York: Basic Books.

Fraiberg, S. and Adelson, E. (1975) 'Self-representation in language and play', in Lenneberg, E. and Lenneberg, E. (eds) *Foundations of Language: a multidisciplinary approach 2*. New York: Academic Press.

Freeman, B.J. *et al.* (1978) 'The Behavior Observation Scale for autism: initial methodology, data analysis and preliminary findings on 89 children', *Journal of American Academy of Child Psychiatry* **17**, 576–88.

Friedman, E. (1969) 'The autistic syndrome and phenylketonuria', *Schizophrenia* **1**, 249–61.

Frith, C (1992) *A Cognitive Approach to Schizophrenia*. Cambridge: Cambridge University Press.

Frith, C.D. and Frith, U. (1991) 'Elective affinities in schizophrenia and childhood autism', in Bebbington, P.E. (ed.) *Social Psychiatry: Theory Methodology and Practice*. New Brunswick NJ: Transaction.

Frith, U. (1970) 'Studies in pattern detection in normal and autistic children II: Reproduction and production of colour sequences', *Journal of Experimental Child Psychology* **10**, 120–35.

Frith, U. (1989a) *Autism: Explaining the Enigma*. Oxford: Blackwell Science.

Frith, U. (1989b) 'A new look at language and communication in autism', *British Journal of Disorders of Communication* **24**, 123–50.

Frith, U. (1991a) 'Translation and annotation of "Autistic psychopathy" in childhood by Asperger, H.', in Frith, U. (ed.) *Autism and Asperger Syndrome*. Cambridge: Cambridge University Press.

Frith, U. (1991b) 'Cognitive development and cognitive deficit', *The Psychologist* **5**, 13–9.

Frith, U, *et al.* (1991) 'The psychological basis of a biological disorder: autism', *Trends in Neuroscience* **14**, 433–8.

Frith, U. *et al.* (1993) 'Research into the earliest detectable signs of autism: what parents say', *Communication* **27**, 17–8.

Frith, U. and Happé, F.G.E. (1994) 'Autism: beyond theory of mind', *Cognition* **50**, 115–32.

Frith, U. and Snowling, M. (1983) 'Reading for meaning and reading for sound in autistic and dyslexic children', *British Journal of Developmental Psychology* **1**, 329–42.

Gagnon, L., *et al.* (1997) 'Questioning the validity of the semantic-pragmatic syndrome diagnosis', *Autism: The International Journal of Research and Practice* **1**, 37–56.

Gedye, A. (1991) 'Frontal lobe seizures in autism', *Medical Hypotheses* **34**, 174–82.

Geller, E. *et al.* (1982) 'Preliminary observations on the effect of fenfluramine on blood serotonin and symptoms in three autistic boys', *New England Journal of Medicine* **307**, 165–9.

Gerland, G. (1997) *A Real Person: life on the outside*. London: Souvenir Press.

Gibson, J.J. (1979) *The Ecological Approach to Visual Perception*. Boston: Houghton Mifflin.

Gillberg, C. (1989) 'Asperger's syndrome in 23 Swedish children', *Developmental Medicine and Child Neurology* **31**, 520–31.

Gillberg, C. (1992) 'The Emanuel Miller Memorial lecture 1991: Autism and autistic-like conditions', *Journal of Child Psychology and Psychiatry* **33**, 813–42.

Gillberg, C. and Coleman, A. (1992) *The Biology of the Autistic Syndromes,* 2nd edn. London: McKeith Press.

Gillberg, C. and Farsell, S. (1984) 'Childhood psychosis and neurofibromatosis – more than a co-incidence?', *Journal of Autism and Developmental Disorders* **14**, 1–8.

Gillberg, I.C, *et al.* (1994) 'Autistic behaviour and attention deficits in tuberous sclerosis: a population-based study', *Developmental Medicine and Child Neurology* **36**, 50–6.

Gillberg, C, *et al.* (1986) 'The autism-fragile X syndrome (AFRAX): a population-based study for 10 boys', *Journal of Mental Deficiency Research* **30**, 27–39.

Gillberg, C. and Rasmussen, P. (1982) 'Perceptual, motor and attentional deficits in seven-year-old children: background factors', *Developmental Medicine and Child Neurology,* **24**, 752–70.

Gillberg, I. C. (1991) Autistic syndrome with onset at age 31 years (unpublished paper).

Goldman-Rakic, P. (1987) 'Development of cortical circuitary and cognitive function' *Child Development* **58**, 601–22.

Goode, S. *et al.* (1994) 'A 20 year follow-up of children with autism', paper to the 13th-biennial meeting of ISSBD. Amsterdam, Netherlands.

Gordon, S.B. (1994) *Meeting the ADD Challenge: a practical guide for teachers.* London: Research Press.

Grandin, T. (1995) 'How people with autism think', in Schopler, E. and Mesibov, G.B. (eds) *Learning and Cognition in Autism.* New York: Plenum Press.

Grant, D. and Berg, E. (1948) 'A behavioural analysis of degree of reinforcement and ease of shifting to a new response on a Weigl type card sorting problem', *Journal of Experimental Psychology* **38**, 404–11.

Green, W.H. *et al.* (1984) 'A comparison of schizophrenic and autistic children', *Journal of the American Academy of Child Psychiatry* **23**, 399–409.

Green, L. *et al.* (1995) 'Cognitive functioning in autism: an overview', in Schopler, E. and Mesibov, G.B. (eds) *Learning and Cognition in Autism.* New York: Plenum Press.

Hammes, J.G.W. and Langdell, T. (1981) 'Precursors of symbol formation and childhood autism' *Journal of Autism and Developmental Disorders* **11**, 331–46.

Happé, F.G.E. (1993) 'Communication and theory of mind: a test of relevance theory', *Cognition* **48**, 101–19.

Happé, F.G.E. (1994a) *Autism: an Introduction to Psychological Theory.* London: UCL Press.

Happé, F.G.E. (1994b) 'An advanced test of theory of mind: understanding of story characters' thoughts and feelings by able autistic, mentally handicapped and normal children and adults', *Journal of Autism and Developmental Disorders* **24**, 129–54.

Happé, F.G.E. (1995a) 'The role of age and verbal ability in the theory of mind task performance of subjects with autism', *Child Development* **66**, 843–55.

Happé, F.G.E. (1995b) 'Autism: theory of mind and beyond', in Lindfoot, G. (eds) Psychological Perspectives in Autism: Proceedings of Durham Conference 5-7 April 1995 Sunderland: Autism Research Centre.

Happé, F.G.E. (1996) 'Studying weak central coherence at low levels: children with autism do not succumb to visual illusions: A research note', *Journal of Child Psychology and Psychiatry* **37**, 873–7.

Happé, F. and Frith, U. (1995) 'Theory of mind in autism', in Schopler, E. and Mesibov, G.B. (eds) *Learning and Cognition in Autism*. New York: Plenum Press.

Harris, P. (1989) *Children and Emotion*. Oxford: Oxford University Press.

Harris, P. (1993) 'Pretending and planning', in Baron-Cohen, S. *et al.* (eds.) *Understanding Other Minds: Perspectives from Autism*. Oxford: Oxford University Press.

Harris, P. and Muncer, A. (1988) 'The autistic child's understanding of belief and desire', Paper to BPS Developmental Psychology Conference, Harlech, September 1988.

Hauser, S.L. *et al.* (1975) 'Pneumographic findings in the infantile autism syndrome: a correlation with temporal lobe disease', *Brain* **98**, 667–88.

Hermelin, B. and Frith, U, (1971) 'Psychological studies of childhood autism: can autistic children make sense of what they see and hear?', *Journal of Special Education* **5**, 107–17.

Hermelin, B. and O'Connor, N. (1970) *Psychological Experiments with Autistic Children*. Oxford: Pergamon Press.

Hermelin, B. and O'Connor, N. (1985) 'Logico-affective states and non-verbal language', in Schopler, E. and Mesibov, G. (eds) *Communication Problems in Autism*. New York: Plenum Press.

Hobson, R.P. (1984) 'Early childhood autism and the question of egocentricism', *Journal of Autism and Developmental Disorders* **14**, 85–104.

Hobson, R.P. (1986a) 'The autistic child's appraisal of expressions of emotion', *Journal of Child Psychology and Psychiatry* **27**, 321–42.

Hobson, R.P. (1986b) 'The autistic child's appraisal of expressions of emotion: A further study', *Journal of Child Psychology and Psychiatry* **27**, 671–80.

Hobson, R.P. (1987) 'The autistic child's recognition of age- and sex-related characteristics of people', *Journal of Autism and Developmental Disorders* **17**, 63–79.

Hobson, R.P. (1989) 'Beyond cognition: A theory of autism', in Dawson, G. (ed.) *Autism: Nature, Diagnosis and Treatment*. New York: Guildford Press.

Hobson, R.P. (1990a) 'On acquiring knowledge about people and the capacity to pretend: A response to Leslie', *Psychological Review* **97**, 114–21.

Hobson, R.P. (1990b) 'On the origins of self and the case of autism', *Development and Psychopathology* **2**, 163–81.

Hobson, R.P. (1991) 'Against the theory of "theory of mind"', *British Journal of Developmental Psychology* **9**, 33–51.

Hobson, R.P. (1993a) *Autism and the Development of Mind*. London: Erlbaum.

Hobson, R.P. (1993b) 'Understanding persons: the role of affect', in Baron-Cohen, S. *et al.* (eds) *Understanding Other Minds: Perspectives from Autism*. Oxford: Oxford University Press.

Hobson, R.P. (1995) 'Blindness and psychological development 0–10 years', Paper to Mary Kitzinger Trust Symposium, September 1995, University of Warwick.

Hobson, R.P. and Lee, A. (1989) 'Emotion-related and abstract concepts in autistic people: evidence from the British Picture Vocabulary Scale', *Journal of Autism and Developmental Disorders* **19**, 601–23.

Hocking, B. (1990) *Little Boy Lost*. London: Bloomsbury.

Holroyd, S. and Baron-Cohen, S. (1993) 'Brief report: how far can people with autism go in developing a "theory of mind"?', *Journal of Autism and Developmental Disorders* **23**, 379–85.

Horvath, K. *et al.* (1998) 'Improved social and linguistic skills after secretin administration in patients with autistic spectrum disorders', *Journal of the Association for Academic Minority Physicians* **9**, 9–15.

Horwitz, B. *et al.* (1988) 'The cerebral metabolic landscape in autism: intercorrelations of regional glucose utilisation', *Archives of Neurology* **45**, 749–55.

Hotopf, M. and Bolton, P. (1995) 'A case of autism associated with partial tetrasomy 15', *Journal of Autism and Developmental Disorders* **25**, 41–9.

Howlin, P. (1997) *Autism: Preparation for Adulthood*. London: Routledge.

Hughes, C. *et al.* (1998) 'Trick or treat?: uneven understanding of mind and emotion and executive function in "hard to manage" pre-schoolers', *Journal of Child Psychology and Psychiatry* **39**, 981–94.

Hughes, C.H. and Russell, J. (1993) 'Autistic children's difficulty with mental disengagement from an object: its implication for theories of autism', *Developmental Psychology* **29**, 498–510.

Humphrey, N. (1984) *Consciousness Regained*. Oxford: Oxford University Press.

Humphrey, N. (1986) *The Inner Eye*. London: Faber and Faber.

Humphrey, N. (1993) *A History of the Mind*. London: Vintage.

Hunt, A. and Dennis, J. (1987) 'Psychiatric disorder among children with tuberous sclerosis', *Developmental Medicine and Child Neurology* **29**, 190–8.

Hurlburt, R.T. *et al.* (1994) 'Sampling the form of inner experience in three adults with Asperger's syndrome', *Psychological Medicine* **24**, 385–95.

Iversen, S.D. (1996) 'Schizophrenia: the dark side of the mind', *International Journal of Psychology* **31**, 328.1.

Jarrold, C. *et al.* (1993) 'Symbolic play in autism: a review', *Journal of Autism and Developmental Disorders* **23**, 281–307.

Johnson, D.J. and Myklebust, H.R. (1971) *Learning Disabilities*. New York: Grune & Stratton.

Johnson, M.H. *et al.* (1992) 'Can autism be predicted on the basis of infant screening tests?', *Developmental Medicine and Child Neurology* **34**, 316–20.

Joliffe, T. and Baron-Cohen, S. (1997) 'Are people with autism and Asperger syndrome faster than normal on the embedded figures test?', *Journal of Child Psychology and Psychiatry* **38**, 527–34.

Jordan, R.R. (1985) 'Signing', *Communication* **19**, 19–24.

Jordan, R.R. (1989) 'An experimental comparison of the understanding and use of speaker-addressee personal pronouns in children with autism', *British Journal of Disorders of Communication* **24**, 169–79.

Jordan, R.R. (1993) 'The nature of the linguistic and communication difficulties of children with autism', in Messer, D.J. and Turner, G.J. (eds) *Critical Influences on Child Language Acquisition and Development*. London: St Martins Press.

Jordan, R.R. (1996) 'Teaching communication to individuals within the autistic spectrum', *REACH – Journal of Special Needs Education in Ireland* **9**, 95–102.

Jordan, R.R. (1998) 'Is autism a pathology? Reflections from theory, research and practice', in Linfoot, G. and Shattock, P. (eds) *Psychobiology of Autism: Current Research and Practice. Proceedings of Conference, Durham April 15–17 1998*. Sunderland, Autism Research Unit.

Jordan, R.R. *et al.* (1995) 'Theories of autism: do they matter?', *School Psychology International* **16**, 291–302.

Jordan, R. *et al.* (1998) *Educational Interventions for Children with Autism: a literature review of recent and current research*. Sudbury: DfEE.

Jordan, R.R. and Jones, G. (1996) *Provision for Children with Autism in Scotland: report of a research project for the SOEID*. Birmingham: School of Education, University of Birmingham.

Jordan, R. and Libby, S. (1997) 'Developing and using play in the curriculum', in Powell, S. and Jordan, R. (eds.) *Autism and Learning: a guide to good practice*. London: David Fulton Publishers.

Jordan, R.R. and Powell, S.D. (1990) *The Special Curricular Needs of Autistic Children: Learning and Thinking Skills*. London: The Association of Head Teachers of Autistic Children and Adults.

Jordan, R.R. and Powell, S.D. (1991) 'It's all in the mind: an investigation of understanding of false belief and false photographs in autistic children', British Psychological Society Conference 16–17 December 1991: London.

Jordan, R.R. and Powell, S.D. (1992) *Investigating Memory Processing in Children with Autism*. British Psychological Society Conference 15-16 December 1992: London.

Jordan, R.R. and Powell, S.D. (1994) 'Whose Curriculum? Critical notes on integration and entitlement', *European Journal of Special Needs Education* **9**, 27–39.

Jordan, R.R. and Powell, S.D. (1995a) *Understanding and Teaching Children with Autism*. Chichester: John Wiley and Sons.

Jordan, R.R. and Powell, S.D. (1995b) 'Factors affecting school choice for children with autistic spectrum disorders', *Communication* **29**, 5–9.

Jordan, R. and Riding, R (1995) 'Autism and cognitive style', in Shattock P. (ed.) *Proceedings of the International Conference: Psychological Perspectives in Autism, Durham, 1995*. Sunderland: Autism Research Unit/NAS.

Kanner, L. (1943) 'Autistic disturbances of affective contact', *Nervous Child* **2**, 217–50.

Kanner, L. (1946) 'Irrelevant and metaphorical language in early infantile autism', *American Jornal of Psychiatry* **103**, 242–5.

Kanner, L. (1973) 'How far can autistic children go in matters of social adaptation?', in Kanner, L. *Childhood Psychosis: Initial studies and new insights*. Washington: VH Winston.

Kanner, L. and Eisenberg, L. (1956) 'Early infantile autism 1943–1955', *American Journal of Orthopsychiatry* **26**, 55–65.

Kasari, *et al.* (1990) 'Affective sharing in the context of joint attention: interaction of normal, autistic and mentally retarded children', *Journal of Autism and Developmental Disorders* **20**, 87–100.

Kasari, C, *et al.* (1993) 'Pride and mastery in children with autism', *Journal of Child Psychology and Psychiatry* **34**, 352–62.

Kaufman, B.N. (1994) *Son Rise: the Miracle Continues*. California: H.J. Kramer.

Kaufman, B.N. and Kaufman, S. (1976) *To Love is to be Happy With*. London: Souvenir Press.

Kay, P. and Kolvin, I. (1987) 'Childhood psychoses and their borderlands', *British Medical Bulletin* **43**, 570–86.

Kemper, T.L. and Bauman, M.L. (1993) 'The contribution of neuro-pathological studies to the understanding of autism', *Behavioural Neurology* **11**, 175–87.

Klauck, S.M. *et al.* (1997) 'Serotonin transporter (5-HTT) gene variants associated with autism?', *Human Molecular Genetics* **6**, 2244–8.

Klin, A. *et al.* (1992) 'Autistic social dysfunction: some limitations of the theory of mind hypothesis', *Journal of Child Psychology and Psychiatry* **33**, 861–76.

Klinger, L.G. and Dawson, G. (1992) 'Facilitating early social and communicative development in children with autism', in Warren S.F. and Reichle, J. (eds) *Causes and Effects in Communication and Language Intervention.* Baltimore, MD: Brookes.

Knivsberg, *et al.* (1990) 'Dietary interventions in autistic syndromes', *Brain Dysfunction* **3**, 315–27.

Knobloch, H. and Pasamanick, B. (1975) 'Some etiological and prognostic factors in early infantile autism and psychosis', *Pediatrics* **55**, 182–91.

Kubicek, L.F. (1980) 'Organisation in two mother-infant interactions involving a normal infant and his fraternal twin who was later diagnosed as autistic', in Field, T.M. *et al.* (eds) *High Risk Infants and Children: Adult and Peer Interactions.* New York: Academic Press.

Kugler, B. (1998) 'The differentiation between autism and Asperger syndrome', *Autism: the International Journal of Research and Practice* **2**, 11–32.

Landry, S.H. and Loveland, K.A. (1988) 'Communication behaviours in autism and developmental language delay', *Journal of Child Psychology and Psychiatry* **29**, 621–34.

Langdell, T. (1978) 'Recognition of faces: an approach to the study of autism', *Journal of Child Psychology and Psychiatry* **19**, 235–68.

Lazarus, R.S. (1991) *Emotion and Adaptation.* Oxford: Oxford University Press.

LeCouteur, A. (1996) 'The clinical manifestations of the broader phenotype in autism – evidence from the British twin and family studies', in *Therapeutic Intervention in Autism: perspectives from research and practice.* Sunderland: Autism Research Unit/NAS.

LeCouteur, A, *et al.* (1996) 'A broader phenotype of autism: the clinical spectrum in twins', *Journal of Child Psychology and Psychiatry* **37**, 785–801.

Le Couteur, A. *et al.* (1989) Autism Diagnostic Interview: a semi-structured interview for parents and caregivers of autistic persons', *Journal of Autism and Developmental Disorders* **19**, 363–87.

Leekam, S. *et al.* (1997) 'Eye-direction detection: a dissociation between geometric and joint attention skills in autism', *British Journal of Developmental Psychology* **15**, 77–95.

Leekam, S.R. *et al.* (1998) 'Targets and cues: gaze following in children with autism', *Journal of Child Psychology & Psychiatry* **39**, 951–62.

Leekam, S. and Perner, J. (1991) 'Does the autistic child have a metarepresentational deficit?', *Cognition* **40**, 203–18.

Leekam, S. and Prior, M. (1994) 'Can autistic children distinguish lies from jokes? A second look at second-order belief attribution', *Journal of Child Psychology and Psychiatry* **35**, 901–15.

Leslie, A.M. (1987) 'Pretence and representation: the origins of theory of mind *Psychological Review* **94**, 412–26.

Leslie, A.M. (1991) 'The theory of mind impairments in autism: evidence for a modular mechanism of development?', in Whitten, A. (ed.) *The Emergence of Mindreading.* Oxford: Blackwells.

Leslie, A.M. (1994) 'Pretending and believing: issues in the theory of TOMM' *Cognition* **50**, 211–38.

Leslie, A.M. and Frith, U. (1988) 'Autistic children's understanding of seeing, knowing and believing', *British Journal of Developmental Psychology* **6**, 315–24.

Leslie, A.M. and Happé, F. (1989) 'Autism and Ostensive Communication: The relevance of metarepresentation', *Development and Psychopathology* **1**, 205–12.

Leslie, A.M. & Roth, D. (1993) 'What autism teaches us about representation', in Baron-Cohen, S. *et al.* (eds) *Understanding Other Minds: Perspectives from Autism.* Oxford: Oxford University Press.

Leslie, A.M. and Thaiss, L. (1992) 'Domain specificity in conceptual development: evidence from autism', *Cognition* **43**, 225–51.

Lesser, M. and Murray, D. (1998) 'Mind as a dynamical system: implications for autism', in Linfoot, G. and Shattock, P. (eds) *Psychobiology of Autism: current research and practice. Proceedings of conference Durham April 15–17 1998.* Sunderland: Autism Research Unit.

Leuger, R.J. and Gill, K.J. (1990) 'Frontal lobe cognitive dysfunction in conduct disordered adolescents', *Journal of Clinical Psychology* **46**, 696–706.

Lewis, V. and Boucher, J. (1988) 'Spontaneous instructed and elicited play in relatively able autistic children', *British Journal of Developmental Psychology* **6**, 325–39.

Lewis, C. and Osborne, A. (1990) 'Three year olds' problems with false belief: conceptual deficit or linguistic artefact?', *Child Development* **61**, 1514–19.

Libby, S. *et al.* (1997) 'Imitation of pretend play acts by children with autism and Down's syndrome', *Journal of Autism and Developmental Disorders* **27**, 365–83.

Libby, S. *et al.* (1998) 'Spontaneous play in children with autism: a re-appraisal *Journal of Autism and Developmental Disorders* **28**, 487–97.

Lister-Brooke, S. and Bowler, D. (1992) 'Autism by another name? Semantic and pragmatic impairments in children', *Journal of Autism and Developmental Disorders* **22**, 61–82.

Livoir-Petersen, M.F. (1995) 'Constraint and necessity for sameness in normal and autistic development', in Lindfoot, G. *et al.* (eds) *Psychological Perspectives in Autism: Proceedings of Durham Conference, 5–7 April 1995.* Sunderland: Autism Research Unit/ National Autistic Society.

Lord, C. (1991) 'A cognitive-behavioural model for the treatment of some communicative deficits in adolescents with autism', in McMahan, R.J. and Peters, R.D. (eds) *Behaviour Disorders of Adolescence.* New York: Plenum Press.

Lord. C. (1993) 'Early social development in autism', in Schopler, E. *et al.* (eds) *Preschool Issues in Autism.* New York: Plenum Press.

Lord, C. *et al.* (1989) 'Autism Diagnostic Interview Schedule: a standardised observation of communicative and social behaviour', *Journal of Autism and Developmental Disorders* **19**, 185–212.

Lord, C. and Schopler, E. (1987) 'Neurobiological implications of sex differences in autism', in Schopler, E. and Mesibov, G. (eds) *Neurobiological Issues in Autism.* New York: Plenum Press.

Lotter, V. (1966) 'Epidemiology of autistic conditions in young children: Prevalence', *Social Psychiatry* **1**, 124–37.

Lovaas, O.I. (1987) 'Behavioural treatment and normal educational and intellectual functioning in young autistic children', *Journal of Consulting and Clinical Psychology* **55**, 3–9.

Lovaas, O.I. *et al.* (1971) 'Selective responding by autistic children to multiple sensory input', *Journal of Abnormal Psychology* **77**, 211–22.

Loveland, K.A. (1991) 'Social affordances and interaction II: autism and the affordances of the human environment', *Ecological Psychology* **3**, 99–119.

Loveland, K.A. and Landry, S.H (1986) 'Joint attention and language in autism and developmental language delay', *Journal of Autism and Developmental Disorders* **16**, 335–49.

Luria, A.R. (1966) *Higher Cortical Functions in Man*. London: Tavistock.

MacDonald, H. *et al*. (1989) 'Recognition and expression of emotional cues by autistic and normal adults', *Journal of Child Psychology and Psychiatry* **30**, 865–79.

McEvoy, R.E. *et al*. (1993) 'Executive function and social communication deficits in young autistic children', *Journal of Child Psychiatry* **34**, 563–78.

McHale, S.M. *et al*. (1980) 'The social and symbolic quality of autistic children's communication', *Journal of Autism and Developmental Disorders* **10**, 299–310.

Massie, H.N. and Rosenthal, J. (1984) *Childhood Psychosis in the First Four Years of Life*. New York: McGraw Hill.

Maurer, D. (1993) 'Neonatal synaesthesia: implications for the processing of speech and faces', in Boysson-Bardies, B. de (ed.) *Developmental Neurocognition: Speech and Face Processing in the First Year of Life*. New York: Kluwer.

Mead, G. (1934) *Mind, Self and Society*. Chicago: Chicago University Press.

Meltzoff, A.N. (1990) 'Towards a developmental cognitive science: the implications of cross-modal matching and imitation for the development of representation and memory in infancy', *Annals of the New York Academy of Sciences* **608**, 1–37.

Meltzoff, A. and Gopnik, A. (1993) 'The role of imitation in understanding persons and developing a theory of mind', in Baron-Cohen, S. *et al*. (eds) *Understanding Other Minds: Perspectives from Autism*. Oxford: Oxford University Press.

Mesibov, G.B. (1993) 'Treatment issues with high functioning adolescents with autism', in Schopler, E. and Mesibov, G.B. (eds) *High Functioning Indidviduals with Autism*. New York: Plenum Press.

Miller, P.J. *et al*. (1992) 'The narrated self: young children's construction of self in relation to others in conversational stories of personal experience', *Merrill-Palmer Quarterly* **38**, 45–67.

Millward, C. *et al*. (in press) 'Recall for self and other in autism: children's memory for events experienced by themselves and their peers', *Journal of Autism and Developmental Disorders*.

Minshew, N. (1991) 'Indices of neural function in autism: clinical and biological implications', *Paediatrics* **31**, 774–80.

Minshew, N.J. *et al*. (1992) 'Neuropsychological functioning in non-mentally retarded autistic individuals', *Journal of Clinical and Experimental Neuropsychology* **14**, 749–61.

Minshew, N. and Goldstein, G. (1993) 'Is autism an amnesic disorder? Evidence from the California verbal learning test', *Neuropsychology* **7**, 209–16.

Mitchell, P. (1997) *Introduction to theory of mind: Children, Autism and Apes*. London: Arnold.

Morgan, H. (1996) *Adults with Autism*. Cambridge: Cambridge University Press.

Morgan, S.B. *et al*. (1989) 'Do autistic children differ from retarded and normal children in Piagetian sensorimotor functioning?', *Journal of Child Psychology and Psychiatry* **30**, 857–64.

Moore, C. and Frye, D. (1991) 'The acquisition and utility of theories of mind', in Frye, D. and Moore, C. (eds.) *Children's Theories of Mind*. New Jersey: Erlbaum.

Morton, A. (1980) *Frames of Mind*. Oxford: Clarendon Press.

Morton, J. and Frith, U. (1995) 'Causal modelling: a structured approach to developmental psychopathology', in Cichetti, D. and Cohen, D.J. (eds) *Manual of Developmental Psychopathology*. New York: John Wiley & Sons.

Mottron, L. *et al.* (1995) 'High functioning subjects present particularities in visual processing Lindfoot, G. *et al.* (eds) *Psychological Perspectives in Autism: Proceedings of Durham Conference 5–7 April 1995.* Sunderland: Autism Research Unit/National Autistic Society.

Mottron, L. *et al.* (1999) Perceptual processing among high functioning people with autism', *Journal of Child Psychology and Psychiatry* **40**, 203–13.

Mottron, L. and Bellville, S. (1993) 'Study of perceptual analysis in high level autistic subjects with exceptional graphic abilities', *Brain & Cognition* **23**, 279–309.

Mottron, L. and Bellville, S. (1995) 'Perspective production in savant autistic draughtsman', *Psychological Medicine* **25**, 639–48.

Mundy, P. *et al.* (1986) 'Defining the social deficits of autism: the contribution of non-verbal communication measures', *Journal of Child Psychology and Psychiatry* **27**, 657–69.

Mundy, P. *et al.* (1993) 'The theory of mind and joint attention deficits in autism', in Baron-Cohen, S. *et al.* (eds) *Understanding Other Minds: Perspectives from Autism.* Oxford: Oxford University Press.

Narayan, M. *et al.* (1993) 'Cerebro-spinal fluid levels of homovonicillic acid and 5-hydroxyindoleacetic acid in autism', *Biological Psychiatry* **33**, 630–5.

Neumann, C.J. and Hill, S.D. (1978) 'Self-recognition and stimulus preference in autistic children', *Developmental Psychobiology* **11**, 571–8.

Newson, E. (1979) *Diagnosis of Autism* (Unpublished manuscript) Child Development Research Unit: Nottingham.

Newson, E. (1983) 'Pathological demand avoidance syndrome', *Communication* **17**, 3–8

Norman, D.A. and Shallice, T. (1986) 'Attention to action: willed and automatic control of behaviour', in Davidson, R.J. *et al.* (eds) *Consciousness and Self-Regulation: Advances in Research.* New York: Plenum Press.

O'Connor, N. and Hermelin, B. (1967) 'Auditory and visual memory in autistic and normal children', *Journal of Mental Deficiency Research* **11**, 126–31.

O'Gorman, N. (1967) *The Nature of Childhood Autism.* London: Churchills.

Ohta, M. (1987) 'Cognitive disorders of infantile autism: a study employing the WISC, spatial relationship conceptualisation and gesture imitations', *Journal of Autism and Developmental Disorders* **17**, 45–62.

Olsson, I. *et al.* (1988) 'Epilepsy in autism and autistic-like conditions – a population-based study', *Archives of Neurology* **45**, 666–8.

Osterling, J. and Dawson, G. (1994) 'Early recognition of children with autism: a study of first birthday home videotapes', *Journal of Autism and Developmental Disorders* **24**, 247–59.

Oswald, D.P. and Ollendick, T. (1989) 'Role taking and social competence in autism and mental retardation', *Journal of Autism and Developmental Disorders* **19**, 119–28.

Ozonoff, S. (1995) 'Executive functions in autism', in Schopler, E. and Mesibov, G.B. (eds) *Learning and Cognition in Autism.* New York: Plenum Press.

Ozonoff, S. and Miller, J.N. (1995) 'Teaching theory of mind: a new approach to social skills training for individuals with autism', *Journal of Autism and Developmental Disorders* **25**, 415–33.

Ozonoff, S. *et al.* (1990) 'Are there emotion perception deficits in young autistic children?', *Journal of Child Psychology and Psychiatry* **51**, 343–61.

Ozonoff, S. *et al.* (1991a) 'Asperger's syndrome: Evidence of an empirical distinction from high-functioning autism', *Journal of Child Psychology and Psychiatry* **32**, 1107–22.

Ozonoff, S. *et al.* (1991b) 'Executive function deficits in high-functioning autistic children: relationship to theory of mind', *Journal of Child Psychology and Psychiatry* **32**, 1081–106.

Ozonoff, S. *et al.* (1994) 'Executive function abilities in autism and Tourette syndrome: an information processing approach', *Journal of Child Psychology and Psychiatry* **35**, 1015–37.

Park, C.C. (1986) 'Social growth in autism: a parent's perspective', in Schopler, E. and Mesibov, G.B. (eds) *Social Behaviour in Autism*. New York: Plenum Press.

Parkin, L. (1995) 'Re-examination of the understanding of the appearance/reality distinction in children with autism', in Lindfoot, G. *et al.* (eds) *Psychological Perspectives in Autism: Proceedings of Durham Conference, 5–7 April 1995*. Sunderland: Autism Research Unit/National Autistic Society.

Parkin, L. and Perner, J (1994) 'Wrong directions in children's theory of mind: what it means to understand belief as representation' (unpublished manuscript). Laboratory of Experimental Psychology: University of Sussex.

Parks, S.L. (1983) 'The assessment of autistic children: a selective review of available instruments', *Journal of Autism and Developmental Disorders* **13**, 255–67.

Paul, R. (1987) 'Communication', in Cohen, D.J. *et al.* (eds) *Handbook of Autism and Pervasive Developmental Disorders*. New York: John Wiley and Sons.

Peeters, T. (1997) *Autism: from theoretical understanding to educational intervention*. London: Whurr.

Perner, J. (1991) *Understanding the Representational Mind*. Cambridge MA: MIT Press.

Perner, J. (1993) 'The Theory of Mind deficit in autism: rethinking the metarepresentation theory', in Baron-Cohen, S. *et al.* (eds) *Understanding Other Minds: Perspectives from Autism*. Oxford: Oxford University Press.

Perner, J. *et al.* (1987) 'Three-year olds' difficulty with false belief: The case for a conceptual deficit', *British Journal of Developmental Psychology* **5**, 125–37.

Perner, J. *et al.* (1989) 'Exploration of the autistic child's theory of mind: Knowledge, belief and communication', *Child Development* **60**, 689–700.

Perner, J. and Wimmer, H. (1985) '"John thinks that Mary thinks that" Attribution of second-order beliefs by 5–10-year-old children', *Journal of Experimental Child Psychology* **39**, 437–71.

Peterson, C. and McCabe, A. (1992) 'Parental styles of narrative elicitation: effect on children's narrative structure and content', *First Language* **12**, 299–321.

Peterson, C.C. and Siegel, M. (1995) 'Deafness, conversation and theory of mind', *Journal of Child Psychology and Psychiatry* **36**, 459–74.

Phillips, W. (1993) Understanding intention and desire by children with autism. PhD thesis, Institute of Psychiatry: University of London.

Phillips, W. (1994) 'Understanding intention in normal development and in autism – the 'lucky breaks' test *Proceedings of the British Psychological Society* **2**, p.14.

Powell, S.D. and Jordan, R.R. (1993a) 'Diagnosis, intuition and autism', *British Journal of Special Education* **20**, 26–9.

Powell, S.D. and Jordan, R.R. (1993b) 'Being subjective about autistic thinking and learning to learn', *Educational Psychology* **13**, 359–70.

Premack, D. (1990) 'Do infants have a theory of self-propelled objects?' *Cognition* **36**, 1–16.

Prior, M. *et al.* (1998) 'Are there subgroups within the autistic spectrum? A cluster analysis of a group of children with autistic spectrum disorders', *Journal of Child Psychology and Psychiatry* **39**, 893–902.

Prior, M. and Hoffman, W. (1990) 'Brief report: Neuropsychological testing of autistic children through an exploration with frontal lobe tests', *Journal of Autism and Developmental Disorders* **20**, 581–90.

Prizant, B.M. (1983) 'Language acquisition and communicative behaviour in autism: toward an understanding of the "whole" of it', *Journal of Speech and Language Disorders* **48**, 296–307.

Prizant, B.M. and Wetherby, A.M. (1993) 'Communication in preschool autistic children', in Schopler, E. *et al.* (eds) *Pre-School Issues in Autism*. New York: Plenum Press.

Rapin, I. and Allen, A. (1983) 'Developmental language disorders: nosological considerations', in Kirk, U. (ed.) *Neuropsychology of Language, Reading and Spelling*. London: Academic Press.

Reichelt, K.L. *et al.* (1981) 'Biologically active peptide-containing fractions in schizophrenia and childhood autism', *Advances in Biochemical Psychopharmacology* **28**, 627–43.

Reichler, R.J. and Lee, E.M.C. (1987) 'Overview of biomedical issues in autism', in Schopler, E. and Mesibov, G.B. (eds) *Neurobiological Issues in Autism*. New York: Plenum Press.

Reiss, A.L. *et al.* (1986) 'Autism and genetic disorders', *Schizophrenia Bulletin* **12**, 724–38.

Rett, A. (1966) 'Ober ein eigenartiges hernatropfiches syndrom bei hyperammonmie im kinderalter', *Weiner Medecinsche Wochenschrift* **116**, 723–6.

Reynolds, R. and Druce, P. (1996) Quality assurance and accreditation of services for people with autism. In P. Shattock and G. Linfoot (eds) *Autism on the Agenda*. London: National Autistic Society.

Richer, J. and Cross, R. (1976) 'Gaze aversion in autistic and normal children', *Acta Psychiatrica Scandinavica* **53**, 193–210.

Ricks, D.M. (1972) 'Vocal communication in pre-verbal normal and autistic children', in O'Connor, N. (ed.) *Language, Cognitive Deficits and Retardation*. London: Institute of Research into Mental Handicap Study Group 7, IRMH/Butterworths.

Riding, R.J. (1991) *Cognitive Styles Analysis*. Birmingham: Learning and Training Technology.

Riding, R.J. and Cheema, I. (1991) 'Cognitive styles: an overview and integration', *Educational Psychology* **11**, 193–215.

Riding, R.J. and Pearson, F. (1994) 'The relationship between cognitive style and intelligence', *Educational Psychology* **14**, 413–25.

Rimland, B. (1964) *Infantile Autism*. New York: Appleton Century Crofts.

Rimland, B. (1971) 'The differentiation of childhood psychosis: an analysis of checklists for 2,218 psychotic children', *Journal of Autism and Childhood Schizophrenia* **1**, 161–74.

Rincover, A. and Koegel, R.L. (1975) 'Setting generality and stimulus control in autistic children', *Journal of Applied Behaviour Analysis* **8**, 235–46.

Ripley, K. (1996) 'The semantic pragmatic debate', *NAPLIC newsletter* **32**, 8–11.

Rogers, S.J. and Pennington, B.F. (1991) 'A theoretical approach to the deficits in infantile autism', *Development and Psychopathology* **3**, 137–62.

Rogers, S.J. and Pulchalski, C.B. (1984) 'Development of symbolic play in visually impaired infants', *Papers in Early Childhood Special Education* **3**, 57–64.

Roth, D. and Leslie, A. (1991) 'The recognition of attitude conveyed by utterance: a study of preschool and autistic children', *British Journal of Developmental Psychology* **9**, 315–30.

Rugg, M.D. (ed.) (1997) *Cognitive Neuroscience*. Hove: Psychology Press.

Rumsey, J.M. (1985) 'Conceptual problem-solving in highly verbal non-retarded autistic men', *Journal of Autism and Developmental Disorders* **15**, 23–36.

Rumsey. J.M. *et al.* (1985) 'Brain metabolism in autism: resting cerebral glucose utilisation rates as measured by positron emission tomography (PET)', *Archives of General Psychiatry* **42**, 448–55.

Rumsey, J.M. and Hamburger, S.D. (1988) 'Neuropsychological findings in high-functioning men with infantile autism residual state', *Journal of Clinical and Experimental Neuropsychology* **10**, 201–21.

Rumsey, J. and Hamburger, S.D. (1990) 'Neuropsychological divergence of high level autism and severe dyslexia', *Journal of Autism and Developmental Disorders* **20**, 155–68.

Russell, J. (1995) 'Agency and early development', in Bermudez, J. *et al.* (eds) *The Body and the Self.* Cambridge: MA. MIT Press.

Russell, J. (1996) *Agency and its Role in Development.* London: Erlbaum.

Russell, J. and Jarrold, C. (1995) 'Executive deficits in autism', Paper to Society for Research in Child Development: Indiannapolis 1995.

Russell, J. *et al.* (1991) 'The window task: a measure of strategic deception in pre-schoolers and autistic subjects', *British Journal of Developmental Psychology* **2**, 101–19.

Ruttenberg, B.A. *et al.* (1966) 'An instrument for evaluating autistic children', *Journal of the American Academy of Child Psychiatry* **5**, 453–78.

Ruttenberg, B.A. *et al.* (1977) *Behaviour Rating Instrument for Autistic and Other Atypical Children.* Philadelphia: Developmental Center for Autistic Children.

Rutter, M. (1978) 'Diagnosis and definition of childhood autism', *Journal of Autism and Childhood Schizophrenia* 8, 139–61.

Rutter, M. (1979) 'Language, cognition and autism', in Katzman, R. (ed) *Congenital and Acquired Cognitive Disorders.* New York: Raven Press.

Rutter, M. (1999) 'Autism: two-way interplay between research and clinical work', *Journal of Child Psychology and Psychiatry* **40**, 169–88.

Rutter, M. *et al.* (1971) 'Autism: a central disorder of cognition and language?' in Rutter, M. (ed.) *Infantile Autism: Concepts, Characteristics and Treatment.* London: Churchill Livingstone.

Rutter, M. *et al.* (1988) 'Diagnosis and sub-classification of autism: concepts and instrument development', in Schopler, E. and Mesibov, G.B. (eds) *Diagnosis and Assessment in Autism.* New York: Plenum Press.

Rutter, M. *et al.* (1990) 'Genetic factors in child psychiatric disorders: II. Empirical findings', *Journal of Child Psychology and Psychiatry* **31**, 39–83.

Rutter, M. *et al.* (1997) 'Genetic influences and autism', in Cohen, D.J. and Volkmar, F.R. (eds) *Handbook of Autism and Pervasive Developmental Disorders.* New York: John Wiley and Sons.

Rutter, M. *et al.* (1999) 'Quasi-autistic patterns found following severe early global deprivation', *Journal of Child Psychology and Psychiatry* **40**, 537–50.

Rutter, M. and Bailey, A. (1993) 'Thinking and relationships: mind and brain – some reflections on theory of mind and autism', in Baron-Cohen, S. *et al.* (eds) *Understanding Other Minds: perspectives from autism.* Oxford: Oxford University Press.

Rutter, M. and Schopler, E. (1987) 'Autism and pervasive developmental disorders: conceptual and diagnostic issues', *Journal of Autism and Developmental Disorders* **17**, 159–86.

Sacks, O. (1995) *An Anthropologist on Mars.* London: Picador.

Schmidt, K. (1997) 'It was my genes guv', *New Scientist,* 8 November 1997, 46–50.

Schopler, G. Andrew, C.E. and Strupp, K. (1979) 'Do autistic children come from upper-class parents?' *Journal of Autism and Developmental Disorders* **9**, 139–52.

Schopler, E. *et al.* (1980) 'Toward objective classification of childhood autism: childhood autism rating scale (CARS)', *Journal of Autism and Developmental Disorders* **10**, 91–103.

Schopler, E. *et al.* (1983) 'Teaching strategies for parents and professionals', Baltimore: University Park Press.

Schopler, E. and Mesibov, G.B. (eds) (1985) *Communication Problems in Autism.* New York: Plenum Press.

Schopler, E. and Mesibov, G.B. (eds) (1987) *Neurobiological Issues in Autism.* New York: Plenum Press.

Serra, M. *et al.* (1995) 'Emotional role-taking abilities of children with a pervasive developmental disorder not otherwise specified', *Journal of Child Psychology and Psychiatry* **36**, 475–90.

Shah, A. *et al.* (1982) 'Prevalence of autism and related conditions in adults in a mental handicap hospital', *Applied Research in Mental Handicap* **3**, 303–17.

Shah, A. and Frith, U. (1993) 'Why do autistic individuals show superior performance on the block design task?', *Journal of Child Psychology and Psychiatry* **34**, 1351–64.

Shapiro, T.D. *et al.* (1987) 'Attachment in autism and other developmental disorders', *Journal of the Academy of Child and Adolescent Psychiatry* **26**, 480–4.

Shattock, P. *et al.* (1998) 'Vaccination programmes and autism: some observations', in Linfoot, G. and Shattock, P. (eds) *Psychobiology of Autism: Current Research and Practice, Proceedings of Durham Conference 1998.* Sunderland: Autism Research Unit.

Shattock, P. and Lowdon, G. (1991) 'Proteins, peptides and autism Part 2: Implications for the education and care of people with autism', *Brain Dysfunction* **4**, 323–34.

Sherratt, D. (submitted) 'Teaching symbolic play to children with autism and severe learning difficulties', submitted to *Autism: the International Journal of Research and Practice.*

Siegal, M. and Beattie, K. (1991) 'Where to look first for children's understanding of false beliefs', *Cognition* **38**, 1–12.

Siegal, M. and Peterson, C.C. (1994) 'Children's theory of mind and the conversational territory of cognitive development', in Lewis, C. and Mitchell, P. (eds) *Children's Early Understanding of Mind: Origins and Development.* Hove: Erlbaum.

Sigman, M. (1998) 'Change and continuity in the development of children with autism', *Journal of Child Psychology and Psychiatry* **39**, 817–27.

Sigman, M. *et al.* (1986) 'Social interactions of autistic mentally retarded and normal children and their caregivers', *Journal of Child Psychology and Psychiatry* **27**, 647–56.

Sigman, M. *et al.* (1988) 'Cognition in autistic children', in Cohen, D.J. *et al.* (eds) *Handbook of Autism and Pervasive Developmental Disorders.* Chichester: John Wiley and Sons.

Sigman, M. and Mundy, P. (1989) 'Social attachments in autistic children', *Journal of the American Academy of Child and Adolescent Psychiatry* **28**, 74–81.

Sigman, M. and Ungerer, J.A. (1981) 'Sensorimotor skills and language comprehension in autistic children', *Journal of Abnormal Child Psychology* **9**, 149–65.

Sigman, M. and Ungerer, J.A. (1984) 'Attachment behaviours in autistic children', *Journal of Autism and Developmental Disorders* **14**, 231–244.

Sigman, M.D. *et al.* (1992) 'Responses to the negative emotions of others by (1992) autistic, mentally retarded, and normal children', *Child Development* **63**, 796–807.

Sigman, M.D. *et al.* (1995) 'Social and cognitive understanding in high functioning children with autism', in Schopler, E. and Mesibov, G.B. (eds) *Learning and Cognition in Autism.* New York: Plenum Press.

Sinclair, J. (1992) Personal account in Schopler, E. and Mesibov, G.B. (eds) *High Functioning Individuals with Autism.* New York: Plenum Press.

Skuse, D.H. *et al.* (1997) 'Evidence from Turner's syndrome of an imprinted X-linked locus affecting cognitive function', *Nature* **387**, 705–8.

Smalley, S.L. (1997) 'Genetic influences in childhood onset psychiatric disorders: autism and attention deficit hyperactivity disorder', *American Journal of Human Genetics* **60**, 1276–82.

Smalley, S.L. *et al.* (1988) 'Autism and genetics: A decade of research', *Archives of General Psychiatry* **45**, 953–61.

Smalley, S.L. and Asarnow, R.F. (1990) 'Cognitive subclinical markers in autism: brief report', *Journal of Autism and Developmental Disorders* **20**, 271–8.

Smalley, S.L. *et al.* (1992) Autism and tuberous sclerosis', *Journal of Autism and Develeopmental Disorders* **22**, 339–55.

Snow, *et al.* (1987) 'Expression of emotion in young autistic children', *Journal of the American Academy of Child and Adolescent Psychiatry* **26**, 836–8.

Sodian, B. and Frith, U. (1992) 'Deception and sabotage in autistic retarded and normal children', *Journal of Child Psychology and Psychiatry* **33**, 591–605.

Sparling, J.W. (1991) 'Brief report: A prospective case report of infantile autism from pregnancy to four years', *Journal of Autism and Developmental Disorders* **21**, 229–36.

Sparrevohn, R. and Howie, P.M. (1995) 'Theory of mind in children with autistic disorder: evidence of developmental progression and the role of verbal ability', *Journal of Child Psychology and Psychiatry* **36**, 249–63.

Sparrow, S. *et al.* (1984) *Vineland Adaptive Behaviour Scales survey form.* Circle Pines, American Guidance Services.

Sperber, D. and Wilson, D. (1986) *Relevance: Communication and Cognition.* Oxford: Blackwell Science.

Spiker, D. and Ricks, M. (1984) 'Visual self-recognition in autistic children: developmental relationhips', *Child Development* **55**, 214–25.

Starr, E. (1993) 'Teaching the appearance-reality distinction to children with autism', Paper presented at the British Psychological Society Developmental Section Annual Conference, Birmingham.

Stefanik, K.G. and Balazs, A. (1995) 'Mirror self recognition and developmental deficits in autistic children', in Lindfoot, G. *et al.* (eds) *Psychological Perspectives in Autism: Proceedings of Durham Conference, 5–7 April 1995.* Sunderland: Autism Research Unit/ National Autistic Society.

Steffenburg, S. (1991) 'Neuropsychiatric assesssment of children with autism: a population-based study', *Developmental Medicine and Child Neurology* **33**, 495–511.

Steffenberg, S. and Gillberg, C. (1986) 'Autism and autistic-like conditions in Swedish rural and urban areas: a population study', *British Journal of Psychiatry* **149**, 81–7.

Steffenberg, S. and Gillberg, C. (1990) 'The eitiology of autism', in Gillberg, C. (ed.) *Autism Diagnosis and Treatment.* New York: Plenum Press.

Stern, D.N. (1977) *The First Relationship: Infant and Mother.* Cambridge: MA Harvard University Press.

Stern, D.N. (1985) *The Interpersonal World of the Infant.* London: Basic Books.

Stone, W.L. *et al.* (1990) 'Play and imitation skills in the diagnosis of autism in young children', *Paediatrics* **86**, 267–82.

Stone, W.L. *et al.* (1999) 'Can autism be diagnosed accurately in children under three years?', *Journal of Child Psychology and Psychiatry* **40**, 219–26.

Stone, W.L. and Lemanek, K.L. (1990) 'Parental report of social behaviours in autistic preschoolers', *Journal of Autism and Developmental Disorders* **20**, 513–22.

Sun, Z. and Cade, R. (1999) 'A peptide found in schizophrenia and autism causes behavioural changes in rats', *Autism: the International Journal of Research and Practice* **3**, 85–96.

Sun, Z. *et al.* (1999) 'B-casomorphin induces Fos-like immunoreactivity in discrete brain regions relevant to schizophrenia and autism', *Autism: the International Journal of Research and Practice* **3**, 67–84.

Swettenham, J. (1996) 'Can children with autism be taught to understand false belief using computers?', *Journal of Child Psychology and Psychiatry* **37**, 157–65.

Szatmari, P. *et al.* (1993) 'Lack of cognitive impairment in first degree relatives of children with pervasive developmental disorders', *Journal of American Archives of Child and Adolescent Psychiatry* **32**, 1264–73.

Szatmari, P. and Jones, M.B. (1991) 'IQ and the genetics of autism', *Journal of Child Psychology and Psychiatry* **32**, 897–908.

Tager-Flusberg, H. (1981) 'On the nature of linguistic functioning in early infantile autism', *Journal of Autism and Developmental Disorders* **11**, 45–56.

Tager-Flusberg, H. (1989) 'A psycholinguistic perspective on language development in the autistic child', in Dawson, G. (ed.) *Autism: Natural Diagnosis and Treatment*. New York: Guildford.

Tager-Flusberg, H. (1993) 'What language reveals about the understanding of mind in children with autism', in Baron-Cohen, S. *et al.* (eds) *Understanding Other Minds: Perspectives from Autism*. Oxford: Oxford University Press.

Tager-Flusberg, H. (1996) 'Evidence for a basic theory of mind mechanism from studies of children with neurodevelopmental disorders', *International Journal of Psychology* **31**, 212–13.

Tager-Flusberg, H. and Sullivan, K. (1994) 'Predicting and explaining behaviour: a comparison of autistic, mentally retarded and normal children', *Journal of Child Psychology and Psychiatry* **35**, 1059–76.

Tan, J. and Harris, P. (1991) 'Autistic children understand seeing and wanting', *Development and Psychopathology* **3**, 163–74.

Tanoue, Y. *et al.* (1988) 'Epidemiology of infantile autism in southern Ibaraki Japan: differences in prevalance rates in birth cohorts', *Journal of Autism and Developmental Disorders* **18**, 155–66.

Tantam, D.J.H. (1988a) 'Lifelong eccentricity and social isolation: I Psychiatric social and forensic aspects', *British Journal of Psychiatry* **153**, 777–82.

Tantam, D.J.H. (1988b) 'Lifelong eccentricity and social isolation: II Asperger's syndrome or schizoid personality disorder?', *British Journal of Psychiatry* **153**, 783–71.

Tantam, D.J.H. (1991) 'Asperger's syndrome in adulthood', in Frith, U. (ed.) *Autism and Asperger Syndrome*. Cambridge: Cambridge University Press.

Taylor, M. (1988) 'The development of children's understanding of the seeing-knowing distinction', in Astington, J.W. *et al.* (eds) *Developing Theories of Mind*. New York: Cambridge University Press.

Taylor, T.J. and Cameron, D. (1987) *Analysing Conversation: Rules and Units in the Structure of Talk*. Oxford: Pergamon Press.

Tinbergen, N.K. and Tinbergen, E. (1994) *Autism: new hope for a cure*. Hemel Hempstead: Allen Unwin.

Trevarthen, C. (1979) 'Communication and co-operation in early infancy: a description of primary intersubjectivity', in Bullowa, M. (ed.) *Before Speech*. Cambridge: Cambridge University Press.

Trevarthen, C. *et al.* (1996) *Children with Autism: Diagnosis and interventions to meet their needs*. London: Jessica Kingsley.

Turner, M. (1999) 'Generating novel ideas: fluency performance in high functioning and learning disabled individuals with autism', *Journal of Child Psychology and Psychiatry* **40**, 189–202.

Ungerer, J. and Sigman, M. (1981) 'Symbolic play and language comprehension in autistic children', *Journal of the American Academy of Child Psychiatry* **20**, 318–37.

Uzgiris, I.C. and Hunt, J. McV. (1975) *Assessment in Infancy: ordinal scales of psychological development*. Urbana Il: University of Illinois Press.

Volkmar, F.R. (1998) 'Categorical approaches to the diagnosis of autism', *Autism: the International Journal of Research and Practice* **2**, 45–59.

Volkmar, F.R. *et al.* (1989) 'An examination of social typologies in autism', *Journal of the American Academy of Child and Adolescent Psychiatry* **28**, 82–6.

Volkmar, F.R. and Nelson, I. (1990) 'Seizure disorders in autism', *Journal of the American Academy of Child and Adolescent Psychiatry* **29**, 127–9.

Vygotsky, L.S. (1962) *Thought and Language*. Cambridge: MA. MIT Press.

Wagstaff, J. (1995) 'Do children with autism understand referential opacity?', *Proceedings of the British Psychological Society* **3**, 13.

Walker, A.S. (1982) 'Intermodal perception of expressive behaviours by human infants', *Journal of Experimental Child Psychology* **33**, 514–35.

Walker, A. (1998) 'What is the point of autism?', in Linfoot, G. and Shattock, P. (eds) *Psychobiology of Autism: Current research and practice. Proceedings of Durham Conference 1998*. Sunderland: Autism Research Unit.

Wang, P.P. and Bellugi, U. (1993) 'William's syndrome, Down's syndrome and cognitive neuroscience', *American Journal of Diseases of Children* **147**, 1246–51.

Waring, R. and Ngong, J.M. (1993) 'Sulphate metabolism in allergy-induced autism: relevance to the disease aetiology', in Shattock, P. and Lindfoot, G. (eds) *Biological Perspectives in Autism: Proceedings of an International Research Conference in Autism, Durham 1993*. Sunderland: Autism Research Unit/NAS.

Waterhouse, L. and Fein, P. (1982) 'Language skills in developmentally disabled children', *Brain and Language* **15**, 307–33.

Weeks, S.J. and Hobson, R.P. (1987) 'The salience of facial expression for autistic children', *Journal of Child Psychology and Psychiatry* **28**, 137–52.

Weintraub, S. and Mesulam, M.M. (1983) 'Developmental learning disabilities of the right hemisphere: Emotional interpersonal and psychological components', *Archives of Neurology* **40**, 463–5.

Wellman, H.M. (1990) *The Child's Theory of Mind*. Cambridge: MA. MIT Bradford.

Wellman, H.M. (1991) 'From desires to beliefs: acquisition of a theory of mind', in Whiten, A. (ed.) *Natural Theories of Mind*. Oxford, Blackwell Science.

Wellman, H.M. and Bartsch, K. (1988) 'Young children's reasoning about beliefs', *Cognition* **30**, 239–77.

Wellman, H.M. and Estes, D. (1986) 'Early understanding of mental entities: a re-examination of childhood realism', *Child Development* **57**, 910–23.

Welsh, M.C. *et al.* (1980) 'Neuropsychology of early-treated phenylketonuria: specific executive function deficits', *Child Development* **61**, 697–713.

Wetherby, A. (1984) 'Possible neurolinguistic breakdown in autistic children', *Topics in Language Disorders* **4**, 39–58.

Wetherby, A.M. and Prutting, C.A (1984) 'Profiles of communicative and cognitive-social abilities in autistic children', *Journal of Speech and Hearing Research* **27**, 364–77.

Whiteley, P. *et al.* (1999) A gluten-free diet as an intervention for autism and associated spectrum disorders: preliminary findings', *Autism, the International Journal of Research and Practice* **3**, 45–66.

Williams, C. *et al.* (1991) 'Proteins, peptides and autism Part 1: Urinary protein patterns in autism as revealed by sodium dodacylsulphate polyactylamide gel electrophorasis and silver staining', *Brain Dysfunction* **4**, 320–2.

Williams, D. (1992) *Nobody Nowhere.* New York: Time Books.

Williams, D. (1996) *Autism; an Inside-Out Approach.* London: Jessica Kingsley.

Wing, L. (1976) *Early Childhood Autism.* New York: Pergamon Press.

Wing, L. (1981) 'Asperger's syndrome: A clinical account', *Psychological Medicine* **11**, 115–29.

Wing, L. (1984) Letter: Schizoid personality in childhood. *British Journal of Psychiatry* **145**, 444.

Wing, L. (1988) 'The continuum of autistic characteristics', in Schopler, E. and Mesibov, G.B. (eds) *Diagnosis and Assessment in Autism.* New York: Plenum Press.

Wing, L (1991) 'The relationship between Asperger's syndrome and Kanner's autism', in Frith, U. (ed.) *Autism and Asperger Syndrome.* Cambridge: Cambridge University Press.

Wing, L. (1996) *The Autistic Spectrum: a guide for parents and professionals.* London: Constable.

Wing, L. (1997) 'The history of ideas on autism: legends, myths and reality', *Autism: the International Journal of Research and Practice* **1**, 13–24.

Wing, L. *et al.* (1977) 'Symbolic play in severely mentally retarded and autistic children', *Journal of Child Psychology and Psychiatry* **18**, 167–178.

Wing, L. and Gould, J. (1978) 'Systematic recording of behaviours and skills of retarded and psychotic children', *Journal of Autism and Childhood Schizophrenia* **8**, 79–97.

Wing, L. and Gould, J. (1979) 'Severe impairments of social interaction and associated abnormalities in children: Epidemiology and classification', *Journal of Autism and Developmental Disorders* **9**, 11–29.

Wing, L. and Wing, J.K. (1971) 'Multiple impairments in early childhod autism', *Journal of Autism and Childhood Schizophrenia* **1**, 256–66.

Witkin, H.A. and Goodenough, D.R. (1981) *Cognitive Styles: Essence and Origins.* New York: International University Press.

Wolff, S. (1995) *Loners: the life path of unusual children.* London: Routledge.

Wolff, S. and Chess, S. (1964) 'A behavioural study of schizophrenic children', *Acta Psychiatrica Scandinavia* **40**, 438–66.

Wolff, S. and Cull, A. (1986) '"Schiziod" personality and antisocial conduct: A retrospective case note study', *Psychological Medicine* **16**, 677–87.

World Health Organisation (1978) *Mental Disorders: A glossary and guide to their classification in accordance with the 9th revision of the International Classification of Diseases (ICD–9).* Geneva: World Health Organisation.

World Health Organisation (1993) *Mental Disorders: A glossary and guide to their classification in accordance with the 10th revision of the International Classification of Diseases (ICD–10)*. Geneva: World Health Organisation.

Yirmiya, N. *et al.* (1992) 'Empathy and cognition in high functioning children with autism', *Child Development* **63**, 150–60.

Yirmiya, N. *et al.* (in press) 'Meta-analyses comparing theory of mind abilities of individuals with autism, individuals with mental retardation, and normally developing individuals', *Psychological Bulletin*.

Zaitchik, D. (1990) 'When representations conflict with reality: The preschoolers' problem with false belief and "false" photographs', *Cognition* **35**, 41–68.

Zelazo, P.D. *et al.* (1996) 'Theory of mind and rule use in individuals with Down's syndrome: a test of the uniqueness and specificity claims', *Journal of Child Psychology and Psychiatry* **37**, 479–84.

Index

ABC (Autism Behaviour Checklist) 42
ADD/ADHD (attention deficit disorder/attention deficit hyperactivity disorder) 18
ADI (Autism Diagnostic Interview) 43
ADOS (Autism Diagnostic Observation Schedule) 43
adaptive behaviour 121–2
aetiology 49, 52–3, 57
age
  at diagnosis 43–4, 117
  of onset 11, 12, 14, 20, 44–5
agency, sense of 101, 102, 103–6, 111, 112
appearance-reality distinction 67, 71
Asperger, H., work of 8, 22–5, 39, 53 see also Asperger's syndrome
Asperger's syndrome
  in Bishop's model 17, 17
  and depression 21–2
  description by Asperger 22–3
  diagnostic criteria 23–5, 132–3, 137–8
  and executive function 97
  and feelings 90
  and other autistic conditions 25
  prevalence rate 38
  and schizophrenia/schizoid personality disorder 20–21, 23
  and theory of mind 65–6, 68
  and understanding of mental states 31, 65–6
  brief mentions 8, 15, 18, 26, 30, 88, 98, 122
  see also Asperger, H., work of
attachment 115–6, 118
attention
  attention-switching problem 125
  bizarre focus of 122
  deficit disorders see ADD/ADHD
  see also SAM (shared attention mechanism)
Autism Behaviour Checklist (ABC) 42
Autism Diagnostic Interview (ADI) 43
Autism Diagnostic Observation Schedule (ADOS) 43
Autism Europe: charter of rights 127, 128–9
autistic continuum 14
autistic spectrum 14, 15–16
autosomal recessive gene 53

BOS (Behaviour Observation Scale for Autism) 42

BPVS (British Picture Vocabulary Scale) 84
BRIAACC (Behaviour Rating Instrument for Autistic and Atypical Children) 42
BSE (Behavioural Summarised Evaluation) 43
behaviour
  adaptive 121–2
  and age of diagnosis 43–4
  and age of onset 44–5
  and diagnostic criteria 35–6, 41, 132, 133, 136, 137–8
  and diagnostic systems 41–3
  differences in 40–1, 60, 113–4
  and education and management 111, 115–9, 120–21, 122
  and epidemiological basis for autism 36–7
  misleading interpretations of 2, 29, 30–31
  repetitive and stereotyped 26, 37, 119, 132, 133, 136, 137–8
  spontaneous 9
  and studies of early development 45–7
Behaviour Observation Scale for Autism (BOS) 42
Behaviour Rating Instrument for Autistic and Atypical Children (BRIAACC) 42
Behavioural Summarised Evaluation (BSE) 43
biology
  absence of single cause for autism 2
  birth problems 52
  brain abnormalities 54–7 see also brain
  evidence for organic cause 50–51
  genetic factors 2, 51–4
  needs arising from 125
birth, difficulties at 52
Block Design Test 93, 94
bonding 116
boys see males
brain
  abnormalities 54–7
  chemistry 56–7
  damage or dysfunction 50, 50–51, 79
  and executive function 97–101
  and food metabolism 53–4
  functional abnormalities 55–6
  structural differences 54–5
British Picture Vocabulary Scale (BPVS) 84

CARS (Childhood Autism Rating Scale) 42
CHAT (Checklist for Autism in Toddlers) 41–2, 44, 46
central coherence 93–7, 111–2
cerebral palsy 51
change, resistance to, 22, 23 *see also* sameness, preservation of/insistance on
charter of rights 127, 128–9
Checklist for Autism in Toddlers *see* CHAT
checklists/ratiing scales 42–3
Childhood Autism Rating Scale (CARS) 42
childhood disintegrative disorder 137
Children's Embedded Figures Test 93–4, 96
chromosome 15, 53
classification *see* nature and definition of autism
cognitive impairments 25, 62, 83, 119–21
cognitive style 95–7
cognitive teaching 110
cognitive theories 62–80, 86
communication
    Bishop's model of relationship between social communicative disorders 17, 17–18
    deficits and difficulties in autism 12, 26, 40, 63–4, 122–5, 132, 135–6
    and epidemiological basis for autism 37, 37, 38
    and metarepresentation 69
    non-verbal 23, 24, 124
    and semantic-pragmatic disorder 16
compensatory approach 32, 110, 111
compulsion 22
creativity, lack of 24
culture 106, 109
curriculum 32

DAMP (disorders of attention, motor coordination and perception) 18
DISCO (Diagnostic Interview Schedule and Childhood Operation) 43
DSM-IIIR 15
DSM-IV 13, 15, 41, 44, 135–8
Damasio and Maurer neurological model 98
deception 64, 72, 100
decoupling 69, 70, 74
deficits 33–4
definition *see* nature and definition of autism
depression 21–2, 126
design stance 76
desire 64, 65, 77
development
    autism as developmental disorder 125–6
    early 23, 45–7
    'growing out of' autism 4–5
diagnosis
    age at 43–4, 117
    as clue to psychological functioning 30–2
    criteria 11–13, 23–5, 35–6, 131–8
    definition for practice 25–6
    history of 3, 7–27
    importance in education and care 29–34, 114–5
    labels 26–7
    necessary and sufficient features 14–15
    systems 41–7
    tests 41–3
Diagnostic Checklist for Behaviour-Disturbed Children 42

Diagnostic Interview Schedule and Childhood Operation (DISCO) 43
diet 2, 54, 57, 125
disorders of attention, motor coordination and perception (DAMP) 18
Down's syndrome 63, 65, 67, 75
drugs 2, 56–7, 125

EDD (eye-direction detector) 77–8, 79, 80
EEG abnormalities 56
echolalia 9, 10, 26, 37, 37, 45, 91, 96, 97, 122, 123
'ecological view' 102
education
    central role of 32–3
    challenge for 33–4
    and communication problems 124–5
    and management 115–9, 120–1
    and psychological theories 110-111
efference copying 101, 103, 104, 105
emotions 80, 82, 84–6, 87, 88–9, 92, 99, 106, 110, 111, 118–9, 131
empathy 89–90
environmental factors 2
epidemiology 36–9
    epidemiological basis for autism 36–8
    of autistic spectrum disorders 38–9
epilepsy 50, 125
Europe
    European Parliament Written Declaration on the Rights of People with Autism 127
    Autism Europe charter of rights 127, 128–9
evolutionary theory 76–80
executive function 97–101, 102, 104, 111, 120
exogenous causes 53
'experiencing self' 92–3, 102, 105, 111, 112
explanation, types of 1–3
explicit/implicit knowledge 70–71
expressions, facial 82, 84–5, 88, 118, 119
extended phenotype 52
externality 102
eye contact 22, 35, 77, 117
eye-direction detector *see* EDD

false perception, study of 88–9
facial expressions 82, 84–5, 88, 118, 119
false belief 62, 63, 64, 65, 67, 69, 71, 72, 73, 75
fascinations 105
fathers 23, 53 *see also* parents
females 39, 53
flexibility
    and adaptive behaviour 121–2
    lack of *see* change, resistance to; interests, narrow/special; sameness, preservation of/insistence on
fluency disorder 99
food metabolism 53–4
fragile-X syndrome 52

generalisation, lack of 121–2
genetic factor 2, 39, 51–4
gestures 63
Gibson's 'ecological view' 102
girls 39, 53
'growing out of' autism 4–5

Heller's syndrome 19
hierarchisation deficit 95
Hobson's theory 80–90, 110

IBSE (Infant Behavioural Summarised Evaluation) 43
ICD-9 15, 20
ICD-10 13, 15, 25, 41, 44, 131–3
ID (intentionality detector) 76, 78, 80
ice cream van test 65, 66
imaging techniques 56
imagination deficits 37, 40
imitation 90, 91–2, 99, 118
implicit/explicit knowledge 70–71
incidence 38, 39
inclusion 29–30 see also integration
individuals 3, 113–29
   autism as disorder throughout life 125-6
   cognitive impairments 119–22
   communication 122–5
   individualism 3, 113–4
   needs 114–5, 125
   and provision 126–9
   problems in education and management 115–9
Infant Behavioural Summarised Evaluation (IBSE) 43
integration 115 see also inclusion
intelligence
   appearance of 8, 9
   levels of 13
intention 65, 66
intentional stance 76
intentionality detector see ID
interactions 23, 24, 26, 80–81, 82, 83, 86, 105–6
interests, narrow/special 23, 24, 26, 114, 132, 133, 136
internal representation 99
interpersonal relationships, failure to develop 12
intersubjectivity theories 80–93, 101, 102, 108, 110, 111, 112
Irish Society for Autism 127
isolation 11

joint attention 42, 79, 86-7, 90, 117

Kanner's syndrome
   identification of 7
   and intelligence 9, 13
   Kanner's description of 8–10, 91
   later Kanner views 10–11
   and modern identification of autism 14, 15
   and parents 7, 10, 23, 49
   prevalence rate 38
   and social class 39
   and work of Asperger 22, 23, 24

labels
   range of 26–7
   use and misuse of 30
language
   and Asperger's syndrome 25
   and communication problems 122–5
   and diagnosis 8, 9, 10, 11, 12, 13, 23, 131, 132, 135, 136
   differences between individuals 40, 122
   difficulties caused by nature of 72

and education 124–5
processing 96–7
see also echolalia; mutism; pronouns; semantic-pragmatic disorder; speech
learning difficulties
   and autism 5, 13, 40, 50–51, 107, 121, 123
   non-autistic individuals with 46, 72, 75, 84, 85, 116
Leslie's representation theory 68–70, 110
   criticisms of 70–76, 80
lies 73

M-representations 78
males 23, 37, 39, 53
meaning, difficulty in extracting 120
medical model 29–30, 33
memory
   cued 120
   personal episodic 92, 93, 120
   rote 8
mental states 31, 62, 63, 64, 65, 66, 67, 70, 73, 76, 78, 79, 82, 111
metaphorical substitutions 10
metarepresentation 69, 70, 71, 73–4
mindreading 76, 79
mothers 7, 10, 23, 44, 49, 52, 53, 108 see also parents
motivation towards people 117
motor coordination/movement 23, 24, 98
mutism 8, 9, 11, 37, 37, 40, 122

narrative theory 106–9, 112
National Autistic Society mission statement 126–7
nature and definition of autism 7-27
   Asperger's work 8, 22–5
   autistic spectrum 15–16
   definition for practice 25–6
   diagnostic criteria 11–13
   diagnostic features 14-16
   Kanner's work 7, 8–11
   range of lables 26–7
   related conditions 18–22
   and semantic-pragmatic disorder 16–18
   triad of impairments 13–14
needs
   arising from biology of autism 125
   recognising 114–5
   see also education; provision, principles for
neurotransmitters 56
non-verbal communication 23, 24, 124
normality in relation to autism 3–4, 5–6

objects, skilful relationship to 8, 10
obsessive rituals 22
obsessive compulsive disorder (OCD) 22
organic cause 50–51
'other' perception 81, 82, 102
oversensitivity, sensory 8, 9–10

PL-ADOS (Pre-Linguistic Diagnostic Observatin Schedule) 43
pathological demand avoidance syndrome(PDA) 19, 22
paranoia 21

parents
    Asperger's view of 23
    and child's early development 43, 44, 46, 118
    Kanner's view of 7, 10, 23, 49
    not a cause of autism 4, 7, 49
    see also fathers; mothers
perceptions/perceptual input 101, 105
pervasive developmental disorder 138
physical stance 76
piagetian theory 101–6
play 26, 37, 37, 42, 69, 74, 90, 99, 100, 121, 131, 132, 135, 136
Pre-Linguistic Autism Diagnostic Observation Schedule (PL-ADOS) 43
pregnancy, problems during 52
pretence 69, 74
pretend play/activity 37, 37, 42, 69, 99 *see also* play
prevalence rates 38, 39
prognosis 25, 110 *see also* 'growing out of' autism
pronouns 9, 81
    reversal 10, 11, 26
prospective data/studies 44, 45–6
prosthetic environments 30, 110, 122
provision, principles for 126–9
psychogenic theories 49
psychological funtioning 30–32
psychological level 2–3, 4
psychological theories 59–112

questionnaires 42–3

rating scales/checklists 42–3
refrigerator mothers 4, 7, 10, 49
remedial approach 32, 110, 111
repetitive behaviour 26, 37, 119, 132, 133, 136, 137–8
representation permanence 102
representation theory *see* Leslie's representation theory
retrospective studies 43, 45
Rett's syndrome 15, 18–19, 137
rituals 12, 22
Rogers and Pennington's theory 90–92

SAM (shared attention mechanism) 78, 79, 111, 112
sabotage 64, 72, 100
'Sally-Ann' task 62–3, 66, 67, 68, 70, 72, 73
sameness, preservation of/insistence on 8, 11, 12
    see also change, resistance to
savant abilities 5
scans 56
schizoid personality disorder 20–21, 22
schizophrenia 19–20, 21, 23, 65, 104
    childhood 11, 19
self
    role of narrative in construction of 108
    sense of 81–2, 92–3,102, 104, 105, 106, 111, 117
semantic-pragmatic disorder 16–18
sensitivity see oversensitivity; stimulus over-selectivity hypothesis
shared attention mechanism see SAM
situation theory 74
skills, special or savant 5

social
    affordances 80, 81
    avoidance of social demands 19
    brain 79
    class 39
    development 83–4
    and diagnosis 12, 13, 13, 26, 131, 133, 135, 137
    difficulties, 12, 13, 13, 19, 26, 37, 37, 38, 38, 41, 46, 112, 115–9
    effectiveness 14
    interactions 23, 24, 26, 80–81, 82, 83, 86, 105–6
    knowledge 86–7, 104, 118
    skills 66, 67, 113
social communicative disorders, relationship between 17, 17–18
socialisation 106, 109
speech, 23, 24, 37, 38, 40 *see also* language
special skills 5
spontaneous behaviour, lack of 9
stereotyped behaviour 26, 37, 119, 132, 133, 136, 137–8
stereotypies 22
stimulus over-selectivity hypothesis 14
stress 120, 122
symbolic play/activity 26, 37, 38, 38, 74, 90, 100, 121, 131, 135 *see also* play

TEACCH 32
TOMM (theory of mind module/mechanism) 69, 70, 74, 78–9, 80
theory of mind 15, 31, 90, 94, 95, 100
    theory 62–76, 80, 102–3, 111
thinking, rigidity/lack of flexibility in 12, 13, 26, 37, 38, 40
trauma 4
treatment
    diet 2, 54, 57, 125
    drugs 2, 56–7, 125
triad of impairments 3, 13, 13-14, 15, 26, 27, 36, 38
tuberous sclerosis 52

Vineland Adaptive Behaviour Scales 84

William's syndrome 19
'windows' task 100
Wisconsin Card Sorting Test (WCST) 98
withdrawal 8

World Autism Organisation 129

X-linked gene 53